PRIVATE ISLAND

Also by James Meek

NOVELS

McFarlane Boils the Sea
Drivetime
The People's Act of Love
We Are Now Beginning Our Descent
The Heart Broke In

SHORT STORIES

Last Orders and Other Stories
The Museum of Doubt

PRIVATE ISLAND

Why Britain Now Belongs to Someone Else

James Meek

VERSO
London • New York

This revised edition first published by Verso 2015
First published by Verso 2014
© James Meek 2014

Earlier versions of the following chapters originally appeared in
the *London Review of Books*: Chapter 1 in vol. 33, no. 9; Chapter 3
in vol. 30, no. 15; Chapter 4 in vol. 34, no. 17; Chapter 5 in vol. 33,
no. 18; Chapter 6 in vol. 36, no. 1; Chapter 7 in vol. 36, no. 19
An earlier version of Chapter 2 appeared in the *Guardian*
under the headline 'The £10bn Rail Crash'

3 5 7 9 10 8 6 4 2

Verso
UK: 6 Meard Street, London W1F 0EG
US: 20 Jay Street, Suite 1010, Brooklyn, NY 11201
www.versobooks.com

Verso is the imprint of New Left Books

ISBN-13: 978-1-78478-206-1
eISBN-13: 978-1-78168-695-9 (UK)
eISBN-13: 978-1-78168-291-3 (US)

British Library Cataloguing in Publication Data
A catalogue record for this book is available from the British Library

Library of Congress Cataloging-in-Publication Data

Meek, James, 1962–
Private island : why Britain now belongs to someone else / James
Meek. – First Edition.
    pages cm
   ISBN 978-1-78168-290-6 (paperback) – ISBN 978-1-78168-291-
3 (ebook) – ISBN 978-1-78168-291-3
1. Privatization–Great Britain. 2. Great Britain–Economic
conditions–21st century. 3. Great Britain–Social conditions–21st
century. I. Title.
HD4145.M44 2014
338.941'05–dc23

2014012255

Typeset in Minion Pro by MJ & N Gavan Ltd, Truro, Cornwall
Printed and bound by
CPI Group (UK) Ltd, Croydon, CR0 4YY

*This book is dedicated to Sophy, and to the
memory of Chris Geering, master builder.*

Contents

Introduction

One winter's morning in 1991 I loaded a guitar, a condensed edition of the *Oxford English Dictionary* and a Teach Yourself Russian course into an old Volkswagen, left the house near Edinburgh where I'd been staying and drove to Kiev. Five days passed on the road. I left the familiarity, order and prosperity of Britain, the island where I'd grown up, and travelled east to wait for the Soviet Union to dissolve. I didn't have to wait long. A few weeks after I arrived, it ceased to be. Russia and Ukraine went their separate ways. The Kiev traffic policeman waving down my foreign-plated car had time to utter the words, 'What are you doing in the Soviet Union?' before the colour left his face, his mouth went dry, and he turned away, lost, a bully orphaned of his corporate father. A seventy-year experiment to test whether the ethos of the commune could be imposed on a transcontinental empire of hundreds of millions of people was over, long after the answer was in (it couldn't). I wasn't sorry to see Soviet communism go. Despite all that's happened since, I still don't mourn it. There was hope in the beginning that something fine would grow in the gap that was left. It was a while before I realised the cynical, grasping figures who moved in to take possession of the ruins were not, as I'd hoped, transitional symptoms of change, but the essence of that change.

This book about Britain started there, in Ukraine and Russia. Watching the vultures come to feast on the carcass of the world's largest state-owned, planned economy, I began to find the terms to question what had been done by politicians, economic theorists, lobbyists and business people in my own country. I had thought, when I left Scotland, in the unconscious way certainties are stowed in one's mind, that I knew Britain; that some essential way of being would be resilient to Margaret Thatcher's rearrangements, which must, as transient policies, be superficial. I had to go home by way of Kiev and Moscow to see that I was wrong, to begin to see how, and how deeply, she and her followers altered Britain.

With hindsight, 1991 was a pivotal year. When it began, the free market economic belief system, with its lead proselytisers Thatcher and Ronald Reagan, had been pushing back for more than a decade against various attempts to impose levelling communitarianism around the world. The Berlin Wall had fallen, as had communist regimes in Poland, Czechoslovakia, Hungary, Romania and Bulgaria. The market belief system, which holds that government is incompetent by default, that state taxation is oppressive, that the desire for wealth is the right and principal motivator of achievement and that virtually all human wants can best be met by competing private firms, was becoming entrenched in the non-communist world, from Chile to New Zealand. Made bold by a popular public perception that government overspending and selfish organised labour was to blame for economic stagnation and high inflation in the 1970s, Thatcher and Reagan had taken on powerful trades unions, and won. Barriers to the international movement of goods and money had fallen; the European Union was, on paper, a single marketplace. In Britain, restrictions on how much ordinary people could borrow to finance their everyday needs had been scrapped, and millions had acquired credit cards. Volumes of regulations controlling how banks were allowed to use people's deposits had been torn up, and unimaginably vast sums were being moved privately from country to country. Government spending had been cut, as had income tax and corporation tax. Sales tax and fees for everyday services had been raised. Council houses and big state enterprises had been privatised, with more on the way, leading to hundreds of thousands of redundancies. Thatcher's programme in Britain was an inspiration for the IMF and the World Bank as they experimented with the conditions they attached to bail-out loans to developing countries.*

But at the end of 1990, the triumph of marketism seemed to hang in the balance. Reagan and Thatcher had relinquished the stage to less fervent, less charismatic successors. The man who'd introduced the market economy to China, Deng Xiaoping, had been blamed by traditional communists for fostering the Tiananmen Square protests, and was in disgrace. In the Soviet Union Mikhail Gorbachev, the great hope of free marketeers, was facing a similar backlash from hardliners, and the Baltic countries' hopes of escape from the USSR looked bleak. Saddam Hussein, dictator of semi-socialist Iraq, had invaded semi-capitalist Kuwait.

Yet the following year conviction began to grow among the marketeers that the final defeat of centrally planned, communitarian government was at hand, the sense that seemed to confirm such ideas as America having 'won' the Cold War, and the 'end of history'. Early in 1991 it became clear that the Soviet leadership had lost the necessary unanimity and ruthlessness to keep Lithuania within the USSR. The humiliating collapse of the coup against Gorbachev that summer presaged recognition of Baltic independence, Ukraine's vote to go the same way, and the end of the Soviet Union. In Kuwait at the beginning of

---

* In the aftermath of the oil price rises of the 1970s, the countries of the Gulf, awash with cash, lent it to banks in north America and Europe, which, in turn, lent it to countries in Latin America, Africa and the Caribbean for ambitious infrastructure projects. Later these poorer countries found they couldn't pay back the loans, and turned to the IMF and World Bank for help.

the year I saw experienced British war correspondents squabble for reporting billets among the frontline troops with the ferocity of those who believe something is being offered for the last time; we thought British and American armies might never fight another war. Few doubted Saddam would be beaten, and he was. That November, as I drove off the ferry at Ostend, heading east, it seemed a racing, expanding tide of victorious free marketism flickered at my wheels, a tide that has gone by many names – consumer capitalism, Reaganism, Thatcherism, neoliberalism, the Washington Consensus. Though the watchtowers still stood at the old border between two Germanys, the border was gone. In eastern Germany, the narrow cobbled streets of medieval towns had jammed solid with second hand cars. I passed a field where an impatient western German DIY chain, unwilling to wait for steel and breeze blocks, had erected a vast, circular retail marquee, blazing with lights. The canvas superstore seemed to have landed, like a spacecraft from a flashier civilisation, come down to offer shrink-wrapped packs of rawl plugs and a choice of bathroom fittings. In Poland, I got lost in fog near Wrocław, and saw how small shops had sprung up everywhere, even in the tiniest villages. In the middle of the night, in the middle of nowhere, in damp, coal-scented murk so thick I wasn't sure which way my car was pointing, I came across an entrepreneur hawking coffee from a roadside kiosk; the best coffee I ever tasted. He was like a champion of Thatcherite values, the small businessman standing ready to serve at all hours, in all weathers, making up for lost time under communism, silently mocking the market-questioning scepticisms I'd brought with me from Scotland. Then I crossed the border into Ukraine, where the USSR had a month left to run.

The effect on me of witnessing the unplanned collapse of a planned economy, where there'd been virtually no private property or private enterprise, was a series of viscerally direct lessons in economics. I saw how badly the Soviet communist system had failed on economic grounds alone, quite apart from its denial of personal freedoms. Long before the end, there was a hopeless housing shortage. Multiple households were sharing two-roomed flats; families were living in dormitories. Apartments seized from their bourgeois owners after the 1917 revolution were still unrepaired more than seventy years later. The infrastructure was rotten; there were cities and suburbs built around factories in the 1960s and 1970s where homes only had mains water for a few hours a day. Surpluses of goods nobody wanted (copies of the complete works of Soviet politicians, busts of Lenin) prevailed beside shortages of goods everybody wanted (cheese, coffee, sausage) because the element sticking together demand for a thing and the amount of trouble it took to produce and deliver it – the price – had been scraped out of transactions and replaced with a made-up figure concocted by planners in Moscow. Inequality was rampant, reflected not just in monetary wealth or property but in the degree to which you actually had access to the cheap goods everyone was supposed to have access to. One consequence of food and drink being allocated by civil servants according to central decrees, rather than by price, was that the restaurant business became an incubator for the black market and organised crime. Airports and railway stations looked like refugee camps because tickets cost virtually nothing, yet there weren't enough flights or trains to move the people who wanted to take them. The first response of the Russian and Ukrainian authorities after independence was to massively increase the production of a single essential item that people were chronically short of: money. Hyperinflation resulted, and millions of people had their savings wiped out.

The other side of the collapse of communism, along with the post-Soviet boons of freedom of movement, freedom of expression and freedom of initiative, was the flourishing of enterprise. Armies of tough middle-aged women made epic journeys to the bazaars of Poland, Turkey and China and returned to Ukraine and Russia with clothes to dress a handsome people as they'd yearned to dress, in jeans, leather and gold. Shops, restaurants, bars, cafés and night clubs opened up; book and music stalls were everywhere. Foreign firms brought wonders: a tampon factory, international direct dialling. Kiev went from a place where you couldn't buy anything to a place where you could buy anything, if you had the means.

Contempt for the planned economy, a new appreciation of the danger of printing excess money, gratitude to the entrepreneurs – there were times, in those early months in Kiev, that I asked myself whether I was becoming a Thatcherite. I can't pinpoint the moment when it soured for me. It might have been the sight of a solid rank of impoverished pensioners, some several hundred respectable old ladies, standing shoulder to shoulder in the freezing winter darkness outside Belarus Station in Moscow, each holding a single sausage for sale – the free market as desperation. Or a visit to the Arctic mining city of Vorkuta, where miners were being paid in sandwiches while their bosses pocketed the money from the coal they were earning free market prices for. Or meeting Roger Gale, head of the Moscow mission of the International Finance Corporation, a branch of the World Bank, where he'd been talking up Russia's programme to privatise businesses by issuing vouchers to all its citizens which they could use – and must only use – to buy shares. I left his office, went to a kiosk selling foreign chocolate, nuts and fizzy drinks, and, non-Russian that I was, bought a voucher for thirteen pounds cash, no ID required. One government estimate was that each supposedly one-off voucher was used, on average, between two and three times.

Or was it the time in 1995 I visited a privatised factory in Volgograd, the former Stalingrad, which once employed ten thousand, whose boss was in jail awaiting trial on embezzlement charges, where the few remaining workers hadn't been paid for several months? One of the plant's former party officials showed me round. I met her in her office, where the busts of revolutionary communist heroes and yellowing mountains of old Pravdas were thick with dust, and the complete works of Marx and Lenin languished untouched in locked glass cabinets behind her. At one point I asked an old worker, who'd been waiting for a council flat for twenty years and got to second place in the queue when perestroika happened, why, if he wasn't being paid, he didn't go on strike. 'If I'd known you were going to ask that kind of question,' the party woman, heir to Lenin, hissed at me, 'I never would have let you come in here.'

In the first stages of disillusionment, it didn't seem obvious to me to make connections between the extremes of marketisation and privatisation in the former Soviet Union and the partial privatisation of a British economy which had always been mainly private anyway. I still assumed some fundamental distinction between two worlds. After all, where Britain had a series of regulators to set rules for the privatised industries – Ofcom, Ofwat and so on – the principal regulator of privatisation in Ukraine and Russia, at least in the early days, was murder. In Russia in particular, a small number of individuals quickly became fantastically rich when they took private control of state producers of petrochemicals and metals. They were grotesquely over-rewarded, or grotesquely undertaxed, and money which should have gone to rebuild roads or hospitals or schools went instead towards yachts, property in London and foreign football teams. But that had nothing in common with privatisation in Britain – did it?

I began to notice something odd about the British and American business people and financial advisers I met in Ukraine and Russia in the 1990s. It was no surprise, I suppose, that they cared more about businesses being overtaxed than undertaxed, more about protection of private property than about protection of pensioners; that they didn't care how weak and bullied the local trades unions were. Besides, their Russian interlocutors kept being assassinated. What was revealing was how many of these emissaries of the capitalist way seemed to believe the myth that all that was good in the British and American economies had been constructed by the free market. They seemed to believe, or talked, made speeches, wrote papers as if they believed, that the entire structure of their own wealthy modern societies – the roads, the electricity grids, the railways, the water and sewage systems, the universal postal services, the telecoms networks, housing, education and health care – had been brought into being by individual entrepreneurs driven by desire for gain, with the occasional lump of charity thrown in, and that a bloated, parasitical state had come shambling onto the scene, seizing assets and demanding free stuff for its shirker buddies. I don't want to absolve the Russians or Ukrainians of responsibility for their handling of the aftermath of communism, but the template they were handed by the fraternity of the Washington Consensus was based on fake history. If this is what the triumphalists of Wall Street and the City of London told the Russians about the way of the capitalist world, I thought when I moved back to Britain in 1999, what have they been telling us? And what came of it?

When Margaret Thatcher's Conservatives came to power in Britain in 1979, much of the economy, and almost all its infrastructure, was in state hands. Exactly what gloss you put on 'in state hands' depends on your political point of view. For traditional socialists, it meant 'the people's hands'. For traditional Tories, it meant 'in British hands'. For Thatcher and her allies, it meant 'in the hands of meddling bureaucrats and selfish, greedy trades unionists'. How much of the economy? A third of all homes were rented from the state. The health service, most schools, the armed forces, prisons, roads, bridges and streets, water, sewers, the National Grid, power stations, the phone and postal system, gas supply, coal mines, the railways, refuse collection, the airports, many of the ports, local and long-distance buses, freight lorries, nuclear fuel reprocessing, air traffic control, much of the car-, ship- and aircraft-building industry, most of the steel factories, British Airways, oil companies, Cable & Wireless, the aircraft engine makers Rolls-Royce, the arms makers Royal Ordnance, the ferry company Sealink, the Trustee Savings Bank,

Girobank, technology companies Ferranti and Inmos, medical technology firm Amersham International and many others.

In the past thirty-five years, this commonly owned economy, this people's portion of the island, has to a greater or lesser degree become private. Millions of council houses have been sold to their owners or to housing associations. Most roads and streets are still under public control, but privatisation has reached deep into the NHS, state schools, the prison service and the military. The remainder was privatised by Thatcher and her successors. By the time she left office, she boasted, 60 per cent of the old state industries had private owners – and that was before the railways and electricity system went under the hammer.

The original background to Thatcher's privatisation revolution was stagflation, a sense of national failure, and a widespread feeling, spreading even to some regular Labour voters, that the unions had become too powerful, and were holding the country back. Labour, and Thatcher's centrist predecessors among the Conservatives, had tried to control inflation administratively, through various deals with unions and employers to hold down wages and prices; Labour had, under pressure from the IMF, cut spending. But Thatcher and her inner circle planned to go further, horrifying moderates in their party with the radicalism of their intentions.

The late Alan Walters, her chief economic adviser, believed a key source of inflation and the weak economy was the amount of taxpayers' money being poured into overmanned, old-fashioned, government-owned industry. Just as in the Soviet Union, he thought, Britain's state industries concealed their subsidy-sucking inefficiency through opaque, idiosyncratic accounting techniques that took little account of how much time and effort were required to do and make things, or what people actually wanted to buy, or how much they were prepared to pay for it. As long as the subsidies kept coming, neither managers nor workers had much incentive to come up with smarter working methods or accept new technology, because that would mean fewer jobs, which would mean less power for the bosses and a smaller union. Yes, Walters knew, his protégée would slash spending on steel and coal and power and all the rest, yes, hundreds of thousands of workers would be sacked, but that wasn't enough. As many state-owned companies as possible must be privatised – be divided up into shares and sold to the public. They'd no longer be subsidised; they'd have to borrow money like any private company, account meticulously to shareholders for every penny they spent or earned, and strive to make a profit. The bigger the profit, the more efficiently the firm would be doing its job, and the more management would be rewarded. Most importantly, they'd have to compete with other firms. If they fell behind their competitors, they'd risk bankruptcy. Managers would face incentives for success and penalties for failure. British industry would become more competitive internationally. It would serve citizens better. Government would save the taxpayer money. The sacked workers would get redundancy payments; they'd go off and start businesses, or find other, more useful jobs once the economy was working properly. Everyone would win, except the lazy, and Arthur Scargill.

Millions did buy shares. Most Britons, bemused by the process, assumed the main reason for privatisation was to raise cash for a desperate government. Harold Macmillan, who before his death provided a snarky Wodehousian commentary from the wings on the work of the grocer's daughter, observed in an often paraphrased line: 'The sale of assets is common with individuals and states when they run into financial difficulties. First, all the Georgian silver goes, and then all that nice furniture that used to be in the saloon. Then the Canalettos go.'

Another leal privatiser, Nigel Lawson, a minister in the Thatcher government from the beginning almost to the end, dismissed the idea that the government cared about the price it was getting for selling off the family silver. Having many ordinary people owning shares, he writes in his memoirs, was the point. 'The prime motives for privatisation were not Exchequer gain,' he declares, 'but an ideological belief in free markets and a wider distribution of private ownership of property.'

Neither Walters nor Lawson, nor other allies like Keith Joseph, the ex-communist Alfred Sherman or Nicholas Ridley, would have been able to implement their ideas without the pre-hubris Thatcher herself, her extraordinary sense of the way the political wind was blowing, her conviction of her own rectitude, and the stamina and persistence with which she was able to go on insisting on something until her opponents in government gave in. Hers was a different emphasis to Walters, who saw the curbing of 'bloody-minded trades unions' as a useful side effect of privatisation. For Thatcher, privatisation, in the beginning at least, was simply one of many weapons to use in her battle against the unions, which was, in turn, a single episode in her war to exterminate socialism, to be fought in one unbroken front from Orgreave Colliery to Andrei Sakharov's place of exile in Gorky. Her great political inspiration, apart from her father, was the Austrian economist Friedrich Hayek's 1944 book, *The Road to Serfdom*, written in Cambridge during the war. Hayek was regarded as an able economist; he eventually won a Nobel Prize for it. But *The Road to Serfdom* isn't an economics book. It's a book about society, the recent past and human nature that bears the same relation to sociology, history and psychology as *Atlas Shrugged* bears to literature. It is devoted to the idea that Winston Churchill later nodded to, catastrophically for him, in the 1945 election campaign, when he said Labour would have to fall back on 'some form of Gestapo' to implement its welfare and nationalisation programme. Churchill was thrown out of office, and Labour won a huge majority.

The Road to Serfdom claims that socialism inevitably leads to communism, and that communism and Nazi-style fascism are one and the same. The tie that links Stalin's USSR and Hitler's Germany, in Hayek's view, is the centrally planned economy – as he portrays it, the attempt by a single central bureaucracy to direct all human life, to determine all human needs in advance and organise provision, limiting each to their rationed dole and their allotted task. Such a bureaucracy will no more tolerate dissent and deviation than the engineers tending a vast production line will accept a pebble jamming the gears. Confusingly, Hayek denies he is a pure libertarian, and declares the free market must have rules; he also says it is acceptable for government to 'provide an extensive system of social services'. Yet this is in contradiction to his main message, which is that there can be no mixture of state planning and free market competition. To him they are mutually exclusive. 'By the time Hitler came to power, liberalism was dead in Germany,' he writes. 'And it was socialism that had killed it.' Even to *try* to make socialism work, according to Hayek, is dangerous:

> in the democracies the majority of people still believe that socialism and freedom can be combined. They do not realize that democratic socialism, the great utopia of the last few generations, is not only unachievable, but that to strive for it produces something utterly different – the very destruction of freedom itself.

Hayek was proven wrong. As in other western European countries, socialists came and went from power in Britain, introduced a welfare state and took control of large swathes of the economy without democracy and individual freedoms being threatened. The NHS was set up, council houses were built, social security was established, state education was expanded, coal, rail and steel nationalised, yet despite all the planning this required, millions of private businesses, small, medium and large, carried on merrily competing (or co-operating) with each other, flourishing or going to the wall as the market determined. Private doctors kept their clinics on Harley Street, young aristos still ruggered their way across the playing fields of Eton, the private shop windows of Harrods still blazed forth at Christmas time. Bankers and stockbrokers thronged the City, and the farmers owned their land. No one was forced by the government to live in a particular place or do a particular job. Indeed, by abolishing conscription and, albeit rather hypocritically from a male point of view, endorsing greater rights for women, Britain seemed to be coming up with new forms of individual freedom that hadn't occurred to Hayek. There was an argument to be made about how much tax people and businesses paid, and how much of that money government would have been better letting them choose for themselves how to spend. The argument was made, and will always be made; in the end neither the Gestapo, nor the English Hitler, nor the English Politburo appeared, or looked like appearing.

Hayek's work, the work of a frightened refugee in wartime, in the blackouts and shortages of a besieged island, had been superseded by the 1970s. A better framework for understanding the Britain of the time would have been the American Daniel Bell's masterful introduction to his 1976 book *The Cultural Contradictions of Capitalism,* where, though he spoke in general terms, he seemed to capture the actual contemporary problems of the UK:

> A system of state capitalism could easily be transformed into a cor-porate state ... a cumbersome, bureaucratic monstrosity, wrenched in all directions by the clamour for subsidies and entitlements by various corporate and communal groups, yet gorging itself on increased governmental appropriations to become a Leviathan in its own right.

Thatcher, however, never stopped seeing the world through a Hayekian prism. After she defeated the attempt by Britain's coal miners to stave off mass redundancies and pit closures by downing tools, she wrote: 'What the strike's defeat estab-lished was that Britain could not be made ungovernable by the Fascist Left.'

Putting together the words of Walters, Lawson and Thatcher, then, the ostensible aims of the programme to privatise Britain were diverse. Privatised companies, it was said, would be forced to do without subsidies, and wouldn't be bailed out if they ran into trouble. Competing for business and profits with other firms in the marketplace, they'd be forced to cut superfluous workers, invest in new technology and try new ideas. Competition would bring new clarity to the finances and prices of the privatised companies, whose managers, set free from the shackles of political interference and union intransigence, would skip over tired, increasingly socialistic Europe and strut their tigerish entrepreneurial stuff in the wider world. Meanwhile the cuts in subsidies to the privatised firms would mean income tax could be cut, too, so ordinary British people would be better off. No longer would they be subject to the burgeoning control of state central planning, confining them to a faceless bureaucrat's idea of how they should live. They'd select their preferences from the choices in the marketplace – a marketplace whose success they'd have a direct, personal stake in, since millions of them would be shareholders in the privatised firms. 'Privatisation,' wrote Thatcher, 'was one of the central means of reversing the corrosive and corrupting effects of socialism ... the state's power is reduced and the power of the people enhanced ... privatisation is at the centre of any programme of reclaiming territory for freedom.'

About ten years ago, I began to investigate what happened after the early Thatcherite zeal took effect. I looked at four privatised industries, only one of which was completely sold off before Thatcher left office – rail, water, electricity and the Royal Mail – at the biggest privatisation of all, the sale of Britain's council houses, and at an organisation that hasn't been privatised, but has been structured in such a way that it could be, the National Health Service. My curiosity took me to the obscure realm of events that are too fresh for history, but too old for journalism; the murky gap of popular perception that covers the period from two years ago to about twenty-five years back, in which events are well remembered but patterns not easily perceived. It's a period of time long enough for several democratically elected governments of opposing parties to be born and die, yet it's also the shortest period of time in which the long-term effects of the policies of the first of those governments show, and can be seen for what they are.

I was sceptical when I began my inquiries, but I was prepared to be convinced that privatisation in these half-dozen cases had been a success. I learned that it has not been, except, perhaps, in one way – but that way was not touted in advance.

Privatisation failed to turn Britain into a nation of small shareholders. Before Thatcher came to power, almost 40 per cent of the shares in British companies were held by individuals. By 1981, it was less than 30 per cent. By the time she died in 2013, it had slumped to under 12 per cent. What is significant about this is not only that Thatcher and Lawson's vision of a share-holding democracy failed to come to pass through privatisation, but that it undermines the justification for the way the companies were taken out of public ownership. As I saw in the extreme example of the imploding USSR, the problem with big state monopolies is not so much that they're made to serve political ends as that they tend to be captured by their management and workforces, whose loyalties are, in different ways, to the preservation of the power and culture of the institution, in preserving or expanding jobs and winning the maximum financial support from government. There's always cutthroat competition in an economy with a high degree of state ownership, but it's between different branches of industry vying for a share of the government cake, not between different firms chasing the same clients. Having big industries as branches of government isn't necessarily a good way of doing things. Technology does change, and it's hard to justify paying people to do work that doesn't need to be done, unless it is for artistic reasons. Councils no longer employ lamplighters, because there are no lamps to be lit; mainline railways no longer employ firemen, because locomotives have no coal for them to stoke. It's true that the British army still has cavalrymen, even though they can't charge the Taliban on horseback, but a column of Life Guards trotting by in harmless nineteenth-century gear is pleasing to the eye and soul. So is a steel foundry. But it is hard to see how a steel plant employing five thousand could ever have been run on heritage principles. It's quite likely that the big nationalised industries of the 1970s were overmanned; and certainly the unions, quite rationally, were resistant to change that might threaten their members' jobs. There's no doubt that since privatisation the old nationalised industries have sacked colossal numbers of workers and brought in new technology. If efficiency is doing the same job or better with fewer workers, many of the privatised firms are more efficient.

But this simply suggests some or all of the nationalised industries should have been commercialised – that is, had their subsidies shrunk and been removed from direct government control, obliging them to borrow money at commercial rates and operate in a world of market prices without making a loss. Apart from the failed attempt to encourage wider share ownership, there was no obvious reason to privatise them by floating them on the stock market and selling them to shareholders. There are many forms of private ownership. The department store chain John Lewis, an unsubsidised commercial firm in a fiercely competitive market, is owned by its employees. The Nationwide Building Society, an unsubsidised commercial firm in a fiercely competitive market, is owned by its members. The Guardian media group, an unsubsidised commercial firm in a fiercely competitive market, is owned by a trust set up to support its journalistic values and protect it from hostile takeover. And so on. None of the many alternatives to stock market flotation were put up for discussion by either side: it was either shareholder capitalism or the nationalised status quo.

Privatisation failed to demonstrate the case made by the privatisers that private companies are always more competent than state-owned ones – that private bosses, chasing the carrot of bonuses and dodging the stick of bankruptcy, will always do better than their state-employed counterparts. Through euphemisms like 'wealth creation' and 'enjoying the rewards of success'

Thatcher and her allies have promoted the notion that greed on the part of a private executive elite is the chief and sufficient engine of prosperity for all. The result has been thirty-five years of denigration of the concept of duty and public service and a squalid ideal of all work as something that shouldn't be cared about for its own sake, but only for the money it brings. The magic dust of the market was of little use to the bosses of the newly privatised Railtrack in the mid-1990s. They thought they could sack people with impunity – not just signalling and maintenance staff but expert engineers and researchers – and carry out a massive line upgrade cheaply with the most advanced new technology. Unfortunately, as I describe in Chapter 2, the people who could have told them that the new technology didn't exist were the people they'd sacked. As a result, the company went bust in 2002, and had to be renationalised.

Privatisation failed to make firms compete or give customers more choice – said to be the canonical virtues of privatisation. Pretty hard, you'd think, to privatise water companies, when they're all monopolies, with nobody to compete with, and can't offer customers a choice – neither the choice of which supplier to use nor the choice of whether to take a service or not. And yet the English water companies were privatised, and in such a way, as I describe in Chapter 3, that customers have been over-charged ever since. The privatisers loved competition, but the actual privatised competitors hate it. As I show in Chapter 4, the competitive vision of those who designed Britain's electricity privatisation – a rumbustious, referee-supervised free-for-all between sellers and makers of electricity old and new, large and small – has degenerated into an opaque oligopoly of a handful of giant players.

Indeed, the electricity debacle shows how privatisation failed to empower individuals as it was supposed to. It fails to provide the most important thing essential to the functioning of free markets – information. The arcane, incomprehensible pricing systems of the old nationalised electricity industry have been

replaced by the even less comprehensible pricing systems of
the privatised electricity industry. Commercial secrecy is a less
effective protection from public scrutiny for the electricity companies than the tyranny of complexity. When MPs and energy
ministers can't understand how pricing works, what chance do
regular bill payers have of working out the best tariff and the
best supplier, and whether even the cheapest firm is ripping
them off?

Reading Margaret Thatcher's autobiography the impression
grows that she believed the transformational effect of privatisation was such as to turn executives into self-consciously moral,
patriotic, civically minded entrepreneurs like her father; as if a
monopoly on water supply for several million people were a local
grocery shop in a small English town in the 1940s. Privatisation,
she claimed, was 'the greatest shift of ownership and power away
from the state to individuals and their families in any country
outside the former communist bloc.' The reality is that the faceless state bureaucrats of the old electricity boards have been
replaced by the faceless (and better-paid) private bureaucrats
of the electricity companies. Not only are the privatised utilities
big, remote corporations; most of them are no longer British,
and no longer owned by small shareholders. Indeed electricity
and water privatisation could not have failed more absolutely to
foster the emergence of world-beating, innovative British companies. Most of the electricity made and sold in England is now
owned by dynamic, tech-savvy companies from western Europe,
a region doomed, Thatcher thought, by creeping socialism. As
a direct result of the way electricity was privatised, much of it
has now been renationalised – but by France, not Britain. Of the
nine big English water and sewerage firms, six have achieved
the seemingly impossible feat of being privatised a second time,
delisted from the stock market by East Asian conglomerates
or by private equity consortia. Today much of England's water
industry is, it is true, in the hands of individuals and their families, but they don't use English water; they're millions of former

civil servants in Canada, Australia and the Netherlands, investing, unwittingly, through their pension funds.

The National Health Service, which I write about in Chapter 5, is a special case. It hasn't been privatised, and the political parties vie with each other to show that it's safest in their hands. Yet it has been commercialised and repeatedly reorganised, with competition introduced, in such a way as to create a kind of shadowing of an as-yet-unrealised private health insurance system. The story of the transformation of the NHS is part of the wider story of the inheritance of the Thatcher legacy by a Blairite Labour administration over-filled with politicians who struggled to separate their ambitions for Britain from their ambitions for their own and their families' ascent into the six-figure-income class. After their Sisyphean struggles with the Tories and the conservative socialists in their own party, New Labour in power yielded with all too apparent relief to the charms of the business world. It wasn't the creation of foundation trusts for hospitals – or academy schools, or support for housing associations – that was the mistake, rather a lack of awareness that without elaborate safeguards these structures might prove mere waypoints to the next set of privatisations.

What the story of the latter years of the NHS shows is that the most powerful market force eating away at the core of the welfare state is not so much capitalism as consumer capitalism – the convergence of desires between the users of a public service and the private companies providing it when the companies use the skills of marketing to give users a sense of dissatisfaction and peer disadvantage. 'If consumption represents the psychological competition for status,' writes Daniel Bell, 'then one can say that bourgeois society is the institutionalization of envy.' Hip replacement, a procedure invented within the NHS by John Charnley, began as a blessed relief from pain for which patients were, as Charnley said, pathetically grateful. It rapidly progressed to a rationed entitlement. It has now become a competitive market in which a company can design and hard-sell, as a lifestyle choice,

its own, defective variant of an existing artificial hip – an existing hip that does the same job perfectly well.

This points to a difficulty for anti-marketeers. Since 1945,
even if privatisation had never happened, socialism would have
struggled with the move from a world of unsatisfied needs to a
more complex world of unsatisfied wants. Socialism can't unin-
vent artificial hips in order to recreate the benison of going from
a world without hip replacements to a world with. It's the same
with postwar council housing. Having provided all less well-off
Britons with central heating and indoor bathrooms, socialists can't repeat the feat by reinstalling coal fires and back yard
privies and replacing them again. Council housing went from
something that was much better than tenants expected to something much worse than they hoped. The heirs of Adam Smith,
writes Bell,

> assumed that the market was a sufficient arbiter of the public weal;
> there, the differential utilities of individuals and the scarcity of dif-
> ferent goods would come to an equilibrium that harmonised the
> intensity of desires and the willingness to pay the asking price.
> Classical Marxism had an entirely different answer to the problem
> of relative justice in society. It assumed that competition, envy, and
> evil all resulted from scarcity, and that the abundance of goods
> would make such conflicts unnecessary. But what we have come to
> realise is that we will never overcome scarcity. In the post-industrial
> society … there would be new scarcities which nineteenth-century
> utopians could never envision.

The selling off of Britain's municipal housing without replacing it, which I write about in the last section of this book, was
supposed to be a triumphant coming together of the individual
and free market principles. It actually ended up as one of the
most glaring examples of market failure in postwar history. It
wasn't like the other privatisations; its justification as anything
other than an electoral bribe to its relatively well-off beneficiaries
always rang false. It certainly did to Thatcher in the beginning.
She was, she wrote,

wary of alienating the already hard-pressed families who had scrimped to buy a house on one of the new private estates at the market price ... They would, I feared, strongly object to council house tenants who had made none of their sacrifices suddenly receiving what was in effect a large capital sum from the Government.

In the end, she came round, and made the policy her own. But the gap where the economic rationale for privatising council houses should be becomes a window through which it becomes possible to see beyond the individual privatisations to the meta-privatisation, and its one indisputable success: that it put more money into the hands of a small number of the very wealthiest people, at the expense of the elderly, the sick, the jobless and the working poor.

What do we think we know about taxes since the Thatcher revolution? Government spending has been cut, we know that. Income tax is lower than it used to be, we know that. And we might remember that the one time Margaret Thatcher tried to change the principle of progressive taxation, where the amount of tax you pay depends on your income, to a flat fee, where every-one pays the same – when the Conservatives tried to introduce the infamous 'poll tax' on council services – it was the catalyst for her downfall. Low tax was her mantra. Her core political message was this, in her own words: 'I believe the person who is prepared to work hardest should get the greatest rewards and keep them after tax. That we should back the workers and not the shirkers: that it is not only permissible but praiseworthy to want to benefit your own family by your own efforts.'

What we think we know is wrong. Yes, government spend-ing was cut, and, as I write, it is being cut again, by Thatcher's Coalition successors. When the Conservatives came to power in 1979 the top rate of tax was 83 per cent, the basic rate 33. The top rate is now 45 per cent and the basic rate 20 per cent. The message seems clear enough. The Conservatives cut public spending and cut taxes, they kept their promises to working people, and Labour went along with it. But that is not all that happened. At the same time as they cut income tax and public spending, the first Thatcher administration hiked the sales tax, VAT – a flat rate tax far more remorselessly regressive than the poll tax. When they came to power, the main VAT rate was 8 per cent. It is now 20 per cent. And the poorer you are, the harder VAT hits you. A study by the Office of National Statistics in 2010 showed that, for the richest fifth of the population, VAT added an extra 4 per cent to their tax bill. But the poorest fifth, often thought by the better off to pay no tax at all, actually pay 8.7 per cent of their income to the Treasury in VAT. When the Coalition came to power that year, George Osborne raised VAT by 14 per cent.

Where privatisation comes into this is that VAT isn't the only flat-rate tax on the poor. There are others, and they are onerous; they just aren't called taxes, though they should be – private taxes. One of the other ways the Thatcherites tried to balance the books in their first budgets was by hiking the price of gas, electricity and council rents, then all still under state control. After privatisation, above-inflation price rises have continued, in the private sector. A tax is generally thought of as something that only a government can levy, but this is a semantic distortion that favours the free market belief system. If a payment to an authority, public or private, is compulsory, it's a tax. We can't do without electricity; the electricity bill is an electricity tax. We can't do without water; the water bill is a water tax. Some people can get by without railways, and some can't; they pay the rail tax. Students pay the university tax. The meta-privatisation is the privatisation of the tax system itself; even, it could be said, the privatisation of us, the former citizens of Britain. By packaging British citizens up and selling them, sector by sector, to investors, the government makes it possible to keep traditional taxes low or even cut them. By moving from a system where public services are supported by progressive general taxation to a system where they are supported exclusively by the flat fees people pay to use them, they move from a system where the rich are obliged to help the poor to a system where the less well-off enable services that the rich get for what is, to them, a trifling sum. The commodity that makes water and power cables and airports valuable to an investor, foreign or otherwise, is the people who have no choice but to use them. We have no choice but to pay the price the toll-keepers charge. We are human revenue stream; we are being made tenants in our own land, defined by the string of private fees we pay to exist here.

It is not racism that makes the foreign identity of some of the owners of our privatised infrastructure objectionable. It's the selling of taxation powers to foreign governments over whom we have even less democratic control than our own. It is the hypocrisy, in particular, of a party that claims to loathe nothing more than communism and totalitarianism obliging Londoners to pay a tithe to the Chinese government just for turning on the tap; of a party that claims it wants to free Britain from European interference obliging all of us to pay a levy to the French government in order to fund construction of experimental nuclear reactors in Somerset.

The shift of taxation from the rich to the middle class and low paid is reflected in the reverse of the long trend of growing income equality between the wealthy and the less well off. In 1937 the share of national income earned by the richest 1 per cent of Britons, after tax, was 12.57 per cent. This fell steadily until by the eve of Thatcher's coming to power it wasn't much over 4 per cent. It then began to climb steeply. By 2007, it was back to where it had been sixty years earlier – 12.57 per cent.

Beset by high VAT and an array of private taxes their parents didn't have to cope with, the low-paid are being squeezed by their employers, too. The story of the Royal Mail, leading up to its privatisation in 2013, is sometimes portrayed as if it were a textbook case of one new technology (the Internet) destroying an old-fashioned state monopoly while an obstructive trades union blocks the other new technology that might have saved it (new sorting equipment). In fact, as I show in the opening chapter, the Royal Mail is the last in a sequence of trans-European privatisations that is likely to end with the work of a traditional British postman, on the face of it an honourable enough job that ought to draw decent pay, being recategorised as a minimum wage, breadline or pocket money occupation. To see how, I travelled across the North Sea.

1. In the Sorting Office

Privatised mail

Somewhere in the Netherlands a postwoman was in trouble. Bad health, snow and ice and a degree of chaos in her personal life had left her months behind on her deliveries. She rented a privatised ex-council flat with her partner and so many crates of mail had built up in the hallway that it was getting hard to move around. Twice a week one of the private mail companies she worked for, Selektmail, dropped off three or four crates of letters, magazines and catalogues. She sorted and delivered the fresh crates but the winter backlog was tough to clear. She thought her employers were getting suspicious. I counted sixty-two full mail crates stacked up in the hall when I visited. There was a narrow passageway between the wall of crates and her personal pile of stuff: banana boxes, a disused bead curtain, a mop bucket. One of the crates had crept into the study, where the postwoman's computer reared up out of her own archival heaps of newspapers and magazines. Were those two streams of paper to merge they would not have been easily separated. The postwoman hadn't given up. She'd had a similar problem with the other private mail company she worked for, Sandd, a few years earlier. 'When I began at Sandd in 2006 I delivered about fourteen boxes of mail every time,' she said. 'I couldn't cope and at Christmas 2006 I had about ninety of these boxes in the house. By New Year's

[handwritten margin notes: "universal service obligation", "physical delivery is suffering", "privatization → more mail, lower wages", "↑ profits from delivery ↑", "most available pay ↓ → smaller wages", "made it difficult for delivery people"]

Day we had ninety-seven. There were even boxes in the toilet.' The postwoman was paid a pittance to deliver corporate mail. She hadn't done her job well, yet so few people had complained about missed deliveries that she hadn't been found out.

Across the world, postal services are being altered like this: optimised to deliver the maximum amount of unwanted mail at the minimum cost to businesses. In the Internet age private citizens are sending less mail than they used to, but that's only part of the story of postal decline. The price of driving down the cost of bulk mailing for a handful of big organisations is being paid for by the replacement of decently paid postmen with casual labour and the erosion of daily deliveries.

I agreed not to name the Dutch postwoman or to give away any detail that would identify her. Even if she hadn't been sitting on months of undelivered mail Sandd or Selekt could have sacked her in a heartbeat. She worked, she reckons, about thirty hours a week for the two companies, earning about five euros an hour, although the legal minimum wage in the Netherlands is between eight and nine euros an hour. She had no contract. She got no sick pay, no pension and no health insurance. One of the companies gave her a dribble of holiday pay. Selekt gave her a jacket and a sweatshirt but she got no other clothing or footwear and had to pay to maintain her own bike. The company was able to offer such miserable conditions because of loopholes in Dutch employment law. The postwoman was paid a few cents for each item of mail she delivered. The private mail firms controlled their delivery people's daily postbag to make sure they never earned more than €580 a month, the level at which the firms were obliged to give them a fixed contract. Somehow Selekt hadn't noticed it was getting fewer empty crates back than it sent full crates out. When I followed the postwoman to the kitchen, I saw, like some recurring nightmare, twenty more crates filled with letters.

Selekt's crates were yellow and stamped with the black hunting horn logo of Deutsche Post, the former German state mail monopoly that, like its Dutch counterpart, was privatised long ago. For years the two had been locked in a struggle for business on the streets of the Netherlands, part of a fratricidal postal war across northern Europe into which Britain's newly privatised Royal Mail has been drawn. Privatising old state post companies doesn't necessarily make it easier for rivals to compete with them. Privatisation isn't the same as liberalisation. But in Holland privatisation and liberalisation combined have altered the post in a way far beyond anything Britain has so far seen.

At the time I visited the Netherlands, Dutch households and businesses were visited by postmen and postwomen from four different companies each week. There were the 'orange' postmen of the privatised Dutch mail company, trading as TNT Post but about to change its name to PostNL; the 'blue' postmen of Sandd, a private Dutch firm; the 'yellow' postmen of Selekt, owned by Deutsche Post/DHL; and the 'half-orange' postmen of Netwerk VSP, set up by TNT to compete cannibalistically against itself by using casual labour that is cheaper than its own (unionised) workforce. TNT delivered six days a week, Sandd and Selekt two, and VSP one. From the point of view of an ardent free marketeer, it sounded like healthy competition. Curiously, however, none of the competitors was prospering. TNT was being forced by the hedge funds and other transnational shareholders who controlled its destiny to split up, even as it tried to beautify its bottom line by replacing reasonably paid jobs with badly paid ones. Deutsche Post was pulling out of the Netherlands and selling Selekt to Sandd – a company that had never made a profit.

Sandd, set up by a group of ex-TNT managers, pioneered the distinctive Dutch style of private mail delivery. 'Sandd' stands for 'Sort and deliver'. In Britain, as in many other countries with big postal networks, private companies can now collect and sort mail, but delivery, the so-called 'final mile' of a letter's journey, has remained until very recently a Royal Mail monopoly. Mail is delivered from distribution centres to local delivery offices, where salaried Royal Mail postal workers sort it into individual rounds and deliver it by van, bike and on foot. Under the Sandd system, crates of mail are delivered to casual workers' houses. These workers sort the mail, on whatever flat surface they can find, then deliver it on set days at a time of their choosing. Besides slashing the mail companies' overheads, the system has the advantage, from the management's point of view, that there is little danger of the postmen and postwomen meeting each other to swap grievances or talk about joining a union.

I watched the postwoman sorting mail in her kitchen, dividing it up into piles on the steel counter on either side of the sink, carefully dried after the evening's washing-up. It seemed to be mainly Ikea catalogues, the cover showing an exquisitely lit arrangement of blond, cheerful furniture. The Ikea ideal did not include any obvious area for the sorting of mail. As the greasy slap of the catalogues' plastic covers hitting the counter became monotonous, my eye kept being drawn to a row of Smurfs balanced on the copper pipe above the sink. They were covered in a thick layer of black dust. The postwoman knew things were not going well. In an anguished email she sent me after my visit, she wrote: 'Many tears are dropping.'

Another private postman, Joris Leijten, who quit Sandd a few months earlier, told me he used to sort mail on his bed. In a café among the grand villas of Bussum, near Hilversum, he handed me the flyer that Sandd put through his door after he resigned, advertising his job: a picture of four smiling white people in Sandd blue, striding down the road with light sheaves of paper, grinning. 'Keep busy outdoors, in charge of your own time,' it read. 'Ideal for students, housewives and pensioners.' He showed me a day's work from just after Christmas: three rounds, sorting and delivering 323 pieces of mail, weighing a total of 81.4 kilograms, to 279 addresses. Sandd claimed this should take six hours; Leijten said it took eight. For this he was paid a little over twenty-seven euros – not much more than three euros an hour.

Sandd promotes the job as a 'bijbaan', a bit of work on the side for somebody who wants fresh air and exercise and already has a state pension, is studying or has a salaried husband. But Leijten, thirty-two and unable to get the museum job he's trained for, is not alone in relying on several poorly paid bijbaans for his livelihood. I asked whether Sandd had given him anything besides eight cents a letter. Normally, he said, workers had to pay for their uniforms out of their wages. But the company also hands out 'points' every so often, which can be redeemed against a blue Sandd jacket.

In the Netherlands, as in Britain, the postal market has been liberalised in the name of the consumer, as Europe's former citizens are now known: competition, it is said, will benefit everybody. But competition, as Leijten noted, only really exists for large organisations. Private citizens can't post letters in Sandd or Selekt mailboxes. There aren't any. Ordinary Dutch people still had to pay forty-six cents to send a PostNL letter. The Dutch government, meanwhile, had negotiated a deal with Sandd to deliver some of its mail at eleven cents a pop. 'For ordinary people, there's no choice, there's only TNT,' Leijten said. 'The postal system is sick.'

On the eve of my journey to Holland, David Simpson, the earnest Ulsterman who was Royal Mail's chief spokesman, took me to one of the facilities the company is most proud of, the Gatwick mail centre in Sussex. Despite its name, it has nothing to do with the nearby airport. It's a giant mail processing plant, built in 1999, that sucks in and shoots out every letter, packet and small parcel posted from or sent to every address in six hundred square miles of England, from the M25 down to the south coast, from Eastbourne in the east to Littlehampton at the westernmost edge of the county. They sort two and a half million items a day.

Michael Fehilly, Gatwick's manager, strode around in a grey pinstripe suit, brown loafers and an open-necked pink shirt. He's second-generation Irish. 'My dad tells me I'm a plastic Paddy, not a real one,' he said. He grew up on a council estate in Peckham and joined the Post Office as an apprentice postman in 1987, aged seventeen. He hated the early starts and was ready to quit after a few months. Instead they made him a trainee manager. Twenty-four years later he is a company star. Under Fehilly, Gatwick has embraced the philosophy of the Japanese management consultant Hajime Yamashina, which Royal Mail is trying to propel throughout the company. Yamashina visits Gatwick all the time. He was at the mail centre on the day the earthquake and tsunami struck his homeland. Fehilly's eyes shone as he preached the Yamashina way. It starts with safety. All over the mail centre there are cute cartoons of an animal in a white coat and glasses: the Safety Mole. ' "Don't be safety blinded, be safety minded," ' Fehilly said. 'When I started the programme I could guarantee twenty-eight accidents a year – a knock, a bump or a bruise. Last year we had zero accidents.'

The vast industrial space, made of breeze blocks and galvanised steel and filled with trolleys and sorting machinery, is neat and clean, enabling Fehilly to practise his kaizen powers of vision. He stopped suddenly and pointed to a bit of floor that looked spotless to me. 'I can see three rubber bands and a label,' he said. 'That's a defect to me now. Five years ago I would just have accepted that. Now my eyes have improved, that's a defect to me.' Fehilly has worked with the staff to find solutions to problems they didn't know were problems. The Gatwick workforce saved a million pounds a year just by hiring an electric truck to replace the laborious heaving of mail trolleys from one side of the plant to the other. They discovered that certain electric conveyor belts were slowing down the people who worked on them and invented a simple, unpowered device that let gravity do the work instead. They found that, for more than a century, nobody had questioned the number of pigeonholes in the frames that mail sorters use to sort letters by region. Why were there fifty-six? Because there'd always been fifty-six. It turned out that entire man-years of pain and muscle strain, not to mention wasted time, could be saved just by reducing the number of pigeonholes to fifteen and cutting openings at the back as well as the front.

Yet even with such ingenuity and co-operation, even with the closure of post offices and mail centres and the whittling down of the company workforce from 230,000 to 165,000 in nine years, even at relative peace with the union, even earning £9 billion a year, the Royal Mail was struggling, competing for a shrinking quantity of mail with aggressive competitors, first among them Holland's TNT.* Unlike its competitors, it was – and is – obliged to hand-deliver to every home and business in the country, from Lerwick to Penzance, six days a week. It couldn't make more money without modernising faster, and it couldn't modernise faster without more money. Hence the main official justification for privatisation, a familiar one – that a private Royal Mail would be able to borrow money for itself, privately, whereas a publicly-owned Royal Mail couldn't be allowed to borrow and add to the government's debt.

I wondered what Fehilly thought of the Sandd system, and told him I was on my way to the Netherlands to see how their private postmen operated. Fehilly didn't see why it couldn't work in Britain. 'We can prepare the mail for delivery,' he said. 'We can go and deliver a sack of mail to some mother's house who's just dropped her kids at school, she can spend two or three hours delivering mail in her area – it's a model we're aware of and would like to use. We're stuck with a large workforce … [the Dutch model] is a model we've spoken of and would like to do in the future.'

I sensed Simpson, standing at my shoulder, prickling nervously. 'We'd certainly have to agree that with the unions,' he said.

'Of course, yes. But why not?' Fehilly persisted. 'I'd say, in the future, why not look at these models if they're more efficient?'

It's not easy to understand what happened to turn the Netherlands into a test bed for a private postal service. In privatising

---

* Now rebranded as Whistl in Britain, it is a subsidiary of PostNL, which split off from TNT.

their own royal mail the Dutch, who for some reason have an image in Britain and America as vaguely hippyish lefty liberals, went one step further than Margaret Thatcher ever did. The Dutch establishment weaves a subtle web of complicity and patronage that binds its members together over generations, discouraging discussion of the past with outsiders. Ruud Lubbers, who as prime minister from 1982 to 1994 led the free-market charge, declined my interview request. Neelie Kroes, who pushed through the privatisation of the Dutch post office under Lubbers in 1989, had the excuse that she is a European commissioner.

One morning I went in search of the last left-winger to run the Dutch mail, Michel van Hulten, who had the post office in his portfolio until 1977 in the government of Joop den Uyl. I boarded one of the yellow double-decker trains that tick across the Dutch countryside and set out for van Hulten's home in the town of Lelystad. At some point a change in the light made me look up from my book. The landscape had altered. To the right of the train was a flat plain dotted with rows of boxy houses. There was something raw and fresh about the land, like some stretch of the American prairie that had only just been settled by Europeans, and something strangely familiar about the low-rise, flat-roofed, cuboid form of the houses, even the way they were spaced: it looked like Milton Keynes.

To the left, towards the sea, the view was disorientatingly different. It reminded me of an illustration in a book I had as a child of how the north European plain would have looked at the end of the Pleistocene era. Under a grey sky, the flatlands stretched off towards the bright horizon, dotted with isolated trees, bent over by the prevailing wind, like some Friesian veldt. The spring grass, sprouting bright green out of the cold soil, was being cropped by huge herds of deer, shaggy, long-horned kine and wild ponies. It was a primeval scene, a few minutes northeast of Amsterdam; only the mammoths were missing.

This, as van Hulten explained to me in the kitchen of his Lelystad bungalow, was Flevoland. It's artificial, the result of perhaps the most grandiose act of intervention in nature by a twentieth-century government: the creation of new land out of the sea in the form of two great polders, together about the size of South Yorkshire. The kitchen where we sat eating toast and cheese and drinking coffee was, when van Hulten was born in the Dutch East Indies in 1930, several metres under the salt water of the Zuiderzee. The deer, ponies and cattle I saw had been imported and left to run wild in a nature reserve, the Oostvaardersplassen. And Milton Keynes? 'The English new towns were an inspiration for us,' van Hulten said, and he smiled at me kindly as though I were a long-lost relative. He was one of the architects of Flevoland, and one of its early inhabitants. He and his wife were among the first four hundred settlers of this new world in 1972, as his brief political career began. The virgin lands he helped to create are a memorial to the era of government intervention, of belief that the state had the power, the right and the duty to make a better world for its citizens. The building of the dam across the Zuiderzee began as a Great Depression work programme, and the appearance of the polders above the waves coincided with the high-water mark of progressive socialist optimism in the 1960s and 1970s.

'In the beginning, the state did everything,' van Hulten said. 'It was a state enterprise and fully paid from the state budget. When you needed money no one in the Hague was interested why: you got it.' Marxist and New Testament ideas mingled in van Hulten and the spirit of Paris was palpable in Holland in 1968, when the non-aligned group he was one of the leaders of, the Christian Radicals, became a political party, the Political Party of Radicals or PPR. A series of accidents led to his getting a seat in parliament and in 1973 he found himself, to his surprise, the minister for transport in a left-leaning coalition government, responsible for, among other things, the Dutch post office.

In the 1970s the Dutch, like the British, experienced high inflation, rapid industrial decline, strikes, a vague sense of national failure and a reaction against the dirigiste, technocratic governments that built new towns or summoned a Flevoland out of the sea. Locked in a fractious coalition cabinet where the prime minister's trump card was his ability to stay awake in late-night meetings longer than any of his quarrelling ministers, van Hulten saw the growing ideological polarisation of Dutch politics, but didn't realise that the same intellectual currents driving Thatcherite and Reaganite thinkers were at work in the Netherlands. When he took charge of the Dutch post office, it was losing money. His solution was straightforward: he doubled the price of stamps. He still sounds surprised that he was attacked for it from the opposition benches by Neelie Kroes, who accused him of hurting business. His idealism brought him up against the rightist finance minister, Wim Duisenberg, over the post office bank.

'It was one of the richest banks in the Netherlands, 100 per cent owned by the Dutch people,' van Hulten said. 'It was my opinion that we should use the money for social purposes … That was a fight I lost. Duisenberg already favoured making the post bank independent of the post office. I did not understand this at the time as a move to privatisation.' Van Hulten left government and parliament after the 1977 election. His successor, Kroes, set about preparing the ground for the privatisation of the Dutch post office. Not long afterwards, a curious sequence of Nazi-related scandals felled Lubbers's Christian Democrat rivals – one of them, the ex-postal worker Wim Aantjes, forgot to tell anyone that he had joined the SS during the war in order to get out of forced labour as a postman in Nazi Germany – and Lubbers became prime minister, pushing through postal privatisation with Kroes in 1989. Seven years later the privatised company bought the Australian parcels company TNT and took its name.

Van Hulten, now in his eighties, is still an activist, an idealist. The privatisation of the mail depressed him; the latest privatisation, of Holland's local transport networks, made him angry: the three bus companies supposedly competing in Lelystad, he said, were all owned by the same French firm. 'Today's Wednesday, yeah?' he said. 'On Wednesday, we have at least six people coming to the door, all bringing some mail. First was the local paper. Then the other local paper. Then the postman comes. Three more will come later. I think that's the basic defect of post office privatisation. What used to be done by one man is now done by six. They're all underpaid, and the delivery hasn't improved. It used to come in the morning, and now I'm still waiting.'

When the Dutch post office was privatised in 1989, there were reasons to think Lubbers and Kroes had done the organisation a favour. For all their belief in the virtues of the free market, the Dutch were evidently guided by a patriotic sense of national interest when it came to their royal mail. Where Britain sold off the shiniest part of the old Post Office, the telecoms part, as British Telecom in 1984, leaving the mail to fend for itself, the Dutch kept the mail and phones together until 1998, making the company stronger. From 1986 to 1996, when postal services in both countries were making money, the Conservative government borrowed almost all Royal Mail's profits – £1.25 billion – to fill the holes in Britain's budget, while the Dutch post office kept its profits and used them to modernise and to buy TNT. In the late 1990s, when email and the Internet began to destroy paper mail and new European rules exposing the old postal services to competition loomed, the Dutch were in the stronger position. In 2000, TNT had become so powerful relative to Royal Mail that the Blair government held secret talks about merging the British postal service with, or selling it to, its Dutch rival.

That deal fell through. But the regime put in place by New Labour in 2000 to expose Royal Mail to competition had a curious effect. Whereas other European countries, like the Netherlands and Germany, protected their old postal firms by giving them complete commercial freedom long before they had to compete with rivals – privatisation first, to prepare for liberalisation – Britain did it the other way round: liberalisation first, privatisation later. What this meant was that Britain's rules for who could deliver what mail, and for how much – rules that were supposed to protect plucky, nimble entrepreneurs from the pampered monopolistic dinosaur that was Royal Mail – were of most benefit to the only marginally less pampered private monopolies of the Continent. By trying to prevent the small mammals of the postal world getting squashed by the Royal Mail brontosaurus, Labour and their advisers exposed Royal Mail to the raptors of TNT and Deutsche Post, aka DHL.

I asked Martin Stanley, the former civil servant Labour put in charge of exposing Royal Mail to competition from 2000 to 2004, why Britain did it before everyone else in Europe. 'Unilateral disarmament,' he said. 'If we hadn't disarmed first, it would have taken Western Europe much longer to do it. Deutsche Post and TNT didn't face serious competition in their home countries. They were portrayed as these great privatised companies but they were not competing in the bulk mail business, they were simply making huge profits. British policy was, if we don't open up, nobody will.'

Then surely, I said, letting other countries' monopolies take market share from a British monopoly, when the British monopoly couldn't do the same in Holland or Germany, wasn't fair competition?

'I don't think we could have said we have a UK competitor but not a German one,' Stanley replied. 'What really matters is that mail is posted, collected, sorted, transported and delivered by British people: always has been, always will be. Ownership of the company is irrelevant. If we hadn't come along and woken up Royal Mail in the way we did, Royal Mail would now be a horrible basket case.'

Except that a horrible basket case is exactly what Royal Mail did become, according to Richard Hooper, whose successive reports on the organisation – the first appeared in 2008 – gave the government its case for selling the company off. 'Without serious action,' Hooper warned, 'Royal Mail will not survive in its current form and a reduction in the scope and quality of the much loved universal postal service will become inevitable.'

One day in 1979, a British postal functionary settled down to write a five-page instruction called 'Trap Doors in Postal Buildings'. He listed five kinds of permissible trap door. A trap door in category B 'should be strong enough to carry the weight of a man who accidentally steps on the trap door. It must carry a label on self-adhesive vinyl, black on yellow, measuring 250 by 200 mm, saying DO NOT STAND ON THIS TRAP DOOR.' Who was this far-off bureaucrat? Did a superior send him a memo telling him that there was need for a fresh trap-door instruction? Why? Were they constructing postal buildings in 1979, or postal castles? Was the anonymous official, perhaps, the same person who wrote instruction N02F0024, 'Vocabulary of Grey Uniform with Corresponding Outer Clothing', or declared in instruction K07B0400, 'Clocks', that 'Clocks should be provided in cloakrooms that serve more than 50 persons, but not in corridors'?

In the research department of the Communication Workers Union in Wimbledon, whole yards of shelving are taken up by red folders itemising the postal rites of the past, an encyclopedia of forgotten modalities for any postal occasion. 'When I joined,' said John Colbert, now the CWU's communications and campaigns manager, 'you were in a classroom for two months, learning all the different acronyms. There was a postal instruction for everything. What every label meant. At the end of it you had a sorting test. If you passed, you became a Substantive Postman. They don't do none of that no more.'

People have changed. One-time Substantive Postman Colbert, who led a Militant cell in Milton Keynes in the 1980s, talked to me cheerfully about the union hiring a lobbyist who used to work for William Hague, Philip Snape, to press its anti-privatisation case with the coalition. Context has changed too. Even as the old empire of Britain's postal bureaucrats began to

crumble with the split-off of British Telecom under Margaret
Thatcher in 1981, a greater threat to traditional mail was forming.
By 1982, a hundred thousand executives in the US were wired
into a fad called 'electronic mail'. The office system consultants
Urwick Nexos were scornful of this frivolous innovation. 'Who
wants to replace a diary by a thousand pound terminal and have
to learn to type in the process?' a consultant sneered. 'What is
wrong with a memo? About 90 per cent of letters are delivered
next day and that is fast enough for most requirements. If you
want to send an urgent telex you can always go to the telex room
with a handwritten note.' By 1985, the word 'email', initially
spelled with a hyphen, began to replace 'electronic mail'. The US
firm MCI offered a transatlantic service to its American clients.
It only took a minute for the sender's email to flash to MCI's
state-of-the-art receiving centre in Brussels, where it would be
lovingly printed out and hand-carried to its destination by a
Belgian postman.

And then everybody learned to type. Before I started
researching the mails, I thought about trying to set up interviews by post. I didn't think about it very long. I sent no letters,
and received none. I phoned, emailed, texted, Skyped, Vibered,
Gmail chatted and Googled. By Easter, I'd only just used the last
of my Christmas stamps. I sent a card to a friend to thank her
for dinner and she emailed back to thank me for my thank you.
The morning I wrote this, my post consisted of a bank statement
and a credit card statement (which, as my bank keeps telling
me – 'Go paperless!' – I don't need), and a card from Ed Miliband
urging me to go online to tell him my priorities for moving
Britain forward.

Just after the turn of the millennium the growth in the
amount of mail being sent became decoupled from the peaks
and troughs of economic growth. The economy boomed, but the
rate of increase in paper mail fell as email, text messages, web
chat and the Internet in general erased old paper trails. In 2005,
the letters market went into absolute decline, and has fallen ever

since. By 2015, according to the Hooper reports, letter volumes are likely to decline by another 25 to 40 per cent.

Technological shifts are nothing new. In the late eighteenth century, new media meant horse-drawn mail coaches flashing information up and down the country, in the form of newspapers, at the blinding speed of six and a half miles an hour. Fifty years later, the railways came along, and, presumably, a lot of disgruntled mail-coach drivers found themselves looking for alternative employment. What is different this time is that text has broken free of the requirement for it to take material form, and for a human hand, at some point, to feel its weight.

There aren't many large factories in the heart of London. Perhaps Mount Pleasant, hunched battleship-grey on a street corner in Clerkenwell, is the last. When I went there recently more than 1,700 people were employed in this decrepit postal Gormenghast, breathing the ancient institutional smell of its stairwells, treading the worn parquet flooring and flicking paper into dark pigeonholes to the cacophony of clashing music stations. If any postal building had trap doors, surely it was this one.

When in 1889 the Post Office took over the debtors' prison that stood on the site, it didn't demolish the whole jail at once, but edged in beside it, like an impecunious lodger renting half a bed. The building was flooded in a wartime air raid, gutted by one fire after another, then burned out again in 1954. Far beneath it lies the derelict central station of the Royal Mail's defunct underground railway. Some of the mail centre's machinery is twenty-five years old. They used to have twelve letter-sorting machines; now they have eleven and use the twelfth for parts. Mount Pleasant is the Royal Mail's favourite 'before modernisation' exhibit to Gatwick's 'after'. 'I've been here eight years,' said Richard Attoe, the manager who showed me round with David Simpson, 'and it's never had a lick of paint.'

All this is changing. Mount Pleasant is the chosen one: the last mail centre to remain standing in inner London after the South London operation, in Nine Elms, and the East London one, in Bromley-by-Bow, went dark in 2012. The reason they didn't get the same £32 million renovation as Mount Pleasant, Royal Mail said, is that there wasn't enough for them to do. In 2006, London posted 861 million pieces of mail. By 2014, Royal Mail predicts, that will have fallen to 335 million. Across the country a score of mail centres have been or will be shut, including Liverpool, Bolton, Hull, Oxford and Milton Keynes.

On the evening I visited Mount Pleasant, an entire floor had already been cleared, ready for new machinery, Hajime Yamashina and the Safety Mole. While the makeover proceeded, the mail didn't stop. The depot workforce was sorting a flood of census forms and handling two million trade union ballot papers without breaking sweat. Some new machinery had already arrived. One enormous contraption, like a Marcel Duchamp–Philippe Starck collaboration, did nothing but sort A4 envelopes. 'This machine is about five years old. It replaced about 120 postmen. It's an excellent bit of kit,' Attoe said. 'When we get the census forms through, it just bangs them out.'

Simpson gazed through a window into the guts of a machine where endless missives danced hypnotically. 'When you look at it you get a feel of Britain as a nation,' he said. 'There's something unifying about it.'

Besides its huge mail centre operation, Mount Pleasant has a delivery office. It is, in effect, the City of London's mailroom, delivering to all the EC postcodes. One morning I joined a postwoman, Denise Goldfinch, on her round. Postal workers call them 'walks'. As I walked towards the green plastic gills of her sorting frame, her colleagues began to bark like dogs: a postal worker called Prince had just entered the room.

Goldfinch was a petite woman in a sky-blue Royal Mail blouse, with a henna bob and gold hoop earrings. She'd got up at ten to five and caught the 63 bus from Waterloo to start her six a.m.

shift. Her son is BA cabin crew; her husband is a driver. When I met her it was not long after nine and she was sorting her mail down into individual addresses, wrapping them in bundles with red rubber bands, ready to go in her pouch. She had three lots of mail that day. While she was delivering the first batch, a van would be dropping two more bags off at 'safe drops' where she'd pick them up later.

One of the things you realise when you see a postwoman prepping the mail is how much time she has to spend dealing with the global public's incompetence. Goldfinch had more than a hundred undeliverable letters. A single legal firm in New Jersey had sent a dozen to a non-existent company on her walk. Goldfinch had to put a sticker on each one and tick a box explaining why it couldn't be delivered. She went to weigh her first load: it came in at 9.7 kilograms; the maximum is supposed to be 16. 'What it is, because in the Royal Mail everything's done on seniority, because I've got twenty-five years, this is what we'd call a good walk,' she said, meaning it was relatively light. She reckoned it would take her two hours. She skipped her morning break, and we left Mount Pleasant at ten; she'd be finished by noon.

I carried Goldfinch's bag, and we stepped through the turnstile into the spring sunshine of Farringdon Road. It was like being in a promotional film designed to show how wonderful it is to be a postwoman. The leaves were coming out, the air was mild, and old ladies greeted Goldfinch by name, as if they had been looking forward to seeing her, as if they were lonely and might not see anyone else that day. We rang the doorbell at a flat to get a householder to sign for something and after a long delay he came to the door. He looked wan but pleased. 'Sorry about the wait, I'm recovering from a stomach bug,' he said. 'How are you?'

'I'm well, thank you.'

'Nice to see you.' And we moved on to the flower shop. Perhaps the sickly addressee lived alone; a third of British households

have only one member. As long as there is post, at least one
human being comes to the door with something for you.

The sun doesn't always shine on postwomen. It snows. It rains.
Dogs bite (it happened to Goldfinch once). There are stairs to
climb – hundreds, if you work in Edinburgh or Glasgow – and
hills and muddy paths. Most postmen don't get to step straight
out of their delivery offices and into their walk, as Goldfinch does.
And most walks last longer than two hours. Lower-level union
officials and individual postmen complain that Royal Mail is fid-
dling the figures and mail volume is going up, not down; that
the software used to calculate optimum routes for walks doesn't
take reality into account; that postmen are getting ever larger
loads and being bullied into doing ever longer walks. In a barbed
inter-postman discussion on the bulletin board royalmailchat,
postmen talk of daily loads from 120 kg (heavy) to 25 kg (light),
though a postman who claims to have weighed a load of 130 kg
is regarded with scepticism.* On another thread, a part-timer
asks whether other postmen think it is possible for him to walk
eight and a half miles on his round in two and three-quarter
hours, as he is expected to do. The consensus is that it isn't.

'If a postman says to me, "Don't tell me about falling mail
volumes, I'm carrying more than ever," a lot of the time he'll be
correct,' Simpson said. 'But the round is designed to take three
and a half hours, with the last letter delivered at the end of the
round, not the way it would have been five or ten years ago, an
hour after the round started. I think most postmen are working
harder and being paid the same ... They've been used to working
80 per cent of their time, but now they're working 100 per cent.'
Working 100 per cent, as those who have tried it know, involves
shooting for 90 per cent and ending up with 110. The more
precisely Royal Mail management tries to make the mailbag fit
the time and distance allotted, the more likely it is that some

---

* As noted with Goldfinch, postmen and women aren't expected to carry
the entire weight at one time – bags are staged at drop-off points along the
route.

postmen will be pressured into carrying too much too far. Times are tougher for Britain's postmen. But in the opinion of Royal Mail's competitors, not tough enough.

Pre-privatisation, a typical Royal Mail postman outside London earned about £375 before tax – just shy of £20,000 a year – for a forty-hour week, with diminishing prospects for overtime. 'That's a lot of money in current terms,' said Guy Buswell, the chief executive of UK Mail, Royal Mail's only big British-based competitor. 'My drivers who deliver parcels have to struggle to get £300 in their pay packets before tax and they work a lot longer hours than postmen do.' Denise Goldfinch was not only better paid than the private postmen of Sandd and Selekt in the Netherlands: she got five weeks a year paid holiday for long service. She got a uniform and service footwear provided free. In the savage ice and snow of 2010–11, she was given spikes for her shoes. When she retires, it will be with a decent pension.

But it is the Dutch model that competition is pushing the Royal Mail towards. The real battle for postal workers and their sympathisers is not so much to save the jobs that are doomed to fade away ('60,000 people since 2002 is nothing!' Buswell snorted when I mentioned how far Royal Mail had already slimmed down), as to prevent the degradation of the jobs that remain: to prevent the job of postman from becoming something like a child's paper round. 'In real terms, now, "postman" should be a part-time job,' Buswell said. 'If you look at the cost of sorting by hand it's about 2p a letter; by machine, it's 0.1p a letter. Unfortunately that's the way it's going to go. The actual job the postman does in the near future is just delivering. They will deliver for four or five hours and that's done.'

I got a pretty clear line when I phoned Muck, but I had to call my contacts on the island several times while lambs and grandchildren were dealt with. Muck only gets mail four times a week, and I wondered if they minded. 'It seems very reasonable,' said

Lawrence MacEwen, whose family owns the island. 'I would even be quite happy if we had less. About three times a week is probably plenty.'

According to law, the Royal Mail must empty each of Britain's 115,000 postboxes and deliver any letter to any of Britain's 28 million addresses, six days a week, at the same, affordable price, wherever the letter is posted and wherever it's going. The rule's the same for parcels, except with them it's only five days a week. This is the universal service obligation, the USO – 'part of our economic and social glue', as Richard Hooper put it in the reports that framed the debate over Royal Mail privatisation.

There have always been a few exceptions. Muck, a Scottish island two and a half miles long to the south of Skye, is one. There are twelve households on Muck and they get mail when and if the ferry arrives from Mallaig. 'Obviously we are very expensive to the Royal Mail to deliver to,' MacEwen said. Bad weather can cut the ferries down to one a week in winter. There have also been times when the MacEwens put a first-class letter on the early ferry and it reached London the next morning. But Muck now has a satellite dish for broadband Internet. You can even catch a mobile signal in some parts of the island. 'Nowadays email's so important for communication that the post is getting less and less important,' MacEwen said. 'I'm afraid the Royal Mail's in a losing battle.'

If the battle is about keeping the USO – and that is the way Hooper put it – it is underway. At the other end of the British archipelago from Muck, the postal service on Jersey, where Anthony Trollope carried out the first trials of pillar boxes in 1852, announced in 2011 that it was abandoning Saturday deliveries in an attempt to staunch the flow of red on its balance sheet. Five days a week is the current Europe-wide minimum for the USO, according to the most recent postal directive from Brussels. But the then TNT lobbied hard to get that minimum reduced. In 2010 Pieter Kunz, then head of TNT's European mail operations, described the USO as 'a kind of Jurassic Park, and we should get rid of it.' It is easy to imagine, a few years from now, the right-wing British media blaming Eurocrats for cutting the number of weekly deliveries – 'BRUSSELS SOUNDS LAST POST FOR DAILY MAIL' – and the private Royal Mail, with quiet relief, following the Dutch lead. 'If TNT has its way, five days would be reduced to three,' said John Baldwin, the CWU's head of international affairs. 'TNT is the bogeyman of the postal industry but they are not alone. Royal Mail, frankly, isn't going to argue if it's going to be released from the five-day obligation.'

Richard Hooper's first report recommending part-privatisation of the Royal Mail was produced for Labour in 2008; the second, endorsing a sale or flotation, for the Con-Dem coalition in 2010. Both said modernisation and privatisation were essential to stop Royal Mail going bust and to save the USO. Hooper One was unequivocal: 'Now is *not* the time to reduce the universal service. Reducing the number of deliveries each week ... would be in no one's best interests.' Hooper Two was less sure. There was no case for cutting the service, it said, until the Royal Mail was fully modernised. But then, cutting it 'might be justified'. In both reports, Hooper expended much ink and anguish over the highly technical rules that force Royal Mail to deliver the bulk mail its competitors sort at a certain price: a price, Royal Mail says, that obliges it to deliver at a loss.

Hooper is right in that Royal Mail is in a fight for survival with new media, the world of words not written on paper, weightless electronic words. As with music and newspapers, so with letters. It is in a fight with competitors who get guaranteed access to its reservoir of postmen as if they were a water or gas supply. But it is also the subject of a third kind of competition, between two utterly different sets of customers with incompatible needs. A few hundred giant firms and organisations that want to send bursts of millions of letters and catalogues every few days are competing for the same set of postal workers with millions of people who want to send a few Christmas cards and once in a while something that needs a signature. In this competition the power lies with the few, whose priority is cheapness, rather than the many, whose priority is regularity and universality; cheapness wins, and it is the postal workers who suffer.

There's a strange blip between the two Hooper reports. Hooper One is full of laudatory references to the old Dutch and German postal monopolies, TNT and Deutsche Post DHL, which privatised, then modernised, then became free-market champions. There's a chart showing Royal Mail bottom of the class in Europe in terms of profit in 2007, with TNT and Deutsche Post leading the pack, raking in the euros. Two years later, Hooper Two was strangely quiet about the German and Dutch mail stars. No wonder: the equivalent chart for 2009 shows that TNT and Deutsche Post averaged profit margins of only 3.25 per cent, less than Royal Mail.

The bitter postal rumble between the Netherlands and Germany in the late noughties may have had nothing to do with these figures, but it looked like the symptom of something rotten. When I say bitter, I mean bitter. TNT's Almast Diedrich was courteous in the face of my impertinent questions about the company's activities in Britain, but when I asked about one particular German attempt to block TNT's expansion east, his mouth twisted into something almost like a snarl. 'What Deutsche Post did was very clever,' he said between his teeth, 'and typically German.' What the Germans did was not so different from what the Dutch did: they tried to protect their decently paid former state postmen from low-wage competition in their home country, while setting up networks of low-wage private postmen to undermine the former state post in the country next door. At one point, Diedrich said, TNT managers called the offices of the German postal union, noted their principled stance in defence of well-paid Deutsche Post mailmen in Germany, and asked when they were going to take a similar stand in defence of appallingly paid Deutsche Post mailmen in Holland.

'It's very interesting that the Germans compete with the Dutch in Holland not on product, not on the number of days they deliver: they compete solely on wages,' the CWU's Baldwin said. 'And in Germany, the Dutch compete with the Germans solely on wages. And both of them cry like stuck pigs about the other.'

Why, I asked Baldwin, did multinational companies find it so easy to move across European borders, but unions seemed only capable of acting nationally? Why hadn't the postal unions across Europe mounted multinational protests against the casualisation of the post?

'It's partly because everything happened piece by piece,' he said. 'Every country is suffering a loss of postal workers' jobs, partly due to the financial crisis, partly due to e-substitution, partly due to increased automation. Almost all of these countries are managing their reductions by early retirement, voluntary redundancy, redeployment, so the actual impact on any given day just is not the same. To convince ordinary postal workers that they need to take part in a European strike to protect postal services across Europe would be incredibly difficult. Unless they're hit in their own pocket, today, your average worker ... doesn't go to work to worry about the future of the postal services in twenty or thirty years' time.'

While I was in the Netherlands, the Dutch parliament's pressure on the low-wage postal companies, which had been building for years, finally forced them to make a deal. In the small hours of the morning they agreed with the unions that by the end of September 2013, 80 per cent of all postal workers in companies like Sandd must be on proper contracts, meaning they gain some degree of social protection. One of the companies was Netwerk VSP, TNT's low-wage postal subsidiary. Almast Diedrich was the highest-ranking executive prepared to talk to me; the most senior bosses were preparing for the final stage of TNT's break-up, which was stripping the former Dutch post office of the racier acquisitions it made when it was the darling of the markets. I met him in TNT's headquarters on Prinses Beatrixlaan in the Hague, which with its aspirational office blocks, multi-lane highway and elevated tramway has a sort of

Pacific Rim vibe. I asked him about the deal with the unions, and he fessed up. 'Yes, we underpaid, if you want to call it that, in the same way that others did. From early on we said when others agree to come to a labour agreement we will follow. We would not take the lead.'

On the other side of the road, in the lobby of a luxury hotel, I met Egon Groen, one of the union leaders who put his signature to the deal with employers. It was late Friday afternoon and a group of young salarymen were ordering a round of what Joseph O'Neill called 'the gold-and-white gadgets that are Dutch glasses of beer'. Groen stood out with his hoodie and his exhaustion.

'The TNT strategy was "We want to be one of the big players, like FedEx or UPS," and it failed, of course,' he said. 'If you have to split up it means it didn't work. In the end the shareholders were not benefiting and nor were the employees. So there were just a few managers who had a nice adventure and it didn't work out.' The winners from Holland's liberalisation of the postal market, he said, were the big organisations who bulk mailed. 'The losers? Almost everybody else. TNT, the new postal companies, the workers, the government. They liberalised the market and they've had a headache for five years and it's not over yet.'

TNT did experience a postal strike in 2010, after workers balked at union leaders' negotiation of a 15 per cent pay cut. But Groen had no illusions about the way things were going for paper mail. 'Postal volumes are going down much faster than expected. Substitution by email is going up much faster than expected. We had to fill in our tax forms by today so I guess everyone's doing it on the Internet.' Yet Groen is optimistic about the future for the luggers, the heavers, the hefters and the trudgers of society. 'About a third of the workforce is going to retire in ten years. That will be a huge problem which will give people like the private postmen you met more chances. Employers won't be able to be so choosy. We can't import two million people from Ireland or anywhere else. The price of labour will go up.'

*   *   *

Most of Royal Mail was privatised in October 2013. The government kept 38 per cent to sell later and split 10 per cent equally, for free, between the company's 150,000 employees. A few hundred idealists refused to take their allocation, sacrificing a likely future gain (they're not allowed to sell for three years) of thousands of pounds. The remainder of the shares, 52 per cent, were put up for sale at £3.30 each. Investors small and large stampeded to buy a stake; the allotment set aside for private buyers was oversubscribed by seven times, for big institutions, twentyfold. Only the very smallest investors, those with less than £750 to spend, got what they'd asked for, while a single hedge fund and the government of Singapore got large stakes. Those in between were left short. There'd been nothing like it since the speculative frenzy of the big Thatcher-era privatisations in the 1980s. The government made £1.7 billion from the sale; the share price roared upwards till, by December, it had nearly doubled. The government was accused, from both ends of the political spectrum, of naivety and incompetence, of selling a British folk treasure on the cheap. The *Daily Mail* described Goldman Sachs, the financiers handling the sale for the government, as a 'giant Wall Street investment bank that is notorious internationally for its greed' and accused it of prioritising 'its favoured clients in the big City institutions ... it is now clear that the offer price was ludicrously undervalued.'

Politically, it's easy to see why the government sold Royal Mail cheap. Of the two risks to the sale – that eager investors would make a killing, and that the sale would flop because investors thought the price too high – ministers and civil servants knew, because it had happened before, that the first outcome would be a short, intense storm, soon to blow over, whereas the second would haunt the Cameron–Clegg regime forever with the stigma of incompetence. More than that: if you're a politician in favour of privatisation, a debate about the price of shares means you've already won, because the debate about privatisation itself is over. Alternatives to the simple opposition of state ownership versus privatisation – the creation of a Royal Mail Trust, for instance, run on commercial lines but not for profit, or a John Lewis-style, employee-owned enterprise, both of which would have kept the company's debt separate from the government's – were never debated. And while the furore over the share price drew all the attention, in the background, something far more significant for Royal Mail's future was happening.

There was always something fantastical about the flotation. Right up to the moment of its disposal, the company had been portrayed by free marketeers and Tory commentators as a doomed behemoth, a pre-Internet, pre-Thatcher throwback, a state-milking army of overpaid, underworked, Luddite ne'er-do-wells jamming the cogs of the British economy. Suddenly, almost overnight, at the very moment it became too late to have second thoughts about the sale, the Royal Mail became a priceless national asset, its shares like gold, like Apple stock, with hard-nosed moguls from the world of big finance and nerdy stock pickers in suburban bungalows trampling over each other to get a piece. How to explain the dissonance? Was it that privatisation happened to coincide with an upturn in Royal Mail's fortunes, or was there something evidently transformative, in the Midas sense, about privatisation itself?

While I was wondering about it, at home one foggy day in London, a letter slipped through my door. It was from Royal Mail and seemed to offer their answer in support of the first proposition. 'We love parcels,' it said on the outside. It was a circular promoting new sizes and prices for small packages sent by mail. The Internet has devastated the letters business, but you can't send objects down a wire, and the boom in Internet shopping has seen a corresponding boom in parcels, so much so that it looks to be starting to compensate for all those lost letters – so much so that Moya Greene, the head of Royal Mail, has spoken of offering deliveries not six, not five, but seven days a week.

But it is too soon to speak of a new golden age of mail, and the parcels business is subject to ferocious competition. In the

Netherlands, PostNL recently announced it would go down to five-day deliveries, scrapping its Monday service. The US Postal Service wants to stop Saturday deliveries. Most New Zealanders will soon be getting mail three days a week. Much more likely that there was something else that excited investors. Some have suggested the unneeded land and buildings owned by Royal Mail are more valuable than the government's sell-off advisers said they were, offering shareholders a future windfall. Then there was the government's generosity in putting Royal Mail in the private sector, but leaving its massive unfunded pension liabilities – £8 billion – with the Treasury; and the postal regulator Ofcom's largesse, allowing Royal Mail, just before privatisation, to raise first class stamp prices by 30 per cent. There was the recent outbreak of peace with the union, which had been expected to be more militant; and, of course, the prospect of commercial loans pouring in to fund new equipment.

And then there was something else. One of the analyses accusing the government of selling Royal Mail cheap came from a brokerage firm, Canaccord Genuity. If the company could just cut 3 per cent of its workforce and increase sales by 3 per cent, it said, it might be worth £10 billion by 2015, triple what the government sold it for. Tucked away in its investment note was an intriguing coda. 'But the real interest is, what if the company could reduce people costs?' it said. In other words, what if Royal Mail could slash its wage bill, not merely by making much deeper cuts in staff than 3 per cent, but by actually cutting the pay of those who remained, and worsening their conditions? Then the shareholders would really clean up.

Just a few days before privatisation, PostNL's British subsidiary TNT Post announced that it was recruiting a thousand staff in and around Manchester to set up a new delivery service. Building on a similar operation it had already set up in west London, most of the new employees would be postmen and postwomen, delivering mail on orange bicycles. In future, TNT added, it wanted to expand its postal service to employ 20,000.

George Osborne took time to laud TNT. 'Today's news is great for Manchester, and offers real opportunities for young people looking for work and the long term unemployed in this area,' he said. 'It is a vote of confidence in Britain.' The *Manchester Evening News* was even more enthusiastic. 'Postal firm delivers jobs joy,' its headline said.

The enthusiasm was misplaced – or fake, in Osborne's case. If the total amount of physical mail being despatched is falling, as almost everyone agrees it is, and automation requires fewer postal workers, as almost everyone agrees it does, there can be no question of TNT Post 'creating jobs'. All the Dutch company can do is take jobs away from other postal workers. And to do that, it is doing something it is no longer able to do in its home country.

In 2011, when I visited the Netherlands, there was little sign of Royal Mail's competitors looking to recruit private postmen in Britain to challenge the state's de facto monopoly on 'final mile' deliveries, which suggested that – although they wouldn't admit it – the private companies were getting a bargain from using the state postman's shoe leather. 'The general public is not ready to have anybody else delivering to their door. Actually providing a service where Royal Mail ends up delivering it is perfect,' Royal Mail's rival Buswell purred. 'I'm a real fan of Royal Mail and I don't believe anybody else should walk the streets and make deliveries.'

Nonetheless, it was always Royal Mail's fear that the burden of carrying out the USO, having to offer all but the very remotest communities the same level of postal service as the densely packed cities, would leave it vulnerable to 'cherry-picking'. In this scenario a rival would undercut it by recruiting private postmen to do the relatively cheap, easy job of delivering urban mail, leaving Royal Mail withering away, forced to Postman Pat it at unsustainable expense around the glens and dales of rural Britain. Apart from the now long-lost advantage of being an incumbent monopoly, Royal Mail does have important protections against this happening. One is that it is, for the time being, exempt from VAT, while its competitors aren't. Another is that it has some leeway to adjust the prices it charges competitors to use its services. Finally, Ofcom is obliged, by law, to step in if necessary to protect the universal service.

Crucially, however, it is *not* obliged to step in to protect Royal Mail. If cherry-picking rival post companies – which, for the time being, means the Dutch – threaten Royal Mail, one way Ofcom has said it might respond is by taking chunks of country-side away from Royal Mail and giving them to TNT. After 2021, Ofcom has the option of putting the entire USO out to tender, in search of the cheapest bidder. And the cheapest bidder is what TNT is positioning itself to be. Royal Mail postmen and women are on an average base wage of £11.64 an hour in London. According to CWU figures and anecdotal reports, the starting base wage for TNT postmen in London is £7.10 an hour, 39 per cent less than Royal Mail, and 20 per cent below the living wage. In Manchester, TNT is believed to be paying £6.50 an hour, 37 per cent less than Royal Mail. TNT postal workers are on zero hours contracts – in other words, there's no guaranteed minimum number of hours per week – and in terms of pensions, holiday pay and sick pay, they're worse off (and cheaper to the company) than their Royal Mail counterparts. According to the deal Dutch postal operators hammered out in 2011, TNT wouldn't be able to pay postmen so little if it were at home. It may be to TNT's advantage – politically, as well as in business terms – that its competition with Royal Mail is paralleled by inter-union com-petition. Instead of the CWU, TNT has done a recognition deal with Community, the union of betting shop staff, steel workers, carpet weavers, footwear makers and football managers. 'Having campaigned for years to have TNT essentially closed, the CWU have now woken up to the fact that it's not going to happen,' Paul Talbot of Community told me.

The Royal Mail may yet triumph, commercially, as a privatised company. It may be eroded and eventually displaced by TNT, now named Whistl, or another big private mail firm. PostNL, Whistl's parent, could one day buy Royal Mail, or vice versa, or the two could simply merge. Whatever happens, the most intense competitive pressure will be on Royal Mail to squeeze the wages of the postmen who remain, turning low-paid workers into exploited workers. Without a political and ethical breakthrough of the kind that was eventually forced on Holland's post companies – 'we underpaid' – the story of the Royal Mail becomes a paradigm of how technological progress, privatisation and a willingness by the majority to accept minority poverty goes to recreate a past phenomenon, the pool of desperate, hungry labour, mobbing the depot gates, fighting each other for paid hours.

2. Signal Failure

Privatised railways

On a mild, wet February morning, a work gang of ten men moved around a stretch of railway line near the village of Goostrey, between Crewe and Manchester airport. Against the extreme green of fields and the whipped grey of rainclouds their synthetic orange work suits shone out violently, like figures in a psychedelic episode. It was hard work. Using thick, weathered, metal-capped staves, they cranked jacks that raised a stretch of rail, along with its concrete sleepers, up off the bed of stone chips it rested on. A bulldozer on rail wheels purred up on the other line and pawed at the stones. The men were to pack fresh ballast in under the rails with hand shovels.

The year was 2004, and the men were engaged in the single most expensive non-military task ever undertaken by Britain alone: the modernisation of the national rail network's west coast main line. A project that was supposed to cost roughly £1.5 billion had, by the time a version was finished two years late in 2008, consumed £9 billion, much of it from the taxpayer. This was £3 billion more than the White House thought NASA would need at the time to send men back to the moon. For this vast expenditure, Britain got a supposedly modernised railway that over its busiest section, the eighty miles between London and Rugby, had barely had its ancient infrastructure touched, and had, in the words of the rail regulator in 2013, been 'persistently disappointing' ever since. A project that was intended to rebuild a London-to-Scotland railway for the twenty-first century is now casually dismissed by government as 'nine billion pounds worth of improvements north of Rugby', which requires a whole new railway, High Speed 2, to replace it.

The bizarre story of those multiplying billions, reconstructed here from dozens of interviews and documents, ran parallel to the bloodier history of fatal accidents on the railway since privatisation, and contributed, in equal or greater measure, to the ignominious end of the Railtrack era. It is a tale of incompetence, greed and delusion, driven by the conviction that profit and share value is the only true measure of success, and that the ability to chair a meeting or read a balance sheet is always worth more than the ability to understand how machines and materials will best serve human needs.

It is a story, too, with wider implications about the kind of country that Britain has become: a country that has lost faith in its ability to design, make and build useful things, a country where the few who do still have that ability are underpaid, unrecognised, and unadmired.

Watching over the Goostrey work gang, dressed in cleaner, newer versions of the same orange suits, were three of their bosses, all American, from the US construction firm Bechtel, brought in two years previously to rescue the project from the incompetence of the collapsed rail company Railtrack. No British company seemed to have the skills required; nor, after Railtrack's systematic efforts to gut itself of in-house specialists, did Railtrack's quangoid successor, Network Rail.

As an extreme measure to bring the final bill down, the rail industry had agreed to shut the entire stretch of railway we were standing on, from Crewe to Cheadle Hulme, for four months, forcing thousands of travellers on the then First North Western railways to use coaches while 600 orange-suited men and women worked on the line twenty-four hours a day, seven days a week. Without such radical steps, said Tom McCarthy, the Californian who led the Bechtel west coast team, the project could have ended up costing £13 billion.

It could have cost much, much more. The project was a stripped-down version of a fantasy railway which, in 1997, Railtrack locked itself into a brutal contract with Richard Branson's Virgin Trains to build. I sat one day with Stuart Baker, the man brought in by the Strategic Rail Authority in 2002 to survey the wreckage of Railtrack's west coast plans, and read out to him the sequence of growing price tags: £1.5 billion in 1996, £5.8 billion in 1999, £7.5 billion in 2001 …

'None of those numbers delivers the contract,' he said. 'You could talk about numbers six or eight times that. It is into 30 to 40 billion if you were actually to create the infrastructure necessary to fulfil [Railtrack's original] obligations.'

At Goostrey, I encouraged the Americans to talk about why the project turned out to be so much more expensive than its creators thought. Bob Brady, a Texan from Houston who was managing the reconstruction of that part of the route, began to answer: 'I think part of the issue was the politics when it was privatised – '

McCarthy interrupted him. 'Don't go there,' he said.

And Brady didn't. But he was right, which is why McCarthy didn't want him to say any more. The problem with the west coast project was not that it was going to cost £9 billion, but that the original bosses of Railtrack thought it could be modernised at a fraction of the price, and sold this ideology-driven delusion to the public and the City.

Friday, 23 December 1994 dawned foggy and almost freezing in central London. The papers reported on Yeltsin bombing Chechnya, on new developments in the Guinness scandal, and on fresh Labour attacks against the millions of pounds made by directors of recently privatised utilities. On the fifth floor of an office building in Hanover Square, London, a group of fifteen consultants sat in a room carrying out a laborious task. They were writing numbers by hand, in red ink, in the top right-hand corner of a secret 182-page report.

The red numbers were a device to stop the report being leaked, as so many documents were in the course of rail privatisation, the most controversial of all the Conservatives' state sell-offs. That spring, Railtrack, a new organisation, had taken over state-owned British Rail's responsibility for running and maintaining tracks, bridges, signals and tunnels. Railtrack was due to be floated on the stock market. It was essential that it convince the public and the City that it could finance and organise the modernisation of the west coast line – something British Rail (BR) had never been given the money to do – and the report was going to tell Railtrack how it should do it.

Five years later, when the consequences of the report's recommendations became clear but the report itself had been forgotten by the media, a subsequent generation of Railtrack bosses tried to blame it all on BR. In fact, BR had nothing to do with it. Railtrack was determined to prove that it didn't need BR's expertise, so it commissioned a consortium of consultancy firms to do the job.

That Friday, two days before Christmas, the consultants were in festive mood. They'd been working on the report since March and as soon as they had finished with the red numbers, off it would go to the government and Railtrack, the job would be done, and the holidays would begin. 'We had to get it finished by noon, and we finished by eleven,' one of the consultants recalled. 'I think we all went down to the pub afterwards – the kind of jolly, end-of-project thing that happens.'

On the face of it, the consultants had every reason to celebrate. They had approached a gigantic problem, and come up with an elegant solution.

*   *   *

For a culture that has been under constant attack from the public and the media for almost two centuries, the rail industry has a surprising love of misleading jargon. The west coast main line, usually known in the business as the WCML, is a case in point. It doesn't run along the west coast, and it isn't a line. It's a 690-mile network of routes between London and Glasgow, connecting them to Liverpool, Manchester, Birmingham and scores of other large towns in the West Midlands and north-west of England.

It is almost the oldest inter-city railway in the world. It was built higgledy-piggledy over three decades, starting in 1833, by entrepreneurs and hard-drinking, red-waistcoated navigators who, if they died on the job, were sometimes buried where they fell. Its narrow tunnels, lines squeezed together, tight curves and eccentric kinks reflect not just the geography of the land but the speed of contemporary trains – 40 mph max – and the reluctance of powerful landowners to have clanking, smoky iron horses hauling the proletariat across their estates. Robert Stephenson, son of George, who built the London-to-Birmingham stretch, had to make some of his measurements secretly, by night, to avoid being run off the squireocracy's property.

Between 1833 and 1994 the line was modernised, of course, but never rebuilt. Anyone who has lived in a nineteenth-century house will be familiar with the problem. The arcane wiring when electricity came along, the subsequent clumsy rewiring; the cheap flat conversion in the 1960s; the constant saga of patch and mend from occupants who never have the money or vision to remake the whole thing from scratch – all this, and more, was paralleled on the WCML on an enormous scale. When the consultants came in, the WCML had been starved of investment by governments for some twenty years. The only significant reconstruction was in the 1960s, when the railway was modified to take electric trains. Repairs and the skills of Georgian and Victorian engineers enabled train speeds to increase until the mid-1980s. Then the network began to deteriorate quickly.

The greatest problem was the signalling. It had to be replaced, but to remake that system, with its thousands of miles of cables, coloured lights on poles and elderly signal boxes, would be staggeringly expensive. A 1992 document, the Hesketh report, classified at the time but later slipped without publicity into the House of Commons library, recounts in bald language the horrific state of WCML signal boxes, on which the safety of passengers depend. They read like despatches from a war zone. Stockport signal box 1 was 'installed 1896. Roof of relay room lets in rain. Cable route heavily damaged ... very few spares. Signal structures have severe corrosion. Power supplies are suspect.' Brewery Sidings: 'Installed 1894 ... severe structural problems ... incapable of modification ... signal structures have severe corrosion and access by staff is by special arrangement.' Miles Platting: 'Installed 1890 ... box and relay room have serious structural damage with propping by the civil engineer to prevent collapse.'

How could Railtrack do it? How could they do what BR had not done and rebuild this tottering railway? The consultants came up with a remarkable scheme which would, besides modernising the WCML without costing the Treasury a penny, enable trains to whizz between London and Glasgow at the unprecedented – for Britain – speed of 140 mph, and make the west coast line the envy of the railway world.

A new idea was being discussed in rail circles in the 1990s. It was called 'moving block', and it was supposed to do away with conventional signals for ever. It was based on the technology used for mobile phones. Normally, trains run on a fixed-block system. A line is divided into stretches called blocks, with signals controlling the entry and exit to each block. If a block has a train in it, the signals prevent another train entering that block and crashing into it. Moving block abandons conventional signals in favour of computers, track-mounted radio beacons and a cellular radio network. With these, train drivers always know where they are in relation to other trains. They still have a protective block of space around them, but it moves along with the train, and shrinks or grows according to how fast it and the trains in front and behind are going.

Once Railtrack's consultants fed moving block into the equation, the miraculous happened. The numbers made sense. They wouldn't have to remake the signals; they would simply demolish them, and replace them with a few mobile-phone masts and black boxes in existing train cabs, which would be far cheaper to install and maintain. Thanks to moving block, they would be able to squeeze more trains onto the line. The trains could go faster, which would not only justify charging passengers higher fares, but would mean the train operators could run more services with fewer trains. As the final cherry on the cake, the cost of upgrading the route to take 140 mph expresses could be defrayed from the extra profits the express operators would make.

There was only one problem with moving block, but it was a crucial one: moving block for main-line railways did not exist. Even now, almost twenty years later, there is not a single main-line railway anywhere in the world, no matter how sophisticated, that uses moving block. It is used only on a number of urban transit systems, such as the Docklands Light Railway and the Shanghai metro, and the great majority of these had moving block* installed long after the WCML upgrade was due to be finished. For inter-city express trains it remains where it was, on the drawing board. The consultants did not allow this detail to stop them, and nor did Railtrack.

'When I heard about it from outside, I thought: "Wow, they must have had some amazing breakthrough which means this is now a proven bit of kit." And it wasn't,' Chris Green, then head of Virgin Trains, told me. 'It was a wish list. To put that wish list on Europe's third busiest railway really was outrageous.'

*   *   *

---

* Now known as Communications-Based Train Control, or CBTC.

Of the four teams of consultants that prepared the feasibility study, Booz Allen Hamilton was responsible for coming up with the recommended signalling system. No one from the company would comment for this article, but one of the consultants involved in 1994 did talk. Of the eventual core team of eight consultants, only two had experience of British mainline railways, one at a very junior level. Four of them were American or normally based in the US. Not one had expertise in moving-block signalling on railways like the WCML; most of the experimental work on moving block was being done in mainland Europe.

The consultant asked for his real name not to be used. I've called him Arthur. He said of some of his colleagues: 'My personal view was … they hadn't got the knowledge to try and do this in any sensible way. Coming from an intensely professional railway background, I was appalled by this.'

Not knowing what other railways of the world were up to, the consultants did a write-round. 'We did a trawl,' said Arthur. 'We wrote to manufacturers and asked them for information … we asked the Japanese what they'd got [in terms of moving block] and they said: "Well, nothing, really." Which amazed us.' Indeed, this would, a lay person would assume, have given the consultants pause for thought. Neither the Japanese, with their 160 mph bullet trains, nor the French, with their 160 mph TGVs, used moving block in 1994: they still don't.

Yet despite this lack of knowledge, the fact that no railway in the world was using the system, and the fact that the equipment needed wasn't being made by any manufacturer, the Booz Allen team ended up recommending moving block. Why? Arthur hinted that the remit was not to find the most practical solution and ascertain the cost, but to find the solution that would make privatisation financially possible. The cost of conventional signalling, had they been told it, would have frightened investors off and halted privatisation in its tracks.

'The thing that everybody always theorises is, why did you recommend such a highfalutin-type system for the WCML? And that's a fair question,' said Arthur. 'But it's not a fair question when you actually look at what the remit was. The remit was to come up with the most cost-effective solution.'

The Booz Allen consultants came to another conclusion which, in retrospect, seems extraordinary. Even though they knew what the privatised railways would look like, with Railtrack owning the infrastructure, a horde of private train operators running services, and dozens of other private outfits all taking a cut and all trying not to step on each other's contracts, they based their estimates of how much the WCML modernisation would cost on British Rail history — the bargain-basement modernisation of the east coast main line, and the development of a new type of conventional signalling twenty years earlier. It was as if a western oil company based its cost forecasts in Putin's Russia on the pricing practices of the Soviet Union.

'What I hadn't understood,' admitted Arthur, 'was that the restructuring of the railway was going to bring a complexity beyond my wildest dreams.' Nor could the consultants have anticipated that the bosses of Railtrack would go on to cherry-pick their conclusions.

Railtrack was led to privatisation by two men, its chief executive, John Edmonds, and its chairman, the late Robert Horton. Edmonds was a former senior British Rail executive, Horton the former chairman of BP. Yet it was Edmonds, the former public-sector boss, who was the private-sector firebrand. Far from being loyal to BR's way of doing things, his experience on the state railways had inspired in him a scepticism towards in-house engineers and safety experts bordering on contempt. They were, he considered, overcautious, conservative, stuck in the mud. It was this that led him, at Railtrack, to shed its nucleus of in-house expertise, leaving the company unable to understand what its myriad specialist contractors were up to.

Edmonds declined to be quoted for this chapter. A senior rail manager said of him: 'He was the one who got rid of operations managers and engineers because he didn't believe in them. He thought it could all be contracted out and commercialised. He had a desire to break the mould and change. He was always opposed to the traditional railway. He believed there was a golden panacea in the private world where you just free people up and new technology comes in and the markets come in and it all happens. The railway doesn't work like that. You're not manufacturing baked beans.'

Like Edmonds, Horton was an advocate of privatising Railtrack. But although Horton was happy to play the role of swashbuckling private-enterprise shaker-upper, he was no entrepreneurial start-up king. Though he'd studied engineering in the 1950s he was no engineering wizard, either. He was, essentially, a highly paid private bureaucrat who made his reputation in the offices of a post-imperial semi-state oil company. He did not make BP; BP made him. It was already a vast, sprawling corporation when he arrived in 1957, and it was still a vast, sprawling corporation when he was sacked in 1992, no matter how much he changed it. He did, at least, know about the oil business. But he didn't know much about trains.

'He wasn't close enough to the railway to know what was going wrong,' said one rail industry source. 'So he was great at privatising, great with the City, good at getting private investment into industry. He didn't understand that he'd lost all his key operators, lost all his key engineers, and was chasing technology that wouldn't work.' Horton, who died in 2011, also declined to be interviewed. In a brief email, he told me: 'I think it is important to understand that the scope of the project changed enormously over time as did the decisions on the technology to be used.'

In 1994, Edmonds, Horton and the latest in a blurry succession of Conservative transport secretaries, Brian Mawhinney, all wanted to hear from the consultants that the WCML could be modernised with privately raised money, by a private railway company. Yet there was still an opportunity for someone to persuade them that the risk they were taking was unacceptably high.

The key expert standing between Railtrack and the catastrophic decision to go for moving block was Rod Muttram, the firm's new director of electrical engineering. But he too knew little about the railways: he'd been headhunted from the arms industry, where he'd been involved in developing weapons systems, including a new type of artillery rocket. He believed moving block could work, in theory. As to whether it could work in practice, on such a complex rail network, he was dependent on what the consultants told him. (Muttram declined to make a public statement to me.)

Yet British Rail still existed in 1994 and 1995, and its board thought the consultants' ideas were far-fetched. John Welsby, then chairman of BR, told me: 'I did have grave concerns about the attempt to integrate a type of technology that had no testing in real, active life in what, in fact, was the most complex railway in the country.'

Welsby wasn't exaggerating his wisdom after the event. A senior Railtrack figure, one of the key men liaising between Railtrack and the consultants, recalled: 'There were huge rows at the time with the British Rail board, who were completely unsupportive of the project. John Welsby, then chairman of BR, was the most vociferous opponent. He said [moving block] could never be done on a railway like this.'

Welsby and his BR colleagues were unable to get the message through to their private sector successors. 'You have to remember that we were all, at that stage, unbelievably busy,' he said. 'All my lads had about three jobs. Firstly, they were running a railway. Secondly, they were breaking it up for sale. Thirdly, they were often preparing a management buyout at the same time. People were working seven-day weeks, twelve-hour days. Our advice was passed across but then it was up to Railtrack to take that advice or not, as they wished ... of course they would have resented it anyway. The climate has to be remembered: we were big, bad BR, being broken up and done away with, because we were anathema to the government, so the new order was not necessarily going to look very favourably on us.'

Another warning came almost as soon as the consultants handed in their report. It came from Europe. The consultants' report – a copy of which I obtained through the Freedom of Information Act – makes little mention of the European dimension. None of the consultants was from mainland Europe. Yet it was clear from speaking to Arthur that they'd assumed other European railways were preparing to introduce the new technology as well, and that Britain, relying heavily on European research, would merely be the first to apply it.

But in January 1995, most of Europe's state-owned railways – nineteen of them – came to the joint conclusion that moving block was not ready to be used in the real world, and a simpler, transitional form of technology should be the next step. Again, Railtrack ignored the warning. In fact, Railtrack may never have heard it: at this time the firm had barely any contact with Europe. It was an extraordinary situation, of which the public was ignorant: a group of Anglo-American consultants and executives took for granted European support to develop a technology which those same Europeans openly declared to be premature.

In March 1995, Railtrack and the government went public with their plans for the west coast main line. Despite the warnings, they endorsed, with few reservations, the consultants' recommendations to make moving block central to the modernisation. John Watts, the Tory rail minister, spoke of an 'innovative signalling and control system' which would be 'at the heart of the proposals' for the WCML. (Interviewed by phone, Watts said he couldn't remember details of this period.)

The consultants' report remained secret. On 22 March Railtrack released what it said was a summary of the report.

By and large, it was. But there were important changes and omissions in what the public was told compared to what the consultants had said. The consultants warned, for instance, that if moving block turned out not to work, and conventional signals had to be used, any attempt to try to get trains to run faster than 125 mph – always Railtrack's intention – would incur 'exceptionally high costs'. This fateful warning, one of the keys to Railtrack's eventual demise, was omitted from the public summary.

At the beginning of March, signalling-company bosses had told MPs that they might – *might* – be able to have moving block working and installed within ten years. In their secret report, the consultants talked, with optimism, of 'a five-year programme' for the development and fitting of moving block. Yet this is what Railtrack told the public: 'The development programme is anticipated to take between three and four years.'

Most surprisingly, Railtrack inserted a line into the public summary that had never appeared in the consultants' report. 'Most of the hardware for this train control system already exists,' it read, 'the technology required being relatively mature.'

I read that line out to Arthur when I met him. He said: 'Mm. That's interesting.'

Did he find it misleading? Arthur paused for a long time. Eventually he said: 'I don't think there's any doubt, sitting here now, that it was not as far developed as we thought it was ... I'm surprised by those words, I really am ... I am amazed at that statement. Because I don't know where they had any proof of that.'

Neither Horton nor Edmonds would comment on the discrepancies. I asked another senior industry figure, with close knowledge of the subsequent attempt to make moving block work, what he thought. 'To say the technology is mature – yes, I think that was a bit adventurous, certainly in 1995.'

What happened? The consultants' report never mentioned it, but there was one other factor in the back of the minds of Railtrack and the Tories. In 1994 there had been a painful strike by railway signalling workers. Bringing in the new technology would be another step towards ending the unions' leverage, by getting rid of thousands of signalling staff.

Some in the rail industry are inclined to give Horton, Edmonds and their colleagues the benefit of the doubt. 'I think dishonesty does matter, but my suspicion is that it wasn't a question of dishonesty, it was more a question of misjudgment,' Michael Beswick, the regulator's director of rail policy until he retired in 2013, told me. 'It was assumed that technology would move very quickly, but it doesn't. That was the problem. That is a bit of an indictment of the calibre of the people running the show at that time in Railtrack.'

Another senior rail industry figure said: 'John Edmonds was keen to get the company privatised and wanted to say things that would encourage people to believe it was bold and dynamic. It was all about creating confidence, which requires bold statements, sometimes.'

Before I knew I would get to see the consultants' report, I spoke to a former senior Railtrack executive. He didn't have a copy of the report, and was trying to remember its conclusions. As I found out later, his memory didn't quite reflect the report; rather, perhaps, it reflected the real back-room conversations going on in Railtrack at the time. 'The basic conclusion was that it was impossible to upgrade the west coast at any sensible cost if you went for conventional signalling,' he said. 'And the only way forward – whether it was feasible or not – was to bring in twenty-first-century signalling technology.' *Feasible or not*: the decision was made, and Railtrack began unconsciously to weave its downfall.

The consultants weren't reckless. They never imagined that Railtrack would manage and finance the WCML modernisation itself. In some detail, they outlined a scheme whereby Railtrack would get a big, experienced civil-engineering consortium to raise money for and manage the project, thereby assuming most of the risk. But when Norman Broadhurst, then

Railtrack's finance director, studied the numbers, he thought the returns looked too juicy to be given away. He thought Railtrack should do it, and talked his colleagues round. One member of the board described how he'd argued against the proposal. 'I said at the time Railtrack did not have the management capability to bring that in house,' he said. He was proved right. No sooner had Railtrack committed itself to moving block than it began to waste time bringing it about. In mid-1995, its rump signalling team had dwindled to the extent that it was possible for it to move office in a single taxi. The following year, a move to Birmingham caused further losses of personnel. One senior Railtrack figure at the time said: 'In resources terms, two years were lost.' It wasn't until March 1996, just a few months before Railtrack was privatised, that the firm picked two consortia of engineering multinationals to develop alternate prototypes of the moving-block system. Soon the consequences of Edmonds' determination to gut Railtrack of its in-house engineering and project-management expertise became apparent. 'What Railtrack did in 1996 was quite exceptional, which was to take a really high-calibre engineering team on the BR system and destroy it,' said Chris Green.

Railtrack had assumed that the two signalling consortia would develop similar types of moving-block technology. It assumed their work could then be pooled to provide the foundation for a system that actually worked. But it didn't happen that way. The consortia saw each other as rivals.

'Not unexpectedly, their work tended to diverge rather than converge,' said a senior figure in the signalling industry at the time. This wouldn't have mattered so much, except that while the moving-block research was meandering, Railtrack made a catastrophic decision. It invited Richard Branson to hold a gun to the company's head.

In February 1997, Richard Branson's Virgin Trains had won the franchise to run fast inter-city services on the WCML. In

October, after the newly elected Labour government backed away from its commitment to renationalise the railways, Branson and Railtrack announced how the WCML project was going to be financed. They painted a wonderful picture for inter-city travellers. Railtrack would spend £1.5 billion to restore the worn-out railway to basic reliability, and, in exchange for a slice of Virgin's profits, would lay out another £600 million to install moving block and other improvements to create a high-speed line. By 2002, new Virgin tilting trains would travel the line at 125 mph; in 2005, they would accelerate to 140 mph. London and Manchester would be only an hour and forty-five minutes apart, London and Glasgow less than four hours. Suddenly, Railtrack found itself locked in a contract with Virgin to deliver a non-existent signalling system on the entire west coast main line by a firm date – 2005 – with crippling financial penalties if it failed to do so.

'They thought, "Oh crumbs, we've just signed [the Virgin deal], we'd better get on with this." There was a realisation the talking had to stop,' said the signalling source.

Yet Railtrack was locked in a catch-22 situation. It couldn't put a contract out to tender to develop a thing if it couldn't specify what the thing was. And it couldn't specify what the thing was until it had signed a contract for somebody to develop it. Meanwhile the two signalling consortia had made the tech-nology look less, rather than more, certain. 'Because we went on divergent routes, because we saw ourselves as rivals, it didn't enable Railtrack to say, "It's obvious, here's the specification,"' said the signalling source. 'What's at the core of this, I think, is that Railtrack did not have its own sufficiently strong in-house knowledge and expertise to be able to use industry for what it was good at, to gather their views in and make a judgment.'

Railtrack did have one ace in the hole. It had, in fact, long since recruited an expert in moving-block signalling. Way back in 1995, the then Conservative government had worried that Rod Muttram's lack of railway experience would put off City investors. At the government's insistence, Railtrack appointed a champion of moving-block technology to be its engineering director. Brian Mellitt was a clever, experienced specialist who'd already supervised the early stage of introducing moving block on London Underground's Jubilee line extension, then under construction.

But in 1997, just when his expertise was most needed, Mellitt's pet project was suffering a horrible public failure. Quite simply, moving block on the Jubilee line didn't work. Computers that were supposed to talk to each other couldn't. Costs soared. Desperately trying to complete the project in time for the opening of the Millennium Dome, engineers had to come up with a crash programme for an old-style conventional signalling system. The number of trains an hour was slashed in half. Westinghouse, the key signalling company responsible, took much of the blame. John Mills, who in 1995 had told parliament that moving block on the west coast main line might be possible in ten years, was removed as chief executive.

Throughout 1998, as news of the problems on the Jubilee line began to emerge, the newly arrived Gerald Corbett – who took over from Edmonds in late 1997 – became increasingly uneasy about the moving-block plan he'd inherited for the west coast. He didn't get on with Mellitt. Corbett was, if anything, even more hostile towards the engineering profession than his predecessor. Railtrack didn't sign a contract to develop the system with the British-French company GEC-Alsthom (later Alstom) until July 1998, more than a year behind schedule. But even this wasn't a proper contract to deliver something; it was a nine-month contract to define the thing that should be delivered.

And the signalling was only part of the WCML modernisation. Much more needed to be done. Tracks needed to be relaid, tunnels modified, bridges altered. This work, too, was behind schedule and over budget. Plans changed constantly. At one point, Railtrack paid £10 million to a contractor to develop a new kind of transformer, only to abandon it later and go back to the original type. With every passing day, contractors were finding out how much more seriously the line had deteriorated than Railtrack and the consultants had understood.

At the same time, because Railtrack had shed so much of its engineering and railway operations expertise, it had little ability to judge whether the prices its myriad contractors were charging were fair. 'It is easy to understand why certain elements within the industry took advantage of that situation,' said one rail industry figure. 'It would have been a great temptation.'

In one iteration of a recurring pattern, Railtrack turned to a US company for project management expertise, but managed to botch that, too. Railtrack hired Brown & Root, a subsidiary of the US engineering group Halliburton, then run by Dick Cheney. Whether Brown & Root, which had grown fat on Pentagon contracts from the Vietnam war and beyond, could have managed the job is unknown, but Railtrack never allowed it to try.

'Railtrack was half in bed with them and half not,' said an executive who saw the process from the inside. 'Brown & Root had a lot of experience in oil and gas contracts. Railtrack said, "Fine, show us how," but they got cold feet and never signed up.'

Meanwhile, Corbett and his team were becoming horribly aware of the other set of baroque errors that had been made by their predecessors: the Virgin contract, presented to the new Railtrack boss on his accession as a fait accompli.

Despite Virgin Trains' initial reputation for lateness, there was a general fondness for the Railtrack-Virgin plan, not just in Railtrack, but among politicians, the media and the public. Tilting trains going at 140 mph; London to Glasgow in time for lunch; it sounded good. It sounded like progress. But there was a severe problem.

Again, the lay observer would think it was obvious: other trains needed to use the same line. And these other trains did not travel at 140 mph. Some of them, freight trains, for example, struggled to reach half that speed. In all, the WCML was used by 120 trains a day. Two thousand different trains travelled up and down its various lines, and another 4,000 crossed it at some point. They were operated by fourteen private train operators, using at least nineteen kinds of locomotive, a mix of regional passenger services, local trains and freight – a contractual nightmare. But contracts had been signed. And, in the course of 1998, Railtrack began to come to the terrible realisation that it couldn't keep to its Virgin contract without breaching some of the others.

The introduction of faster, more frequent Virgin trains on the route meant that Railtrack was obliged to carry out extra work to guarantee the other, slower trains would still be able to do their job and earn their money. When Railtrack began to look more closely at the Virgin contract, and compared it with the work it had promised to do to the railway, it saw that it was unable to draw up future timetables without breaking at least one of its contractual commitments. Or rather, Railtrack looked, but it refused to see. It was the beginning of the end.

'They had committed to the rail regulator and said that it would work, but everybody knew it was impossible,' said Stuart Baker of the SRA. 'A 140 mph train still catches up with a 75 mph freight train or a 50 mph commuter train rather quickly. So it was a bit of an illusion. The capacity wasn't there for the contracted service without a new railway.'

The speed issue was not all. Railtrack was gambling its future on the highly risky maintenance philosophy that said components should be replaced only when they looked about to break, rather than at fixed intervals. When specialists looked into Railtrack's web of contracts with Virgin and other train operators on the WCML after the company collapsed, they were astonished to see that Railtrack had promised to build a railway that would not need any maintenance from 2005 to 2012.

'I don't think anyone denies that the commitment made to [Virgin] was a terrible mistake,' said Michael Beswick. 'It was one of the factors that brought the company down, ultimately.'

In 1999, the bubble burst. When Chris Green, who took over as head of Virgin Trains in February, went out and about to see how the epic west coast reconstruction project was going, he received a shock. 'I was surprised at how little physical activity there was. There was nothing happening on the track. I was looking for the big yellow machines ripping up track and signals being replaced and wires being renewed, but everybody seemed to be in endless debate about the scope of the work. There's no doubt that two years were lost. I think as I arrived it was dawning on Railtrack that this was going to be an incredibly expensive and complicated project.'

He quickly found out about the timetabling crisis. 'The basic railway skill ought to be train timetabling, oughtn't it? Railtrack ought to have been able to timetable it themselves and I'm sure they did. When they found it didn't work, they also found they were in a spectacularly tight contract, with massive penalty clauses, up to £250 million, with Virgin … every time they went round that situation they found they couldn't afford to break the contract. Which is why they had to implode.'

By the spring of 1999, even as Railtrack shares hit a high of more than £17, the project was in turmoil. Brown & Root was dropped and Railtrack drafted in a fresh team of consultants, the Nichols Group, to take stock. The rail regulator was hammering on Railtrack's door, demanding to know how it was going to make the west coast timetables work. Alstom's quest to try to make moving block work was going badly. Nine months of studies hadn't produced a clear design for the system, and amid the uncertainty even Railtrack was not about to give them the £750 million they sought to finish the job. In another blow to the technology, Mellitt quit.

'With him gone, there was nobody championing moving block,' said an insider on the signalling contract, 'and at this time, the Jubilee line was unravelling.'

On 9 December 1999, at a meeting code-named Black

Diamond Day, Railtrack finally took the decision it had avoided for so long. It accepted that moving block, the technology on which the company had staked so much, was a mirage. The Nichols Group report was painful in its clarity. There was no more than one chance in twenty that the system would be ready in time. The Jubilee line fiasco had shown the risks. Alstom had never been able to explain what would happen to a moving-block system in the event of an accident, or if there was a disruption of radio signals. One possibility was that the entire railway network between London and Glasgow would simply grind to a halt.

Nor had Railtrack ever fully grasped the enormous sums it would have to pay train operators for permission to take 2,000 locomotives out of service to fit the new equipment and retrain 4,000 drivers. The implications for Railtrack were catastrophic. They would now have to introduce a different, conventional signalling system, at vastly greater cost. Installing conventional signalling would mean stretches of railway being closed off, which meant huge compensation payments to the train companies. All Railtrack's contracts with train operators were predicated on moving block. The contracts would either have to be torn up – more huge compensation payments – or a costly extra programme of works set in motion to reconfigure the entire railway. Instead of the expected £2 billion, the new headline figure was a staggering £5.8 billion. It quickly turned out that this, too, was a wild underestimate. Without a massive taxpayer bail-out, Railtrack was doomed.

Five days later, on 14 December, Railtrack sent a letter to the rail regulator, Tom Winsor. It was five years almost to the day since those original consultants had explained to Railtrack what a marvellous system moving block was, and more than four and a half years since Railtrack had so misleadingly told the public that it was a 'relatively mature' technology, ignoring the warnings of British Rail, MPs and rail journalists. Now Railtrack wrote: 'No system comparable with [moving block] has been implemented on a main-line mixed-traffic railway anywhere in the world ... the underlying software has never been used previously for a safety critical purpose.' If moving block were installed, Railtrack said, there would be 'a major risk of total disruption' to Britain's most important rail network. At least £65 million, and probably more, had been spent on trying to make moving block work, with nothing to show for it that was any use to Railtrack. The final acts of Railtrack's role in the WCML saga, played out until the company went into receivership in 2001, saw an increasingly isolated Corbett go head to head with Winsor, the regulator, confident in his contempt for Railtrack management. Confident, certainly, in his intimate knowledge of the contract Railtrack had signed with Virgin, because before Tom Winsor became the rail regulator, he was a rail contract lawyer. The central contract whose fulfilment Tom Winsor, government regulator, was insisting on had been drafted by Tom Winsor, commercial lawyer – one and the same man.

Winsor must have known he was contributing to Railtrack's downfall. But he also knew that the Blair government, the public and most of the train companies were fed up with the company, and the City was losing faith. Railtrack's only ally, Virgin Trains, was full of doubt. In the summer, after Railtrack confessed that the £600 million worth of Italian tilting trains he had ordered would not, as promised, be able to reach 140 mph on the new WCML, Richard Branson cheerily told an interviewer: 'Do you know why we're changing the name of Virgin Trains? Cos they're fucked.'

Winsor has published word-for-word transcripts of two meetings with the Railtrack leadership at the rail regulator's offices in Holborn in the spring and autumn of 2000. Corbett, wordy, blustering, pleads for more money, and his company's continued existence.

Winsor and his colleagues sit in judgment, terse and sceptical, like magistrates. 'It would have been incompetent if we had just pressed blindly ahead and tried to get moving block to work,' the transcripts record Corbett saying desperately in May, trying to redefine Railtrack's belated recognition of its problems as a triumph of good management. Corbett goes on to plead for a relaxation of contracts with the other train operators to make way for Virgin. Winsor is not impressed. 'Is it reasonable,' he asks Corbett, 'that a party to a contract should expect to have that contract honoured?'

'Yes,' says Corbett. 'That is reasonable. In the real world' – he pauses for a moment, allowing himself a moment of regret – 'in many senses, the railway is not the real world.'

In June, a fresh horde of consultants, commissioned by the regulator, delivered an indictment of Railtrack's handling of the west coast operation. Some parts of the project, the consultants said, had not been looked at afresh since the original report in 1994. All Corbett could do was choke on the irony that the consultants were from Booz Allen Hamilton – the same firm that provided the experts who, six years earlier, had recommended moving block to Railtrack as a splendid idea.

Away from the WCML, in October 2000, at Hatfield, a Great North Eastern Railway express from King's Cross to Leeds derailed, killing four people, when a broken rail that Railtrack had failed to repair shattered into hundreds of pieces. It was only a year since the Paddington disaster, where thirty-one people were killed and more than 400 injured after a badly trained driver went through a wrongly positioned red light. By the spring of 2001, the railways were in chaos and the estimated cost of the WCML project had gone up to £8 billion. In October, after a last attempt by Railtrack to go behind the backs of the other users of the line and renegotiate the Virgin deal, the government pulled the plug. Railtrack was finished.

As the Strategic Rail Authority, Railtrack's successor Network Rail and, eventually, Bechtel began to investigate the wreckage, the estimated costs of the WCML continued to rise. Twenty billion pounds was even mentioned as a final price tag. Only the retreat to the compromise of a 125 mph west coast line by 2008 brought the price down to £9 billion.

Those who came into Railtrack in the early days, John Edmonds' team, like to blame the fiasco on the Corbett-New Labour era. Dithering over plans, slack financial controls over contractors, political interference, the ever tightening grip of safety regulations – these, they say, added billions to a project that should have cost far less.

Yet all the key decisions that doomed Railtrack were taken before Corbett arrived, before Labour had fully established itself in office, and before the terrible accidents at Paddington and Hatfield: the folly involved in choosing an untried new technology and selling it to the public, the taking over of the WCML by Railtrack instead of letting an experienced engineering consortium handle it, the arrogance displayed in negotiating the Virgin contract.

Throughout Railtrack's existence, the management showed persistent traits – a contempt for engineering wisdom and a steady refusal to confront the decrepitude of the railway they were running into the ground. Even if moving block had come along in time, the rest of the infrastructure would have taken many billions to set right.

'The more we get into it – and facts are still emerging – the more we know the existing infrastructure is completely and utterly worn out,' said the SRA's Stuart Baker. In an imaginary world, if Railtrack had rejected the consultants' advice in 1995 to go for moving block, if it had taken time to investigate the true state of the railway, what would the actual price of WCML modernisation have been? Enough, certainly, to scupper Railtrack's privatisation. And there can be few in Britain today who think that would have been a bad thing. Without privatisation, would the money have been forthcoming to modernise the WCML? Not immediately, perhaps, but sooner or later the Treasury would have had no choice but to put in the billions it is putting in now; and a commercially run, state-owned Railtrack would have been able to borrow more cheaply than the £3.8 billion it paid shareholders and lenders in dividends and interest payments over five years.

One of the disturbing facets of the west coast saga is the failure of democratic government that it represents. Not just of a particular party, but the whole system of government. The administration of John Major created the Railtrack monster. Yet within less than a year of the privatisation of Railtrack, the Conservatives were punished at the polls – and Railtrack, and the WCML project as originally misconceived, went steaming on. No one has answered the question of how governments with five-year terms can be held to account for their stewardship of projects whose lifespan is measured in generations. In the dozens of interviews I carried out for this chapter, it was striking how few rail industry figures mentioned transport ministers or political parties. The only government they recognised was the only government that endures: the unelected Treasury.

And yet it would be wrong to say Britain's elected representatives looked the other way. In mid-February and early March of 1995, after the consultants had delivered their report but while Railtrack and the government were still mulling over it, members of the House of Commons transport committee questioned Edmonds, Horton and the heads of some of the big signalling firms about the WCML project.

The MPs did their job well. Gwyneth Dunwoody, the hard-nosed Labour interrogator on the committee, had been briefed by Richard Hope, an expert railway writer, and knew exactly what was at stake. Accordingly, when their report was published that July, the committee gave an uncannily prescient warning of the risk Railtrack was running.

It warned: 'The renewal of the west coast main line is urgent, and reliance on an as yet unproven train control system to underpin the financial case for investment may lead to unacceptable delays in upgrading the nation's principal intercity route.'

Members of parliament had done what they were elected to do, conscientiously and thoroughly scrutinising a big plan by an unelected organisation with power over the lives and purses of the public. It had pointed out its weaknesses. And nobody paid any attention.

In 1837 Charles Greville, the racehorse owner, political diarist and intimate of the Duke of Wellington, described his first railway journey – on the west coast line between Birmingham and Liverpool – as a 'peculiarly gay' experience. 'The first sensation is a slight degree of nervousness and a feeling of being run away with, but a sense of security soon supervenes and the velocity is delightful,' he wrote. The train travelled at about 20 mph. Greville knew it could go faster. 'One engineer went at the rate of 45 miles an hour,' he recorded, 'but the Company turned him off for doing so.'

It seems unlikely the west coast line will ever become a 140 mph route, unless High Speed 2 – intended to take passengers from Manchester to London at 250 mph, but not till 2033 – is cancelled. When I met Chris Green in 2004, not long before he retired, all he was able to do was take invited guests out on short practice runs in Branson's new red expresses to show them what might have been. 'I went on the 145 mph test run last August and it rode beautifully,' he said. 'It was doing 125, and we said, "Please accelerate to 145," and it shot forward like a sports car … we've got this greyhound train which is going to be running around like a labrador for the next ten years.'

Out in the winter rain on the shut-down Crewe-to-Cheadle line I met a British engineer, Roy Hickman, junior to the Americans from Bechtel but with decades of experience on the railway. He was working for Network Rail: the slogan of anti-engineering Railtrack's successor is 'Engineering excellence for Britain's railways'. It was spending £3 million a day on the WCML project.

'Bechtel are bringing a level of planning we've never seen

before,' Hickman said. 'I think Railtrack, in fact the industry, never really fully understood or anticipated the sheer scope or challenge of building the west coast, and only when work started did we begin to understand just what a huge task it was. It takes twenty years to wreck the infrastructure, and nearly as long to set it right.'

3. Not a Drop to Drink

Privatised water

Looking through the photographs I took in Tewkesbury, I found two pictures of Chuck Pavey and his floodwater hand. There's Pavey, a sixty-six-year-old retired electrician in a hooded Manchester United top, a wispy white pageboy haircut and dark glasses, standing by a wall on the bank of the River Avon. He's holding his right hand horizontally in the air, about thirty centimetres above the top of the wall, which comes up to his waist. The olive-coloured Avon ripples away, three or four metres further below. In the background is an arched pedestrian bridge, a willow tree with its lower fronds stroking the water, and the massive red brick wall of a derelict flour mill. In the next picture, Pavey is standing next to the freshly whitewashed wall of the White Bear pub, looking more agitated, as if he's afraid I still haven't got the point. It's the same stance, except that this time the hand has risen above his head. It hovers about two metres above the road; it comes three-quarters of the way up the casement of the pub window. I did get the point. If you'd tried to stand where Pavey was standing on Monday, 23 July 2007 – the day water levels peaked in Tewkesbury – you'd have been treading water.

At first there seems nothing in the pictures, apart from Pavey's hand, to hint at the fury of the flood that turned the old town of

Tewkesbury in Gloucestershire, at the confluence of the rivers
Severn and Avon, into an island on the banks of a vast brown
waterway resembling the Mississippi Delta. There are clues,
though. In the first picture, you can see two jetties that were
mangled by the torrent and haven't been repaired. The wooden
boards were sucked off and swallowed by the flood, and only the
metal skeleton remains. In the second, the new paint on the pub
indicates that the insurance has paid out and the flood damage
has recently been put right.

There are a couple of A4 sheets of yellow paper stuck in
the pub window. One reads: 'gl20' – the local postcode – 'new
houses no insurance'. The other has a picture of a house, with
a wavy line representing water cutting off its bottom half. The
slogan is 'stop building on flood plain: no more' and then in tiny
letters 'please' and – back to big letters again – 'mr shaw.' This is
a reference to Chris Shaw, then Tewkesbury Borough Council's
director of planning.

Pavey, an activist in the Severn and Avon Valley Combined
Flood Group, a band of concerned citizens who believe that
flooded Tewkesbury was the victim of a greedy, callous government, is one of those people you feel you could trust in a tight
spot. He's a saintly man who is forever a-doing, volunteering,
raising money, inventing practical solutions to concrete problems and helping people out. So it was during the floods, when
a water treatment plant in Tewkesbury belonging to the regional
water company Severn Trent was overwhelmed. It turned out
that the Mythe waterworks was the single, irreplaceable source
of supply for 350,000 people. For ten days, much of urban and
rural Gloucestershire was pushed back in time by a couple of
centuries. It was without running water.

Pavey commandeered a food trolley from Marks and Spencer
and set himself the task of pushing it around the sodden, cracked
streets of central Tewkesbury, delivering hundreds of litres of
bottled water to the aged and infirm, for no reward but thank
yous. 'All that week, when we ran out of water, I delivered water

to all the old people's places who couldn't carry it,' he said as he took me on a tour of his old clients. 'Sometimes they brought you water in little tiny bottles and little old ladies could carry that. But sometimes they brought five-litre bottles that little old ladies had no chance of carrying.'

He introduced me to Gladys Mills, a former farm worker, now eighty-six and living in sheltered housing. 'They said to use bath-water for flushing the loos,' she explained. 'You can't carry much at my age. A little pint bottle is quite heavy.' He introduced me to John Russell, an eighty-eight-year-old ex-engineer in a resi-dential care home. 'I saw one old lady trying to stagger off with six bottles,' Russell said. 'They were carried for her by a complete stranger.' He introduced me to Joan Bufton, whose daughter needs kidney dialysis three times a week; at the height of the floods she was pushed out of Tewkesbury in a wheelchair along a disused railway line. Bufton's husband suffered a stroke after it was over. 'I just think it was the trauma of all this,' she said. 'And he's not the only one ... unless they do something it will happen again, I don't care what anybody says.'

As we walked and talked, Pavey would adopt a scolding tone in his reminiscences: towards the businessman who kept filling five-gallon water containers from the town's emergency sup-plies until he got 'thumped', for instance. He praised others. He didn't seem angry, whereas Dave Witts did. Witts, a fellow Combined Flood Group activist, was calm and polite as he spread documents, reports and evidence out on his kitchen table, but he seethed with victimhood. His house, which is not on the Environment Agency's at-risk flooding map, was flooded the previous July. It took five months to repair. He believed the government had starved Tewkesbury of money for flood protection, while encouraging development in flood-prone areas. The government, he pointed out, was planning to build three million houses by 2020. And why, he asked, did they want so many? 'If you believe the *Daily Express*,' he said, with a look that suggested he was being bold to raise the idea that

I might not, 'we're going to have 600,000 immigrants a year from now on.'*

Ken Powell was sitting with us, listening. He was mayor of Tewkesbury at the time of the floods, though not the only one. The town has two mayors: one representing the borough of Tewkesbury, which covers a number of other communities, has a multi-million pound budget and heavy responsibilities, and is based in a large modern building in Tewkesbury's southern approaches; and one representing the town council of Tewkesbury, which has almost no money, virtually no formal responsibilities and sits in an eighteenth-century town hall on the high street. Powell was the lesser mayor, and it rankled. Being mayor number two, he had to stand behind the borough mayor at municipal events.

'The second-fiddle aspects,' he said, as he drove me back from Witts's house. 'They opened a new heritage centre down the bottom of town. I had to play second fiddle there. We have a thousand years of history with the Mop Fair, and every year it has to be opened by the mayor, but it's the borough mayor, not the town mayor. It just sticks in there a little bit, but there's nothing you can do about it.'

What united Powell, Pavey and Witts? If a visitor from eighteenth-century France had spent time in early twenty-first-century Tewkesbury, and been asked to describe a new Three Estates for the town and other English towns like it, he might reasonably have concluded that Tewkesbury was divided between public servants, private servants and localists. Powell, Pavey and Witts were localists: locals, for sure, in the sense of being long-time residents, but also localists, convinced that local people know better than outside experts – even on highly technical questions – what happens in their town, and what is best for their town; convinced that public servants, the bureaucrats

---

* Since I spoke to Witts, net migration to the UK has fallen to below 200,000 a year.

and Westminster politicians, are being especially mean to Tewkesbury, and doing it on purpose.

The localists made fair criticisms of the status quo in their reports. They complained, correctly, that the Environment Agency, away from coasts, only considered the dangers from fluvial, or river, flooding, and not from pluvial flooding, also known as flash or surface flooding, the kind directly caused by heavy rain.* They complain that local councils will not or cannot resist pressure from wealthy developers who would hem in or even build on flood-prone land. But this doesn't entirely explain the consistent venom of localists towards public servants – almost an assumption of malice – compared to their relatively mild tone when talking of private servants, the representatives of the insurance companies, the big housebuilders and Severn Trent. Nor does it account for the assumption of complete lack of liability on the localists' own part. 'The biggest Confidence Trick by a British Government since the Second World War' was how the Combined Flood Group described the government's guidance for councils on building on flood plains. 'Loss of the life [sic] comes third in the government's priority.'

In Tewkesbury in general there is more hostility towards the government, the council and the Environment Agency for not stopping housebuilders than there is towards housebuilders for building houses, or buyers for buying them. When insurers raise their premiums, more blame is directed at the government for not spending enough on flood defences than at insurers for raising the premiums, or at people who choose to live in a flood-prone valley but don't like paying extra for it. There is more hostility towards the Environment Agency for not warning Severn Trent that the Mythe works was on a flood plain (even though, in fact, it did) than towards Severn Trent for not being prepared for floods.

---

* In 2013 the Environment Agency added areas at risk of surface water flooding to its maps.

I was curious to know how Pavey felt towards Severn Trent, this highly profitable, private monopoly which had chosen not to provide a back-up in case Mythe failed, and whose subsequent mess he, unpaid, had voluntarily helped to cope with. He told me, but only because I asked. 'I suppose I think it should be nationalised,' he said. 'I don't think anybody should have any particular control over water. Everything on earth relies on water to live.'

Categories overlap, and Powell, the ex-mayor, besides being a localist, had been a public servant – he worked for the fire brigade – and was, when I met him, a private servant, working as an electrician for Severn Trent, based at Mythe. After the waterworks was flooded he toiled hard to help get it back on line. Severn Trent gave him £150 as a thank you. 'I gave part of that money to the mayor's charity fund,' he said. 'We were there, doing our job. Trying to get that works back and running so people could have clean water to drink and wash in, and that was our priority. Most of the people who worked there were out of water themselves.'

Since the flood, Severn Trent has spent £36 million on extra flood defences for Mythe and back-up pipelines against future failure. When asked why this hadn't been done before, the company explained that the risk of Mythe failing was too low to justify the expense, and funds for investment were limited.

In July 2007, a few days after the floods arrived, with 350,000 people still cut off from the first necessity of life, Severn Trent held its annual general meeting. It announced profits of £325 million, and confirmed a dividend for shareholders of £143 million. Not long afterwards the company, with the consent of the water regulator Ofwat, announced that it wouldn't be compensating customers: all would be charged as if they had had running water, even when they hadn't. Colin Matthews, chief executive of Severn Trent at the time of the floods, left the company soon after this to head another private monopoly, BAA, arriving just as the baggage-handling chaos at BAA's new

Terminal 5 at Heathrow was peaking. In his last full year as head of Severn Trent, he was paid £1.2 million.

Like many Severn Trent workers, Ken Powell owned shares in the company. I asked him if he hadn't felt bad taking the dividend when his fellow townsfolk's taps were dry. 'I don't see why I should,' he said. 'I went in there and worked hard to give people back their water.'

The Severn is Britain's longest river. It stretches 220 miles from its source in the Welsh hills. When the river makes trouble for Tewkesbury, it begins there, far to the north-west, with downpours that take days to swell the Severn downstream. There's time to act, and usually there's no need; the river bloats out into the meadows of the floodplain for a few days, one or other of the usual handful of houses gets flooded, and the waters recede. That, at any rate, is the standard script. But in July 2007 the source of the trouble was much closer, and hit much faster.

You can see the Cotswold Hills from Tewkesbury, low, amiable-looking bumps on the horizon a few miles to the east, separating the Severn and Thames valleys. Their highest point, Cleeve Hill, isn't much more than three hundred metres off sea level. The Cotswolds are an escarpment. On the eastern side, the land rises gradually from the Thames valley, from the direction of Oxford; on the western side, however, looking towards Cheltenham, Gloucester and Tewkesbury, the hills fall away sharply. When it rains on the Cotswolds, the rivers that run off towards the Thames follow that gentler, slower course. The obscure rivers that take the Cotswold rain towards the Severn and the Avon, in contrast, deliver their load to Tewkesbury in as little as two hours.

Even before July came, 2007 had been a summer of floods, wetter than any since records began, 250 years ago. In Yorkshire and Humberside, 27,000 homes and businesses were flooded in June. In low-lying Hull, pumps failed to cope with the deluge, and a man trying to clear a storm drain died of hypothermia, surrounded by rescuers who couldn't free his trapped leg. A man and a teenage boy were swept away by a flood torrent in Sheffield; the city was cut in half by floodwater. In Gloucestershire itself, schools and roads were closed, and homes and businesses flooded, but the most perilous impact for Tewkesbury of that earlier series of ferocious, unsummer-like storms was more subtle.

The Jurassic limestone of the Cotswolds had started May bone-dry – drier, in fact, than ever previously recorded. But by late July, the soil of the hills just east of Tewkesbury – Bredon, Alderton, Woolstone, Nottingham, Cleeve – was saturated. If more rain fell, the only place for it to go would be down to the valleys. And more rain did fall.

For weeks before 20 July, the weather had been behaving strangely over north-western Europe. If you were to look at a weather map for a regular July, it would show the jet stream – the ultra-fast wind, roaring at high altitude, that marks the boundary between cold polar air and warm tropical air – shooting north-east in a line between Iceland and the UK, across the Faroes. Britain would be comfortably on the mild side of the line, experiencing the benefits of the high-pressure zone centred on the Azores. Look at the same map for July 2007, however, and you see the jet stream take a sharp right turn halfway across the Atlantic and sweep through Brittany before heading across Central Europe into Poland. The whole of the British Isles was on the wrong, low-pressure side of the line. As if this wasn't unpleasant enough, the air and sea temperatures still corresponded to summer. Warm air is capable of carrying more moisture before it falls as rain, leading to the short, intense, highly localised showers that cut short summer picnics and bring out the covers at Wimbledon. The combination couldn't have been worse: saturated ground, the storminess of winter, and the moisture-laden air of summer.

On Thursday, 19 July, a damp, subtropical mass of air rolled from France into a depression over southern England and all but locked into place, like a ball in a cup. When the thick clouds in this air mass burst, they dumped extraordinary intensities of rain. It rained most ferociously on and around the Cotswolds. On Friday afternoon, Pershore, just north of Tewkesbury, was experiencing ten millimetres of rain an hour. Gloucestershire got two months' worth of rain in twenty-four hours. Between Friday and Saturday the worst-hit hills of the Cotswolds had more than 350,000 tonnes of water dumped on them. Much of this water soon found its way west, seeking the Avon and Severn. Normally sleepy brooks and streams became savage torrents. The major obstacle between these suddenly angry watercourses – the Carrant Brook, the Tirlebrook, the Little Fid and the Swilgate – and the two big rivers of the valley was the town of Tewkesbury, its 10,000 inhabitants and the Mythe waterworks.

Gloucestershire's public servants – the councils, the health service, the police and fire service – had been well warned by the Environment Agency and the Met Office that there were likely to be problems with unusually heavy rain on the Friday, although nobody knew exactly where or when. The county's emergency command system, known as Gold Command, opened up at its base in Quedgeley, south-west of Gloucester, on Friday morning, ready for the worst. The private servants knew too: Severn Trent says it issued an 'emergency weather warning' to its managers on Friday. But the company had locked itself into a mindset that precluded the possibility that its waterworks would flood.

Severn Trent periodically commissioned an engineering consultancy, Tynemarch, a spin-off company from Imperial College, to assess the risks to its treatment and supply network. By Severn Trent's own admission, Tynemarch identified Mythe as a critical point of failure in the 1990s: if it shut down there was no back-up. But according to Severn Trent, Tynemarch's most recent report, in 2004, assessed the risk of this happening through floods to be insignificant.

Short of burglary, there is no way to verify what the Tynemarch experts told Severn Trent in 2004, since Severn Trent refused to let me see the report on the basis that it was commercially confidential; and Severn Trent, as a private company, is exempt from the Freedom of Information Act. But here is what Martin Kane, Severn Trent's director of customer relations, said in an interview with Radio Gloucestershire shortly after the floods: 'The risk of flood defences being breached at the Mythe was – I think it was something like a one in a thousand chance of that happening, and the flood defences were considered to be absolutely secure, and we passed the 1947 floods without an issue, and we've had waterworks on the site for over a hundred years without any problem. So in terms of what we were looking for on the site, breaches of the flood defences were not part of the equation.' He went on: 'It was risk assessed, and the [assessment] was that it won't happen. Therefore there wasn't a plan for that.'

The Environment Agency takes a different view of the risk to Mythe. The agency's publicly available flood-plain maps show large parts of the Mythe works covered by water in the event of a once in a hundred years flood – that is, a flood with a 1 per cent chance of happening in any given year. There are two ways of looking at that risk. Severn Trent's way was: it hasn't happened in a hundred years – actually, 137 years; the works opened in 1870 – so it's not going to happen. The other way is: there's a one in a hundred chance of it happening, and it hasn't happened for 137 years, so a catastrophe is well overdue. Hardened gamblers, and statisticians working in the abstract, will tell you that the chance of a coin falling heads or tails in any one flip is exactly the same. But I doubt that even Colin Matthews would take his turn at Russian roulette with a light heart on the basis that a revolver with one round in the cylinder had been fired five times and not gone off once. Mathematically, over 137 years, the chance of at least one flood on a site likely to flood every hundred years is 75 per cent.

What makes Severn Trent's relaxed attitude even more surprising is that the Mythe treatment works did come close to
being catastrophically flooded in 1947 – floodwater entered
basements – and in 2000, when staff got as far as shutting down
key equipment. Then, the Severn peaked at 12.07 metres above
sea level, only 45 centimetres below inundation point. One of
the consequences of Severn Trent's certainty that Mythe was
floodproof is that the county's emergency planners in Quedgeley
had no inkling of how important it was. Severn Trent's managers
hadn't taken part in emergency planning exercises, and when
Gold Command convened at 9.45 a.m. that Friday, nobody
from the water company was there, and nobody remarked on
their absence.

The quickly swollen rivers shooting off the Cotswolds combined with flash floods in unexpected spots, many of them on
higher ground, caused by the sheer local intensity of rain. The
fire service took its first flood emergency call from a business in
Chipping Campden at 11.24 a.m. Less than an hour later they
were dealing with the first threat to life: a group trapped in a car
by rising waters near the village of Adlestrop. By then the emergency services switchboards were lighting up with hundreds
of calls. Minor and major roads across Gloucestershire were
being snipped into unconnected sections by floodwater, just as
the school holidays were beginning. The M5 and M50 motor-
ways began to flood at lunchtime; by late afternoon both were
closed, as were most of the roads that would normally have been
used to bleed off traffic. All trains from London to Cheltenham,
Gloucester, Bristol, Worcester and Birmingham were cancelled.
Thousands of motorists and train passengers were stranded
wherever they happened to be.

In Cheltenham, the River Chelt burst its banks by noon. More
than a hundred roads were underwater by 4 p.m. Some residents were flooded for a second time in a month. In Chipping
Campden, staff at a Ford dealership abandoned their premises
when cars started to float out of the forecourt. In Gloucester,

where most of the city centre was underwater, witnesses saw a
motorist driving through a deeply flooded road crash into the
back of a completely submerged van. In Bishops Cleeve, almost
all roads were impassable. In Moreton-in-Marsh, manhole covers
popped up like the lids on Smartie tubes and sewage gushed out.

In Tewkesbury, the small Cotswold rivers smashed up against
roads and bridges. Following the lines of least resistance they,
and then the rising Avon and Severn, encircled the town. Of the
four thousand homes flooded in Gloucestershire in July, 1,500
were in Tewkesbury. At the height of the floods it was completely
cut off by road. Aerial pictures showed Tewkesbury's medieval
abbey and its grounds seemingly afloat in a sea the colour of
builder's tea, like some fantastic Arthurian vessel attempting to
moor at the half-drowned jetty of the town's old high street.

As it happens, the Environment Agency's main flood-warning
control room for the west of England is on an industrial estate
in Tewkesbury. But the town doesn't use flood sirens, and at the
time the agency's archaic website used text, rather than maps, for
its warnings. Residents got an automatic phone message from
the agency warning of floods only if they'd signed up for one, and
on average only two-fifths of people at risk did sign up. Besides,
as Anthony Perry, flood-risk manager for Gloucestershire,
explained, the key to the 2007 floods was the water pouring off
the Cotswolds, and the agency didn't give warnings for those
small, nippy rivers. 'The limitations are small watercourses,
where they respond very quickly to flash flooding,' he told me.
'It's technically very difficult to provide a flood-warning service
to give a two-hour lead-in time. We don't provide any flood
warnings for the Swilgate or the Chelt at the moment and that's
something we want to do. But it's difficult. Because of the speed.
The rainfall that hits a rain gauge will be into the system and
within the town within a few hours. It's something we're looking
at now: is two hours better than nothing?"

---

* The Environment Agency introduced a flood warning service for the
River Chelt in 2011.

The Environment Agency's flood warning for Tewkesbury – 'Flooding of homes and businesses is expected. Act now!' – didn't come until 6.53 p.m. on Friday. A severe flood warning – 'Act now! Severe flooding is expected with extreme danger to life and property' – followed at 5.45 a.m. on Saturday. By that time, many residents had already been flooded; others had been woken by the sound of rescue helicopters, and the first person in Tewkesbury to die as a result of the floods, nineteen-year old Mitchell Taylor, had drowned while taking a short cut past the abbey on his way home from the pub. Passers-by heard him yelling for help – he couldn't swim – and tried in vain, via mobile phone and the 999 centre, to guide a helicopter to him. His body was found a week later by an Italian hovercraft crew.

Overnight, the waters around Mythe rose with a speed that staggered the flood specialists. Perry showed me a chart plotting the level of the River Severn at the bridge next to the waterworks, sourced from an agency gauge. A red line charted the story of the floods of winter 2000; from a high base the river rose gradually over two days, levelled off for a week, and then slowly sank back. The blue line showing what happened in July 2007 was quite different. The Severn was running relatively low before the rains. At 1.48 a.m. on Saturday, 21 July, the gauge readings began to shoot up almost vertically. In the next seven hours, the water rose 4.4 metres. Soon afterwards, with the water still rising, the gauge broke.

Severn Trent subscribes to the agency's flood warnings and was monitoring them on Friday at its operations centre in Birmingham. But as the rivers swelled, the company and the Environment Agency, without realising it, weren't understanding each other. Despite the agency's severe flood warning at 5.45 a.m. on Saturday, Severn Trent still refused to believe its waterworks would flood. Throughout the day, the company called the agency, asking for updated predictions of what level the river would peak at. The agency obliged; and, since their predictions were lower than Severn Trent's flood point of 12.52

metres, the company didn't feel the need to warn anyone that they were at risk, or what the consequences would be. Severn Trent argues that it based its actions that Saturday on those agency predictions of the exact peak flood levels through the day. The Environment Agency maintains that the predictions were provided as a courtesy, and that what mattered was the earlier severe flood warning.

Perry showed me the agency's flood map for Tewkesbury. 'Half of the [waterworks] site is under water in a one in a hundred year flood,' he said. 'The map shows that. So where we issue a severe flood warning, it is to say half of that site will be flooded. We try to educate [Severn Trent] about what we are here to provide and we made clear to them that we are not here to provide millimetre-accurate warnings at Mythe. We issued a severe flood warning, which includes them, and we expect them to take action. After the 2000 flood, when Severn Trent came close to taking action, there's a requirement for them to have a business continuity plan.'

What Perry meant by 'business continuity plan' was an alternative to Mythe if Mythe failed. But Severn Trent didn't have one. Not until 9.41 p.m. on Saturday night, almost sixteen hours after the severe flood warning, did the company alert Gloucestershire's fire and rescue service to the danger to the waterworks. By that time it was too late. Niall Hall, who was on duty in the Environment Agency's control room on Saturday night, remembers getting a phone call from the fire brigade saying 'Mythe's going to go under.' 'They were saying they had high-volume pumps, where could they pump the water to? I said: "Nowhere, unless you've got hoses that can go four miles."'

Hall recalls a phone conversation with staff at Severn Trent's HQ that night. 'They were panicking,' he said.

'They were struggling,' Perry said. 'They didn't understand how it all worked, really.'

'If you've got infrastructure by a river, there's a risk,' Hall said.

'But it's what level of risk,' said Perry. 'It's having plans, in case, isn't it.'

At midnight, Severn Trent bowed to the inevitable, and at 1.45 a.m. began a controlled shutdown of the plant, to save electrical equipment when the inundation happened. At 2.16 a.m., water gushed in from the Avon side, followed shortly afterwards by water from the Severn side. With the shutdown complete the flooded site was abandoned at 6 a.m.

When he appeared before MPs after the emergency, the head of Gold Command and Gloucestershire's chief constable, Timothy Brain, complained that he and his staff hadn't been told of the Mythe crisis until seven hours after flood water had entered the treatment works. They had no idea that a water cut-off was even a risk until it was about to happen. Severn Trent executives who gave evidence at Gloucestershire County Council's inquiry into the floods said they would have needed at least two days' warning of a severe flood for a temporary barrier to be put up in time to save the waterworks. Yet when, between Sunday and Monday, a similar emergency faced the National Grid at a vital electricity substation in Walham – the failure of which would have triggered the evacuation of half a million people from Gloucestershire – the emergency services and the military managed to complete a temporary barrier to hold back peaking floods less than fifteen hours after the Grid first contacted the fire service for help. On that timescale, had Severn Trent asked for help earlier, Mythe could have been saved.

'The critical thing Severn Trent failed to do was to let Gold Command know in time to protect that vital piece of infrastructure, as National Grid did for Walham,' said Martin Horwood, MP for Cheltenham. 'At Walham, Gold Command brought in the army and protected it, not with much time to spare, but they protected it. Severn Trent never joined up the dots.'

On average, a Severn Trent customer uses 138 litres of water a day. The washing machine, the bath and shower, the tooth-brushing and shaving, the dishwasher and washing-up, the flushing of toilets, the drinking, the cooking, the car-wash, the dozens of times a Briton unthinkingly turns on the tap to wet a cloth or wash hands or boil a kettle: it adds up. As news spread on Sunday that mains water was going to be cut off to much of Gloucestershire, householders rushed to wash clothes and fill baths. Normally the reservoirs would have stored enough for a day and a half, but by noon water was pouring out of Churchdown reservoir so fast the meters could no longer register it, and early on Sunday evening the taps started to cough, rattle and go dry. The phone-tappers, web spooks and cyberwarriors of GCHQ were forced to scale back operations at their new doughnut-shaped building on the edge of Cheltenham. Surrounded by the most advanced technology, reaching out across the globe, GCHQ's five thousand staff could no longer go to the lavatory.

Severn Trent had contingency plans to deal with water cut-offs. Government regulations say the private water industry as a whole should be able to supply 200,000 people with ten litres of water per person per day for seven days. Severn Trent had to supply 350,000 people for between seven and twelve days, and the company soon realised ten litres wasn't enough. One researcher at the post-flood inquiries said her work in African communities dependent on hand-carried well water showed twenty litres was the minimum needed for drinking, cooking and basic hygiene.

The company began buying bottled water in industrial quantities, and scoured the country for bowsers to augment its own depleted stocks. It thought it would need 900; by the end of the crisis it had 1,400 in place, effectively the country's entire inventory. In the early days, the distribution of bottled water was chaotic, and Severn Trent's efforts to keep the bowsers filled were unsuccessful. On Monday, in Longlevens in Gloucester, amid panic-buying, arbitrageurs were spivving water in the Co-op car park for £4 a bottle. The county council was calling contractors in the US, trying to get supplies of a disposable toilet designed for hunters and hikers called a wag bag. On Tuesday, a sixty-nine-year-old woman in Bishop's Cleeve told the *Gloucestershire Echo*: 'We've only got three-quarters of a bucket of water left. We're having to flush the loo with pond water. If we can get drinking water it'll be OK. We just have to give up on washing.'

The big tankers the company normally used turned out to be useless in the narrow, winding streets of Gloucestershire villages, and smaller tankers were in short supply. Severn Trent cobbled together a mixed fleet of beer, milk and water trucks, all of which turned out to have different connectors. A cross-county bowser audit at dawn on Thursday, four days after the flood, found that three-fifths had been drained, vandalised or stolen. Some later turned up on eBay.

The company bodged fixes, opened its corporate wallet – by that Friday it was buying six million litres of water a day, equivalent to the usual daily bottled water consumption for the whole of Britain – and, crucially, turned to the army, which took over much of the organisation and distribution work from a base at Cheltenham Racecourse. The fact that there don't appear to have been any serious public health consequences came down to three factors: Severn Trent trucked special deliveries of water to hospitals and other essential users; the army; and the ad hoc, unpaid generosity of neighbours and volunteers like Chuck Pavey, who helped the elderly and infirm get their water. Tony Wray, who took over as Severn Trent's chief executive after the emergency ended, told MPs: 'We were absolutely inundated with the sheer scale of this.'

Ofwat, the quango regulating the private water industry in England and Wales, accepted Severn Trent's argument that it should be excused the normal compensation rule – which would have given £110 to a household cut off for ten days – on the basis that the floods were an exceptional event, outside the company's control. Tony Wray, who wouldn't be interviewed, has argued that even if Severn Trent had wanted to invest in a back-up to Mythe before the floods, Ofwat would have rejected the plan as

a bad use of the company's scarce capital resources. Yet, like all
England's private water companies, Severn Trent would have
more money to invest in rebuilding and improving the water
system if it didn't pay out such hefty sums in dividends each year
to the shareholders who own it. In 2007, the year Severn Trent
failed its customers catastrophically for the lack of a £25 million
pipeline, then declined to compensate them, it handed over the
equivalent of £38.65 per customer to its shareholders in dividends. Its biggest shareholder, Barclays Bank, got £5.2 million.
That year, Barclays' profits were £7.08 billion.

Supporters of the existing private water regime argue that,
in order to build and renovate facilities in a market economy, a
company has to borrow from somewhere; dividend payments,
the argument runs, are just the price you pay shareholders for
permanently 'borrowing' their cash, in the same way interest
payments are the price you pay banks for temporarily borrowing theirs. (This is a very crude explanation of the difference
between 'equity finance' and 'debt finance' corporate financiers
spend so much time talking about.) That reasoning might work
if Severn Trent were an Internet start-up, or a drugs company
staking its all on a novel medicine. As we shall see, as an
argument about a British water monopoly, it fails.

Edward Warner Shewell, who did most to get the Mythe waterworks built, was a long-lived Conservative patriarch whose career
spanned most of the nineteenth century. With his wife, Emma,
he raised sixteen children at their house in Royal Crescent,
Cheltenham. For many years, with the help of the Tory majority on Cheltenham's Board of Commissioners – the precursor
to the local council – he managed to sustain a glaring conflict
of interest, being both chairman of the commissioners and
chairman of the private water company that had a stranglehold
on Cheltenham's water supply. It was particularly remarkable
because, for decades, the town and the company were bitterly at
odds over where their water should come from.

Many of Shewell's children died before he did. His commercial and political machinations were regularly interrupted by dismal despatches from far corners of the Empire. His brother Frederick, a colonel in the Eighth Hussars, is said to have ridden in the Charge of the Light Brigade with an open Bible on his saddle. Perhaps his contemporaries saw something biblical in the fact that Shewell, so instrumental in getting the Mythe waterworks built, lost three of his sons at sea, two of them drowned.

Water-wise, Cheltenham in the early nineteenth century was, despite being a spa town, not unlike one of the less developed towns in the poor world now, heavily dependent on wells and springs. Unlike present-day Africa, however, which draws well-intentioned rich world aid agencies and profit-seeking rich world multinationals, post-Napoleonic Cheltenham had only localist solutions to its water problems: local entrepreneurs and local campaigners for a cleaner, healthier, more socially just town. The origins of the Mythe waterworks lie in the first avatar of Cheltenham's town commissioners, set up in 1786 to charge the gentry a rate to pay for street lighting and road maintenance. Because the streets needed to be cleaned, and because this demanded a reliable water supply, in 1824 the commissioners set up a private firm – the Cheltenham Waterworks Company – to do the job. Funded by a mixture of shares and loans, the company built a reservoir on the eastern outskirts of Cheltenham, laid a network of pipes into the town and began selling water.

Indoor running water and the novelty of water closets proved popular. The more houses the company supplied, the greater the demand; the greater the proportion of houses with mains water in Cheltenham, the more uncomfortable it became for the town's liberal consciences that the poor couldn't afford it. The company was coming under pressure from three sides: from the town, to supply more water more cheaply; from the springs of the Cotswolds, which couldn't cope with demand; and from its shareholders, who expected profits and dividends to be timely and fat. When government officials arrived from London in

January 1847 to hear about plans for a new reservoir, they walked into this conflict. At the time fewer than half of Cheltenham's 4,700 houses had mains water; the hospital and orphan asylum got water free, but there were no public fountains for the poor; in some of the poorer parts of town, up to ten tenements drew water from a single pump. The company was making a profit of £677, 15 per cent of its turnover. With the national debates that would lead to the 1848 Public Health Act at their height, the government agents told the company that the Act of Parliament needed to get the project going was more likely to get backing if it 'contained some provision for the comforts of the poorer classes'. The company retorted that if the landlords of the poor were prepared to pay for piped water, the poor would get it.

The feud between the Board of Commissioners and the water company went on for years, despite the cross-membership of the two boards, culminating, in the 1860s, in Shewell's long tenure as head of both. On 15 August 1863, Shewell chaired a meeting of shareholders, who voted to pay themselves a massive dividend and bonuses worth 95 per cent of the company's profits, give up the effort to supply more water, and sell out to the ratepayers. The plan had the enthusiastic support of the town's liberal newspaper, the *Cheltenham Examiner*, but a few weeks later the town commissioners – also chaired by Shewell – voted down the plan. One commissioner, who believed like most people in Cheltenham that there was plenty of water in the Cotswolds if the company would only fetch it, declared prophetically: 'There is enough water to be got off the hills to drown Cheltenham twice over.'

Letters from India took about six weeks to reach England at this time and it would have been just after this knock-back that Shewell heard of the death, from illness, of his nineteen-year-old daughter Louisa in the cantonment at Mhow on 27 August, where she was staying with her brother William, an army major. The timing is probably coincidental, but it was in this period that the relationship between Shewell the water company boss and Shewell the top politician in town began to go downhill. Shewell (company) seemed to decide that if Shewell (town) wanted more water, then more water he would have. To the horror of the genteel ratepayers of Cheltenham, it emerged that his water company was planning to make up the supply shortfall by taking water from the River Severn – described by one MP at the time as 'the common sewer of the Midland Counties' – at a place called Mythe, just upstream from Tewkesbury.

'It is thus sought to substitute,' thundered the *Examiner*, 'for the pure and limpid supply we now obtain from the spring head, the contaminated waters of the Severn.' As the town resisted the plan, hostility towards Shewell, and the undemocratic way the commissioners were elected by a minority of citizens in stitched-up contests, deepened. The town begged the company to install double taps for its customers – one with nasty Severn water for washing and flushing, another with nice Cotswold spring water for drinking. The company said it would cost too much. An attempt by the town to buy the company fell through. To Shewell (company's) fury, which Shewell (town) shared and failed to conceal, the other commissioners spent thousands of pounds trying to set up their own, rival water concern.

By October 1865, relations between Shewell and the town commissioners' clerk, George Williams, an indefatigable opponent of the Mythe scheme, had reached the stage of open warfare. Yet in the cosy world of old-time west of England politics, nothing could stop Shewell. In November 1865 he came up for re-election as chairman of the commissioners for the seventh time. He was opposed. One commissioner declared: 'I would not say that Mr Shewell would set up his private interests against the general interests of the town, but human nature is such that private interests must, to a greater or lesser extent, sway the transactions of life.' Nonetheless, Shewell was re-elected by sixteen votes to thirteen, to the cheers of the Tory end of the table, and five years later the Mythe waterworks opened for business.

When, in 2008, I asked Peter Gavan, Severn Trent's director of external affairs, if I could visit the Mythe waterworks, he
said I could not. The floods, he said by way of explanation, were
history; the implication being, I suppose, that history was not a
good thing for a business to have. During the four days I spent
in Tewkesbury a month later I cycled past the works each day
on my way to and from the B&B where I was staying. It was
surrounded by a temporary flood barrier built of components
I'd last seen in Kandahar in Afghanistan in 2006, where they
protected British troops and their allies from attack: textile and
steel-mesh bins, filled with sand or earth, made by the Leeds
company Hesco Bastion.

Edward Shewell's youngest son, Arthur, a lieutenant-colonel,
was killed in Kandahar in 1880, rescuing a wounded comrade
outside the Kabul Gate. His father didn't live long enough to
hear about it; he died in 1878, two years after the town commissioners were replaced by a more democratic council and a
few months before that same council finally bought the water
company out. It would be easy to caricature Edward Shewell
and his cronies as corrupt old Tory buccaneers, damning the
poor and holding back progress. That would be unfair. The ratepayers of Cheltenham could have bought the company out much
sooner than they did, but feared the responsibility, and weren't
ready to accept the principle that universal access to water and
sewers benefited everyone, even if the rich ended up paying
proportionately more for it.

More than that, Shewell, manipulative as he was, was something that his latter-day counterparts, the Colin Matthewses
and Tony Wrays, emphatically aren't: a genuine entrepreneur
and risk-taker, and a localist, deeply embedded in the community he both served and exploited. Even his attempts, through
political control of the town, to establish what Severn Trent has
today – a monopoly of water supply in its area – couldn't fend
off the risk of real competition from other water sources. He and
his partners made fortunes out of selling water to Cheltenham,

but they took a risk to build the Mythe waterworks, and the risk may not have come off. Mythe did open in 1870, but only to supply Tewkesbury – a fraction of the market its backers needed. Cheltenham refused to take Severn water until 1894, long after Shewell was dead and the water company was municipal property. Cheltenham has used it ever since. Shewell's Mythe waterworks entered history as a nineteenth-century private concern, spent 111 years in public ownership, and entered the twenty-first century – much expanded and modernised – as a private asset again. But the private water companies of twenty-first-century Britain are very different creatures.

The privatisation of Britain's water companies in 1989 had nothing in common with the romantic notion of shareholder capitalism, where inventors and entrepreneurs have ideas, start businesses and sell shares to bold investors in order to raise money to help those businesses expand. Far from being exciting new entrepreneurial ventures, the companies involved were settled operations that had been around in one form or another for almost 200 years, and had benefited, for more than half that time, from steady infusions of ratepayers' and taxpayers' money.

The most striking contradiction between water privatisation and Thatcherite free-market romanticism was the monopoly nature of the water companies: millions of customers who have no choice of supplier, no choice but to take the water, and no choice but to pay for it. Millions of captive monthly payments in perpetuity: an investor's dream. Yes, there was a regulator, Ofwat, to limit prices, and to make sure the companies invested in rebuilding the ageing water and sewage systems, but there seemed little danger that the government of Margaret Thatcher would prevent shareholders making a fat return. And so it proved, even unto her successors.

The simplest way to understand the way the water set-up works in England is to think of it as a form of buy-to-let scheme, with us, the customers, as the tenants, paying water bills, like rent; the shareholders as landlords, owning the water companies; and the company staff, like a property management agency, collecting the rent and maintaining the property. Every so often a government inspector – Ofwat – comes round, sets a limit on how much rent the property managers can charge, and tells them they should get a move on with the renovation. But if we don't like the property, the management agency or the landlords, or if we think the rent is too high, we don't have any choice. We can't move to a cheaper property, or a better-run one; we're stuck.

Ofwat argues that English water companies are more efficient than they were before privatisation, pollute less, provide cleaner drinking water and have spent tens of billions of pounds renovating the country's water system. All but the first proposition are true; the first may be too. But that's to compare the privatised water companies with the investment-starved, bureaucratic, centrally funded leviathans of the 1970s and 1980s, not with what they might, or should, have been. In January 2008, the Oxford economist Dieter Helm published a hair-raising analysis of the regulation of Britain's privatised utilities that might have shocked the nation, had its dense technical vocabulary been more comprehensible to MPs and non-economists. Helm argued persuasively that Ofwat had permitted the growth of a system which efficiently ripped customers off, while exposing utility companies to a risk of bankruptcy that has never been higher.

It works like this. When Ofwat decides how much the water companies should be allowed to charge customers, one of the key numbers is how much the regulator thinks it's fair for an investor who puts money into the water industry to get back: the 'return on capital'. But a water company can get investment in two ways. It can get money by selling shares to shareholders – 'equity' – or it can borrow money directly; that is, take on debt. Crucially, equity commands a higher expected rate of return for investors than debt, because shareholders are expected to be more tolerant of risk. The problem Helm identified was that England's water privatisation lumped together two entirely different sides of the business: on the one hand, the existing assets (waterworks, pipeline networks, reservoirs, pumps and so on); and, on the other, operations plus investments in new equipment. The first side was low-risk, and could easily be financed with debt. The second was riskier, and more suitable for finance with a mixture of debt and equity. But Ofwat only has one figure for what it considers a reasonable return on capital: an average of debt and equity.

In other words, Ofwat bases the amount customers pay for water on the assumption that water companies will take on a certain mix of expensive equity financing and cheaper debt financing. But what if water companies simply take on more debt than Ofwat expects? Then the customers will still pay for water according to Ofwat's assumptions, but shareholders will pocket the difference between the two. And that, Helm says, is exactly what happened. 'Investors,' he wrote, 'now contemplate an extraordinary open goal ... The scale of this transfer [from customers to shareholders] is enormous.' In an article in the *Financial Times* inspired by Helm's analysis, Martin Wolf wrote: 'Investors have been able to buy the companies (BAA and the water companies, for example), replace the equity with debt and enjoy a licence to print money. Professor Helm estimates that this financial arbitrage has been worth up to £1 billion a year, at the expense of the customers, predominantly in water. This is, quite simply, a scandal.' As if this wasn't bad enough, Helm pointed out that the huge recent increase in utilities' debt threatened the stability of the riskier side of their business, the day-to-day operations. 'The utilities may not be robust against adverse external shocks,' he said bluntly. 'They might go bankrupt.'

Emma Cochrane, the head of corporate finance at Ofwat, wrote to me in an email that the regulator was familiar with Helm's ideas, had considered them 'very carefully', and rejected them. Helm believes the role of Ofwat itself makes investors in water companies effectively invulnerable to risks where their fixed assets are concerned, passing the risk on to customers; Ofwat disagrees. Cochrane also questioned how easy it would be, as Helm suggests, to split the safe pipes-and-reservoirs side of the water business off from the riskier operate-and-build side. 'You argue that Ofwat has permitted a system that both rips off customers and exposes utility companies to bankruptcy risk. I'm not sure you can argue both,' she wrote.

The Mythe debacle seems to give ammunition for both sides: on the one hand, Ofwat was sufficiently protective of Severn Trent's shareholders to allow the company not to compensate customers for losing their water supply. On the other, Severn Trent lost £14 million as a result of the Mythe failure. Yet on balance, the shareholders seem to win, whatever happens. After the flood, profits were down, but dividends were up, and Severn Trent hadn't lost a single customer, because the customers have nowhere else to go.

On the face of it, Cochrane might seem to be fair in questioning whether a company can be both rapacious and vulnerable. Yet as we saw in the previous chapter, in the five years of Railtrack's sorry existence, the privatised railway infrastructure company sucked in vast amounts of money from government and rail-users, blew out almost £4 billion in debt repayments and dividends, and then collapsed.

It's not as if there aren't other models for water companies. There's the municipal socialism of late nineteenth-century Britain, when business-minded councillors ran networks of utilities as successful commercial concerns, profitable and efficient but publicly owned. Closer to hand, there's Scottish Water – resembling the old water boards in England, but run as a commercial firm, that is to say not subsidised out of general taxation, and with income and expenditure accounted for like a private company. Wales is served, under Ofwat's supervision, by the Welsh water company Glas Cymru, which has no shareholders, but is financed entirely from bonds, borrowings and income from customers. As in France, Glas Cymru puts the actual operation of its water services out to tender to private companies.

A comparison of Scottish Water, Glas Cymru and Severn Trent is instructive. Between 2009 and 2013, Severn Trent gave out almost £1 billion in dividends to shareholders. Had Severn Trent been run as a non-profit, commercial venture, a proportion of those dividend payments would have had to go towards paying interest on debt, but the cash leaked would have been less, and the surplus would have been ploughed back into the business of pipes, sewers and clean water. In the same period Scottish Water, a state-owned, unsubsidised, not for profit organisation, gave away no dividends. Its prices are about the same as Severn Trent – which boasts that it is the cheapest of all English water companies – and yet, over that same five-year period, Scottish Water invested more than £800 per customer, against £475 for Severn Trent. For better or for worse Glas Cymru, meanwhile, actually handed money back to its customers as a form of 'dividend'.

Water privatisation has thrust international generosity on the English public. Popular discontent with the supposed impositions of the European Union is mainstream, yet this discontent finds its strange opposite in the calmness with which English water customers hand billions of pounds over to their monopoly water providers each year, only to see them transmit chunks of it overseas. Anglian Water, for instance, is owned, through a chain of companies registered in Jersey and the Cayman Islands, by a mainly overseas consortium. One consortium partner is the Canada Pension Plan Investment Board. Whenever the captive customers of Anglian turn on the tap they are, in a small way, helping to 'sustain the future pensions of 18 million Canadians', as the CPPIB puts it.

Northumbrian Water, which serves the north-east of England, belongs to Li Ka-shing's Cheung Kong Infrastructure, the same outfit mentioned in the next chapter as having the monopoly on London's underground electricity cables. Southern Water (Sussex and Hampshire) is owned by a Jersey-registered consortium called Greensand Holdings, bringing together various Australian pension funds and the Swiss bank UBS. Ownership of Yorkshire Water is split between various institutional rentiers, including Citibank and the government of Singapore. When the US energy company Enron drowned in its own hype in 2002, it owned Wessex Water, which serves Dorset, Somerset and Wiltshire. Wessex was bought by YTL Power of Kuala Lumpur – its slogan at the time 'World Class Products at Third World Prices'.*

One of the ideals of water privatisation that was most important to its political sponsors – expansion of the number of small shareholders in Britain, the acquisition by ordinary citizens of a direct stake in the financial success of the companies providing them with essential services – hasn't been met. Originally the firms that were privatised became, in the terminology of the markets, 'public' companies, in the sense that they were floated on the stock market, and anyone with money could buy shares in them. Now most of the formerly 'public' privatised firms are only accessible to those who can deal in billions. In market terminology Anglian, Northumbrian, Southern, Thames, Wessex and Yorkshire are 'private companies', no longer traded on the stock market; small shareholders have been bought out by big institutional owners, who occasionally sell great chunks to each other, out of their customer's ken. The only big water companies still listed on the London Stock Exchange are United Utilities, South West (as Pennon Group) and Severn Trent, which fought off a takeover bid in 2013 from a consortium uniting the Kuwait government, a Canadian pension fund and (a rare one, this) the pension fund for British academics.

Thames Water, which holds a monopoly on London's water

---

*   Since changed to 'World Class Products and Services at Very Competitive Prices'.

supply, was 'taken private' – that is, the moment where a privatised but publicly listed company becomes absolutely private property – in 2000 by the German energy company RWE. In 2006 RWE sold it on to a consortium led by an Australian investment bank, Macquarie. At the time of writing Macquarie is the dominant partner – it owns just over a quarter of Thames – with a dozen other institutional owners, only one of which, the British Telecom pension scheme with 13 per cent of Thames, is based in the UK. If you were a resident of London, unhappy with Thames' service, and wanted to stage a protest against its owners, or if you were a British journalist, politician or regulator who wanted to meet them on their home turfs, you'd face a long, expensive trip. The BT pension scheme is based in Chesterfield, England. Macquarie is based in Sydney, Australia, as is the investment house AMP Capital, which has 5.5 per cent of Thames. While you were in Australia, you'd have to visit Brisbane, home of the Queensland Investment Corporation, (8.7 per cent of Thames) and Wollongong in New South Wales, headquarters of the pension fund State Super (2.4 per cent). Your journey would barely have begun. You'd also have to go to Abu Dhabi, base of that sheikhdom's oil investment fund (9.9 per cent of Thames) and Beijing, home to the Chinese government's Chinese Investment Corporation (8.7 per cent). You'd fly trans-Pacific to Canada, where you'd stop off in Victoria, BC (British Columbia Investment Management Corporation, 8.7 per cent); Edmonton (Alberta Investment Management, 3.2 per cent) and Toronto (Aquila Infrastructure, 2.6 per cent, and Optrust, 4.3 per cent). Your last leg would take you across the Atlantic to Holland, home of ABP, based in Heerlen (4.3 per cent) and Stichting Pensioenfonds Zorg en Welzijn of Zeist (2.1 per cent). Truly, the empire of Thames Water investors is one on which the sun never sets.

Macquarie and the rest of the Thames Thirteen are a good example of an attempt to take advantage of weak water industry regulation to suck money out of the taps. In the most recent year for which accounts are available, Thames received £1.8 billion from its customers. The proportion of this which reached the Thames Thirteen was relatively small – only £75 million, which represents, based on some Ofwat data from 2007 about how much of their own money the original members of the Macquarie consortium put into the purchase, a return of just over 3 per cent – pretty meagre. But look at the accounts. The headline figure recorded for dividends to shareholders is much higher – £231 million, or 12.9 per cent of turnover. How to explain the difference? The secret lies in the chain of companies through which the Thames Thirteen owns the actual utility. As that £231 million moves away from the pipes and sewers on its journey to Canada and the Arabian peninsula, it stops off at other entities, like Thames Water Utilities Cayman Finance Limited. Somewhere in the chain it sheds £156 million. This is 'inter-company interest' and relates to the money the Thames Thirteen borrowed in order to buy Thames in the first place. To put it simply, the buyers of Thames Water took out a mortgage to get it, and the money they earn from direct dividends is trivial compared to the amount they think they'll gain when, as they eventually will, they sell the company on.

Think back to the buy-to-let analogy I used earlier. Suppose you received a big inheritance, bought a flat in London as an investment and rented it out. If you paid for the whole flat up front in cash, you'd not be doing too well by capitalist standards. You might earn a few per cent a year on the money you spent – which you would then be taxed on. But what if the flat increased in value? What if you bought the house for half a million and sold it five years later for £600,000? Well, that's a gain of 20 per cent – not bad. However, there's another way. What if you could get a loan for 95 per cent of the flat's value? Then you'd only pay £25,000 up front, use the rent to make the interest payments, and five years later get back £125,000 – a 400 per cent return on your investment. And if you could set the interest payments on the loan off against tax, even better.

That's what private equity consortia like the Macquarie-led Thames Thirteen are doing: borrowing money to buy privatised infrastructure using a small down payment, taking a relatively small dividend directly, and using the rest of the dividend to pay off the loan in the hope that when, after a few years, they sell the water firms/ports/airports/motorways, they'll make an enormous profit. In 2006, when the Macquarie-led consortium beat off rivals to buy Thames (the consortium had a slightly different make-up then) it paid £7.9 billion, at a time when Ofwat, the regulator, reckoned the company's underlying assets were worth £5.9 billion. Based on early Ofwat estimates, most of the loans the consortium borrowed to complete the deal, £4.4 billion's worth, would have gone on the company's books – not an unreasonable amount of debt for a company with a big programme of works to carry out. But a significant additional amount, £1.2 billion, would have been piled onto the accounts of that chain of holding companies, to be paid back through dividends. To buy Thames, then, Macquarie would have borrowed 95 per cent of what Ofwat said the company was worth, and paid, in all, 134 per cent.

The Thames Thirteen, in other words, believe the company is worth much more than Ofwat does. Where did the consortium hope the extra money was going to come from – the extra money to meet its high mortgage payments, and to increase the company's price so it could make a profit when it sold it on? Macquarie may be a super-efficient manager, but a generation after privatisation, it was never going to be able to sack enough people, sell enough land or transform working practices radically enough to make up the difference. There would be limits, too, on how far Thames might be able to drag its feet on the vast programme of pipe and sewer replacement Ofwat demanded. The only give in the programme was the possibility that Thames customers were paying much more for the water system and its renewal than Macquarie's cost of capital – its mortgage rate – required. This is clearly what Macquarie believed, or at least persuaded its fellow investors it believed; and Ofwat didn't seem to mind. Ofwat's attitude is that it doesn't care how much punters pay for a water company, as long as they don't put the company's operations in jeopardy. But this ignores the fact that the overwhelming factor determining a water company's price is Ofwat's own rulings about how much the company can charge customers, and how much it must invest. The Macquarie consortium's bid was a group of sophisticated investors telling the body supposed to protect British citizens' interests that it had screwed up, and it was going to rip them off.

Where does this leave Thames Water's fourteen million customers? Paying more for their water than they should, with a large share of that payment going to remote, unaccountable bodies over whom they have no control, and whom they have no choice but to accept. And regardless of whether it is set at a fair level or not, the obligation to pay, and the lack of choice about whom to pay it too, makes the English water bill, effectively, a tax. I'm all for trade, mutual investment and the exchange of people and ideas between Britain and China. I've nothing against the Chinese. I sympathise with residual anger that Britain waged war against China in the nineteenth century in support of British opium dealers, yet has no popular memory of the fact. But nobody could describe China today as a democracy. It is an authoritarian state that censors free expression and represses campaigners for social justice with a degree of harshness greatly in excess of that currently accepted in Britain. The ruling elite identify themselves as communists, yet have grown personally wealthy by endorsing a version of capitalism. When we Londoners turn on our taps and fill our kettles, it is as if we are taking part in an enactment of the last scene from George Orwell's *Animal Farm*, where the post-revolutionary pigs and the cynical farmers sit down to feast together. A British political party that has traded since I was a child on its claim to patriotism, its belief in freedom and democracy, and in its contempt for communism, has enabled a system in which I am obliged to pay an annual tax to the world's biggest communist country in order to exist.

From the perspective of the Thames Thirteen there's a possible flaw, of course, in the scheme I've described above. It's the same as the flaw in buy-to-let. What if the value of the asset you buy, the house or the water company, doesn't go up? What if it falls? What if interest rates go up, you can't make the loan payments, and you have to sell, just when everybody else is trying to sell for the same reason, driving prices down further? Well, that's bad news for the ultimate owners – but not for everyone.

Look again at the identities of the Thames Thirteen. Apart from Macquarie, which is acting as the agent for another group of smaller institutional investors, and the two sovereign wealth funds, most have something in common: they're investing on behalf of present and future pensioners, and are, or grew out of, pension funds set up for state workforces. The Queensland Investment Corporation began as the pension fund for Queensland state employees; State Super caters for New South Wales civil servants. ABP and Stichting Pensioenfonds Zorg en Welzijn are pension funds for Dutch civil servants, teachers, social workers, doctors and nurses. The Alberta, British Columbia and Optrust funds in Ontario invest on behalf of the public servants of those provinces. BT was once a government firm. Even AMP Capital, never a public outfit, had communitarian origins – a big demutualisation of a non-profit Sydney life insurance firm in 1998.

When you look more closely at what happened to Thames Water, it is not a simple, and potentially chauvinist, tale of exploitation of captive Londoners by cunning foreign capitalists. It is a tale of clever middlemen. On one side, millions of Thames Water customers, paying an inflated private water tax; on the other, millions of Dutch, Canadian, Australian and British pensioners, dependent on their pension funds in their old age, and millions of Chinese and Emiratis, powerless to influence their government's disposition of national wealth. In the middle, an international fraternity of fund managers, telling the Thames customers what a brilliant deal they have with the Thames Thirteen as their tax collectors, and telling the world's pensioners what an extraordinary return they're getting on their stake in Thames Water, so extraordinary that they, the private planners of the fund manager class, need to be rewarded with fat fees, options, salaries and bonuses. It's not possible for both messages to be true. And if the Thames Thirteen lose their shirt on their punt – if Ofwat gets tough, for instance, and they end up selling Thames to the next buyer for less than they paid for it – there'll be no clawing back of the extras, the top 1 per cent renumeration, the beachfront homes, the trophy cars and the vintage wine cellars that the fund managers have gained over the years.

In 2012 the new head of the Ontario civil servants' pension fund Optrust, Stephen Griggs, demanded to know why members of the fund's Private Markets Group – the team responsible for buying a stake in Thames Water – were not paid according to what other Canadian pension fund managers were paid, but according to salaries paid by the likes of Goldman Sachs on Wall Street. Soon afterwards, he was sacked.

One day I went to Worcester to visit Malcolm McMurray, a retired Severn Trent manager who worked for the company in its public and its private incarnations. As a senior union leader, he campaigned against privatisation in the late 1980s, addressing public meetings across the region. After privatisation, Severn Trent showered its workforce with shares. Union organisers from outside the water industry used to complain that when they met unionised water workers, they talked about share prices.

Worcester was drenched in hot sunshine when I walked up to McMurray's house, past the double garage and the shining gold Volkswagen estate to his front door. He let me in. He looked lean and fit.

'Nice house,' I said.

He smiled, a little sadly. 'I'm always grateful I retired while they still had the final salary pension scheme,' he said.

We sat in his long, neat garden, rolling away into trees in the distance. He was sixty-four. He retired in 2000, in his mid-fifties. In 1973, as a regional manager, he was based at Mythe for three months; the then state-owned Severn Trent had tried to save money by changing shift patterns, and the shift workers, then members of the TGWU, were throwing strategic sickies to sabotage the scheme. In the years running up to privatisation, McMurray recalled, investment slumped. He's sure that the Thatcher government deliberately starved the water industry of cash to enhance the case for selling it off. After privatisation, more than half the old workforce of 11,000 lost their jobs. He remembers being shocked at the shift in the public's mood when it was privatised. 'At times of peak demand, we used to be able to use local radio to appeal to our consumers to use less water, to not use hosepipes, and generally they were co-operative, they went along with it. But that suddenly changed when we were privatised. People knew we were only in it to make a profit. It was quite a shock to realise how quickly people's attitude changed.'

I asked McMurray if he knew any union leaders who'd campaigned against privatisation, then taken up company share options.

'Well, I did,' he said. 'It would be easier to say who didn't.'

McMurray's wife came in with their two little blond grandsons, bright in scarlet jumpers and covered in stickers from the school races. They went down towards the trees to play and the sun caught on a small fountain that the couple had installed, chuckling away on a pumped loop in the shrubs in the middle of the garden.

'I had no conscience about it at all,' said McMurray. 'I'd campaigned against privatisation, but we'd lost that particular battle. Privatisation was inevitable. I wasn't going to leave the water industry and so I thought well, I'll buy some shares, and try and continue to serve the public as best I can.'

What kind of overarching narrative have we been constructing?

→ What it means to be British

→ Britain's place in the world → where is power?

→ public vs. private

  ⤷ what does govt involvement look like

  ⤷ welfare state, social democracy, nationalization
      45-79   of industry

4. Taking Power

Privatised electricity

Does it matter that the power Britain relies on to make the country glow and hum no longer belongs to Britain? After all, the lights still shine. The phones still charge. Does it matter that the old electricity suppliers of eastern and north-west England and the English Midlands, the coal-fired power stations of Kingsnorth, Ironbridge and Ratcliffe-on-Soar, the turbine shops at Hams Hall, the oil and gas stations on the Isle of Grain, Killingholme, Enfield and Cottam are the property of E.ON of Düsseldorf? Is it of significance only to sentimental Little Englanders that the former electricity boards of Tyneside and Yorkshire, the power stations at Didcot in Oxfordshire, Fawley in Hampshire, Tilbury in Essex, Littlebrook in Kent, Great Yarmouth in Norfolk, Little Barford in Bedfordshire and Staythorpe in Nottinghamshire belong to RWE of Essen (the last being the only one the German company built itself)? Is it a sign of some atavistic hostility to the Other – nationalism, chauvinism, even racism – to find it strange that the one-time public purveyors of electricity in North Wales, Merseyside and southern Scotland, along with another set of large power stations, are owned by Iberdrola of Bilbao? Are you an enemy of liberal principles if you question the fact that, when local electrical engineers dig up the roads in London, they're working for East Asia's richest man, the Hong Kong-based Li

Ka-shing? In north-east England, they work for Warren Buffett; in Birmingham, Cardiff and Plymouth, the Pennsylvania Power and Light Company; in Edinburgh, Glasgow and Liverpool, Iberdrola; in Manchester, a consortium of the Commonwealth Bank of Australia and a J.P. Morgan investment fund.

More than anyone, you'd think, it would matter to the people who made these arrangements possible in the first place. What has happened is not what they promised or intended when they put Britain's state-owned electricity industry on the block. This is not a trivial issue. When politicians, regulators and corporations decide the future electric life of Britain, they determine how the lights will be kept burning and the wheels turning without severely affecting the world's climate or impoverishing us. But as a result of actions taken a generation ago by Margaret Thatcher's Conservatives – a party whose nationalist programme promised independence from Europe – the decisions aren't Britain's alone. Thatcher promised less state involvement in industry but the future of Britain's energy supply now hinges on companies based in Paris, Electricité de France, better known as EDF, and Areva, maker of nuclear power stations, that are majority owned by the state of France.

Defending her record in Parliament on the day she resigned in 1990, Thatcher spoke in patriotic tones of how, with millions of people buying shares in former state industries, privatisation was giving 'power back to the people', and how competition at home and open markets in Europe would free British enterprise to lead the world. Today it's clear that the result of electricity privatisation was to take power away from the people. Small British shareholders have no influence over the overwhelmingly non-British owners of the firms that generate and distribute power in Britain. The fact that individual households and small businesses can choose to switch from the confusing tariff of one oligopolistic supplier to another doesn't protect them from sharp, unpredictable swings in prices. In overseas chanceries the Thatcher doctrine came up against ambitious leaders who were no less patriotic, but not so arrogant and naive. Unlike Thatcher, they didn't assume that if their country levelled its playing field, others would level theirs. The problem with the ideal of competition is that there are winners and losers. The electricity competition has now been held. It is over, and Britain lost. From the point of view of technology and capital, electric Britain is no longer a centre. It is another centre's province.

The most unexpected consequence of selling the country's electric legacy, the consequence that most directly contradicts what the Thatcherites were trying to do, was the gradual absorption of swathes of the industry by EDF. Beginning with the takeover of London Electricity in 1998, exploiting the Thatcherites' open-door market structures and their decision to split the electricity industry into small, easy-to-swallow chunks, France in effect renationalised the industry its neighbour had so painstakingly privatised. Renationalised it, that is, for France. As well as being one of the six dominant UK suppliers of energy, EDF now owns a fat portfolio of British power stations, including the fleet of nuclear plants that still provides around a sixth of the country's electricity, and is to begin replacing them with new reactors.

It was a setback for the pro-market ideologues. Unlike E.ON and RWE, EDF is a state-owned monolith with a near monopoly on the production and supply of electricity in France, run by technocrats and members of a powerful trade union, the Confédération générale du travail (CGT). Its mission is to empower France in foreign markets, and the government agency that owns it, L'Agence des participations de l'Etat, isn't embarrassed to say so. In her foreword to the agency's 2010 report, Christine Lagarde – then minister for economic affairs in François Fillon's cabinet – boasted that the state would be more active than ever in building 'champions capable of competing with global market rivals'. In Thatcherite terms EDF was a public sector mammoth that would inevitably be hunted to extinction by the hungry and agile competitors of post-privatisation countries like Britain. The laws of economics said so. And yet the opposite happened. The mammoth thrived, and Britain failed to produce new competitors, agile or otherwise.

If the power of EDF in Britain is an embarrassment to neo-liberals, does that mean it's good for their opponents, the pastel-shade socialists of the legacy left? Unison, the British union that represents electricity workers, seems happy. Greg Thomson, Unison's head of strategic organisation, told me that since it crossed the Channel, EDF had gone against prevailing management orthodoxy by reinstating a final salary pension scheme for workers. Unison was given seats with the CGT in an EDF/union body, a 'European Works Council', and enough leverage over EDF management to get union recognition for previously non-union workers at a call centre in Sunderland. 'When London Electricity was privatised, we adopted a policy of returning it to public ownership, and I'm pleased to think I delivered on that,' Thomson said. 'Obviously to the wrong nation, but you can't be too picky.'

Yet EDF's foreign adventures make Unison's French counterparts suspicious. They don't understand why Britain gave away its native electricity industry so easily. A colleague of Thomson's told me that the CGT was 'apoplectic' Unison didn't resist in 2010 when EDF sold off the local networks of cables and transformers it owned in East Anglia, London and south-east England to Li Ka-shing, in order to fund its purchase of Britain's nuclear stations. 'When the sale went through they were absolutely pissed off because we had done nothing to stop it. They voted to man the barricades.' Thomson remembered an early trip to a European Works Council meeting in Paris, when one of the CGT men said to him at lunch: 'There's only one country that's stupid enough to sell off its electricity industry, and that's Britain.'

How did we get here? In 1981, with inflation and unemployment at 10 per cent plus, with the recently elected Conservative government forced to yield to the demands of the miners, public spending cuts provoking general outrage and Thatcher's prime

ministerial career seemingly doomed to a swift, ignominious end, a thirty-eight-year-old economist from Birmingham
University called Stephen Littlechild was working on ways to
realise an esoteric idea that had been much discussed in radical
Tory circles: privatisation. Privatisation was not a Thatcher
patent. The Spanish economist Germà Bel traces the origins
of the word to the German word *Reprivatisierung*, first used in
English in 1936 by the Berlin correspondent of the Economist,
writing about Nazi economic policy. In 1943, in an analysis
of Hitler's programme in the *Quarterly Journal of Economics*,
the word 'privatisation' entered the academic literature for the
first time. The author, Sidney Merlin, wrote that the Nazi Party
'facilitates the accumulation of private fortunes and industrial
empires by its foremost members and collaborators through
"privatisation" and other measures, thereby intensifying central-
isation of economic affairs and government in an increasingly
narrow group that may for all practical purposes be termed the
national socialist elite.'

The gung-ho free marketeers who rode to power with
Thatcher in 1979 don't seem to have been aware of the Nazi
prelude, although they would have known of later privatisations in Pinochet's Chile. Until Bel's recent research it was Peter
Drucker, in his writings about management in the 1960s, who
was said to have coined the term 'reprivatisation'. Nigel Lawson,
a champion of privatisation, attributes the dropping of the 're-'
to a fellow Conservative, David Howell, one of the back-room
Tory ideas men tinkering obscurely with economic models
while Edward Heath and Harold Wilson squared off against
the unions in the 1960s and 1970s. (Howell was Thatcher's first
energy minister. He is, as I write, Baron Howell of Guildford,
Foreign Office minister, and until 2012 remained in government
under his fellow Etonian David Cameron, alongside his son-in-
law George Osborne.)

The 1979 Conservative manifesto barely mentioned privatisation, or denationalisation, as it was sometimes called. In 1968,

when an internal party think tank called the public sector of industry 'a millstone round our necks' and proposed some sell-offs, Thatcher – who had been researching the privatisation of power stations and failed to find 'acceptable answers' – was sceptical. 'One could not have two rival enterprises,' she said, 'seeking to sell electricity in competition one with another.' Littlechild disagreed. And in the ferment of the 1979 election victory, theorists like himself saw a rare chance to test their ideas in a real, live, industrial society of fifty million people. In October 1981 he published a paper in the house journal of the radical free-market think tank the Institute of Economic Affairs called 'Ten Steps to Denationalisation'. Appearing alongside articles with such titles as 'Why Recession Benefits Britain' and 'The Tumbril and the Classroom', Littlechild's proposals would have seemed to most politicians and business people of the time like the ravings of a revolutionary dreamer. As the mainstream right talked warily of selling off parts of the steel industry, Littlechild jumped ahead to what few others imagined could be the future: to the privatisation of the railways and the Post Office. 'What the Post Office needs,' he wrote, 'is an imaginative asset stripper.'

His most extreme ideas, by the standards of the day, were about electricity. In Britain at that time, electricity was produced and distributed by a state organisation with a no-nonsense Attlee-era moniker, redolent of brown paper envelopes and blotched stencils and corridors smelling of disinfectant: the Central Electricity Generating Board, the CEGB. Littlechild suggested splitting the National Grid off from the power-generating side of the CEGB, privatising regional electricity boards, letting private companies build power stations to compete with the state, and forcing the CEGB to sell or lease its coal and nuclear plants. It turned out these were not dreams, but prophecies packaged in an implementable plan; all were to come about within a decade.

As the great shift from public to private ownership of Britain's technological veins and sinews gathered pace through the 1980s – telephones in 1984, gas in 1986, airports in 1987, water in 1989, leading up to electricity and the railways in the 1990s – the public perception was that Britain was becoming more like the United States, where, it was popularly believed, everything, including electricity, was provided by competing private companies. No autobiography of a British free-market thinker was complete without an American epiphany, a journey across the Atlantic to where Ronald Reagan's United States seemed to hum and sparkle in a virtuous free market circle of efficiency and prosperity.

Apart from the reality that, for most Americans, it didn't, the problem was that extreme pro-privatisation Brits like Littlechild thought the US hadn't gone far enough. So radical were the Thatcherite free market evangelicals that they thought America's electricity system all too similar to the neo-Soviet horrors, as they saw them, of the CEGB.

In nineteenth- and early twentieth-century Europe, only the earliest nodes of new-technology networks – piped water, gas, electricity, railways, telegraph and telephone communications, services that societies quickly became dependent on – were built as capitalist ventures. Gradually the networks were taken over, completed and run by national or local government. The United States took a different route. America let private companies carry on providing vital services like electricity; it also let them have local monopolies. But in exchange for being protected from competition, the companies accepted limits on their profits. The limit was worked out as a percentage of the amount the company and its shareholders had invested in the company – in building a power station, for instance – and how much it would have to invest in future to keep the system running. It was called 'rate of return regulation', and it set a ceiling on the profits capitalists were allowed to make on an investment in something society couldn't live without.

It wasn't perfect. There were regular disputes over how much the companies should invest and how much customers should have to pay. But the arrangement gave American society a generally robust set of networks that powered it through its twentieth-century transformation. Looking ahead, in the 1980s, to the great sell-off that few Britons knew was coming, Littlechild concluded that Britain could be more free-market than America. He had a powerful ally in Alan Walters, Thatcher's economic adviser, and when it came to the first of the big privatisations – the sale of British Telecom – Littlechild was commissioned to come up with new rules for governing the private companies on which the country would depend in the new, profit-led world.

The formula he came up with in 1983 sounded benign enough when it was presented to the public. Few knew or cared what it meant, still less how radical a departure it was: it seemed a minor detail compared to the enormity of privatisation itself. Littlechild's formula, known as 'RPI minus X', isn't the only reason Britain's private power industry is now, thirty years later, an overwhelmingly foreign-owned oligopoly. But it is key. The trouble with the American system, Littlechild thought, was that it didn't reward electricity companies (or phone, water or gas companies) for being more efficient: for sacking superfluous workers, using cheaper materials or cutting back on luxuries like research. On the contrary, it encouraged them to invest in high technology and fancy experimental kit, because the more they invested, the more profits the regulator would let them keep. This, in turn, led to higher prices for customers. To an efficiency-obsessed theorist like Littlechild it all smacked of what he saw as the ghastly mix of bureaucrats, engineers, unions and politicians running the CEGB.

Littlechild's solution for Britain was to replace the American ceiling on profits with a ceiling on prices. Privatised companies would only be able to increase their prices each year by an amount equal to inflation, measured by the Retail Price Index, RPI, minus an X-factor, which the regulator would set every five years. Prices were supposed to fall, in real terms, every year: it sounded like a good deal for the customer. But what wasn't obvious to most people was how huge the opportunities were for privatised electricity companies to cut costs, and not just by laying off workers. In *The Queen of the Trent*, published in 2009 to mark the fortieth anniversary of Cottam power station in Nottinghamshire, Robert Davis quotes one of the employees:

> There was so much wastage during the CEGB days. It was like they had money to burn. The stores were always full and we had spares for everything. Bureaucracy was part of the problem. If you signed stuff out of the stores, even if you found you'd got the wrong bits, you couldn't sign them back in. The system didn't allow that. There was nothing to do but put the parts straight in the skip.

Under RPI-X, there was a big incentive for managers to root out such practices. But there was no need for them to pass on the gains to customers in the form of lower prices, or to invest them in research and new plants. As long as they kept their prices in line with the X-factor, managers could bank the profits they made from cost-cutting, or pass them on to shareholders, jacking up their own salaries along the way.

Littlechild, who became the privatised electricity industry's first regulator, thought this was a good thing. He was happy to see the privatised electricity companies make fat profits in the early years, thinking that this would draw in new competitors eager for a slice of the pie. They would build new power stations, eating into the incumbents' profits, poaching customers by offering lower prices. The least efficient electricity firms would go bust, the most efficient would thrive, and electricity would be cheaper. As old power stations wore out, they would be replaced because it was profitable to replace them: the market would organise itself to produce as much electricity as customers were prepared to pay for. To begin with, before full competition was established, he, the regulator, imagined he would act as a surrogate, a kind of State Competitor General, enforcing occasional price cuts to keep the private companies on their toes. In the end, he thought, the need for regulation would wither away.

What Littlechild, an academic with no business experience, didn't fully take on board was that the reason private companies compete with each other isn't that they like competition. They hate it, and will only compete if forced to do so. Rather than competing with a rival on price or product or revenue, they'll try to eliminate the rival firm and take over its territory by buying it; or reach an unwritten agreement on an oligopolistic cartel of a few big firms, carving up the market between them.

Electricity isn't a commodity like copper or coffee or water. It's the only commodity that is both essential to modern life and effectively impossible to store. An electricity system must be able to manufacture and transport as much power as the society it serves demands at every given moment, and not one watt less. The only efficient way to achieve this is for society to invest vast amounts of manpower and resources over generations to plan, build and maintain a network of power stations and supply cables, with excess capacity to deal with breakdowns and peaks in demand.

Britain built just such a network in the mid-twentieth century, and by the time it was privatised it was a creation of devilish intricacy, even before the government sliced it into pieces, replacing central planning with commercial contracts between sellers, makers and transporters of power. The local sellers of electricity, the twelve regional English electricity boards, were privatised as twelve separate companies in 1990. They would now buy their electricity wholesale, supposedly at market rates, mainly from the three big privatised concerns that made it: National Power and Powergen, which took over the CEGB's big coal-fired power stations in 1991, and British Energy, owner of the newest nuclear stations, which was floated on the stock market in 1996. Holding it all together, transporting electricity between power stations and from region to region, was the National Grid, owned jointly at first by the twelve local electricity firms; after 1996, it was an independent commercial player in its own right.

But once the privatisers factored in the costs of spare capacity, and the different profiles of different kinds of power station, they came up with a system for setting the wholesale price of electricity so complicated that the only people who understood it were the people whose interest it was for it to be as high as possible – the people running the electricity firms. In the course of the 1990s, the cost of oil, gas and coal fell and aggressive management made power stations much cheaper to run, mainly by cutting workers. And yet the wholesale price of electricity stayed the same. The big private players found ways to manipulate the market to keep prices high. They were able to game the system by declaring, for instance, that a certain power station was temporarily unavailable to generate electricity. The price of electricity would then rise – at which point the power station magically came back online. One company fingered for doing this – in an early report by Littlechild – was Powergen, headed by Ed Wallis, a former CEGB official who ran the operation to get coal to the power stations during the 1984–85 miners' strike. But however unethically it was behaving, Powergen wasn't breaking any law. It was simply taking advantage of the opportunities for bilking customers that were built in to the rules.

There were many other tactics. In the privatisation carve-up, Powergen inherited two small coal-fired power stations: Hams Hall, outside Birmingham, and Ferrybridge B, near Pontefract. They were used only in emergencies or during maintenance on the local electricity network, when it couldn't handle the voltage from the National Grid. Soon after Powergen took over, it announced that, as a commercial decision, it was going to close both stations. This forced the Grid to upgrade its transformers in the area, to make sure local people and businesses never risked a blackout. But while the upgrade was being carried out, the Grid couldn't be accessed, and Ferrybridge B and Hams Hall became indispensable to Yorkshire and Warwickshire. The stations' electricity had to be bought by suppliers, no matter how much it cost. While similar stations elsewhere in the country were charging between £20 and £30 per megawatt-hour, Powergen hiked Ferrybridge and Hams Hall prices to £120. According to the calculations of Littlechild's statistical elves, this abuse of market dominance brought Powergen an extra £88 million in profits – an extra £88 million, that is, carved out of customers' electricity bills.

Wallis was pilloried in the media in the mid-1990s as the classic bureaucrat-turned-fat-cat for his £460,000 salary and lucrative share options, but his career and establishment reputation don't seem to have been tarnished by the conduct of the company he ran. Until 2014 he was chairman of the Natural Environment Research Council, responsible for handing out government money to scientists researching climate change.

As well as rewarding management and shareholders for cutting costs, RPI-X rewarded them for cutting corners. Unlike water and rail, which badly needed investment when they were privatised, the privatised electricity companies benefited from half a century of high investment in an over-engineered, lovingly maintained power system that produced more electricity than the country needed. In the early years they could slash investment without anyone, apart from their staff, being aware of the effects. Over-investment switched to under-investment, but the consequences of this wouldn't become clear until later.

RPI-X also allowed companies to reap the benefit of windfalls that were the result of luck rather than smart management. Since electricity is one of those things, like food, that people need whether there's an economic slump or not, the companies did relatively well out of the recession of the early 1990s. Their overheads were half what the experts predicted. The companies paid out generous dividends to shareholders and were still swimming in cash. Littlechild could have stepped in to lower prices, but he held back, fearful of intruding on managers' RPI-X nirvana. When he did act, the stock market found the price cuts he ordered so laughably mild that the companies' share prices shot up. In December 1994, the property conglomerate Trafalgar

House tried to buy Northern Electric, one of the privatised electricity companies. It offered £11 a share: four times what the civil servants and City advisers had sold it for a few years earlier. Northern Electric's cash mountain was so large that it was able to give each shareholder a fiver for every share they owned in order to prevent the takeover. The economist Dieter Helm, in his book *Energy, the State and the Market*, writes: 'Northern Electric in effect revealed that it could have given its domestic customers a year without paying any bills and still have been able to finance its functions.'

The privatised electricity companies' minuscule debts and the fat profits they were making under RPI-X drew predators from across the Atlantic, and when the government's golden share in the firms lapsed in 1995, the Americans pounced. Just as California was making the disastrous decision to imitate the British model in opening up its own electricity system to competition, companies from Ohio, Nebraska, Texas, Georgia, Colorado, Louisiana and Virginia spent £10 billion buying up British firms. As the Americans began to flood in, Labour took over from the Conservatives, and Gordon Brown slapped a windfall tax of £1.5 billion on the electricity firms as punishment for their excess profits. It was easy for the Americans to borrow the money to pay, because their new acquisitions had so little debt on their books. But the windfall tax was a sign that US executives, caught up in the more-testosterone-than-sense expansionist passion that brought about the downfall of Enron, had misjudged the risks of investing in British electricity.

They tried the same tricks as their British predecessors. Edison Mission Energy of California, for instance, bought two big coal-fired power stations from Powergen in 1999. In 2000, it announced that it was closing one of the generating units at its Fiddlers Ferry coal station in Cheshire because, it said, it cost too much to run. In fact, it could have been run at a profit. But by taking 500 megawatts of the power it generated off the market, Edison Mission drove up the price of electricity, which meant more money for Edison Mission, and for the other owners of power stations. The customers paid the price. Edison Mission eventually brought the unit back online after pressure from Littlechild's successor as regulator, Callum McCarthy. The writing was on the wall for the Americans. The windfall tax suggested there'd be a tighter regulatory regime under Labour, and shortly after the American buying spree began, wholesale prices for electricity plummeted. There was a rush for the exit. In desperation, the Americans cast around for somebody willing to take their British electricity assets off their hands.

McCarthy was indifferent to the rout of the Americans. He was only interested in price, and claimed partial credit for the sudden cheapness of electricity: he attributed it to Neta, a wholesale electricity trading system that he favoured and the government backed. The New Electricity Trading Arrangements were designed to bring prices down by making the electricity market fairer and more open. On the face of it, Littlechild had cause for satisfaction, too. He could point out that the fate of the Americans – some, notably TXU of Houston, lost their shirts in Britain – gave the lie to the notion that the privatised electricity system was a licence for capitalists to print money. In reality, the fall in the electricity price had little to do with Neta and much to do with Littlechild's endorsement in the late 1990s of the 'dash for gas' – the rapid construction of gas-fired power stations, cheaper to build and run at the time than coal or nuclear. This led at the turn of the century to an electricity glut.

New power stations, an electricity surplus, lower prices, companies going bust because they weren't competitive: it sounds as if everything Littlechild planned had come to pass. Yet the result wasn't at all what he'd imagined. Just because the American companies' shareholders, and their customers back home in the US, got stiffed by their adventures in Britain didn't mean that Britain benefited. In the first place, the electricity surplus was a political and industrial disaster. The new wave of gas-fired power stations took enough market share from the coal and nuclear stations to bring them to the edge of bankruptcy, but didn't have the capacity to replace them if they actually went bust. It wasn't just that the livelihoods of thousands of miners and engineers loyal to Labour were on the line: a system that could bring the country to a halt in a fraction of a second was subjected to market shocks that had no market solution. Blair's government had already intervened to slow down the switch from coal to gas; in 2002 it had little choice but to bail out British Energy, the private company that owned the nuclear stations.

And there was a deeper, less visible problem. Neta was fantastically complex. There is no evidence to suggest that any elected politician has ever understood how it worked (any more than they understood its byzantine predecessor, the 'Pool'). Some specialists believe civil servants don't understand it either. How could they? Its arcane codexes are intelligible only to corporate lawyers and accountants. Yet there was one important clue to how Neta worked: the electricity companies were all for it – this, despite the fact that McCarthy championed it as a means of bringing them to heel. And when Neta – the electricity trading system we still have today – was introduced, it gradually became clear why. It was even more opaque than the Pool. And although its introduction coincided with a sharp fall in wholesale electricity prices, customers saw no change in their bills.

It was true that the 'dash for gas' had brought about a squeeze in profits for the companies that generated electricity. But the main beneficiaries of this weren't customers: they were the firms that distributed and sold the power. Excessive profit margins simply shifted from one set of electricity companies to another. The inevitable next stage was for the companies that distributed electricity to merge with the companies that generated it. This was 'vertical integration', just the kind of cosy arrangement, with all its potential for price-fixing and abuse of market dominance, that Littlechild wished to avoid. The introduction of Neta shed no light on the real costs to companies that sell customers electricity they've 'bought' wholesale from themselves.

There was only one set of companies rich, powerful and experienced enough to take advantage of Britain's burgeoning oligopoly. In 1998, as the Americans began their withdrawal from Britain, Continental Europeans arrived to take their place. The first bid from across the Channel, only seven years after the CEGB was destroyed, came from Electricité de France, the French CEGB.

I met Stephen Littlechild at a hotel in Dorridge, near Birmingham. He's still busy in the obscure world of utility regulation, still attached to Birmingham and Cambridge Universities. Gently sunburned, with white hair and beard, he's almost seventy; he has a Puckish energy, an enthusiasm more postgraduate than professorial, and a way of punctuating his conversation with a falsetto giggle. He once said that instead of RIP, the inscription on his gravestone should read 'RPI-X'.

Privatisation, he told me, had been a matter of achieving clarity. 'In the nationalised industries ... nobody had a clue what anything cost. The government just gave them money, and sometimes didn't ... What has happened is that a price has been put on everything.'

He blamed two groups for the problems that followed electricity privatisation. One was the City analysts who mistakenly characterised investment in long-established public electricity enterprises as 'risky', thus underestimating how cheaply new owners would be able to borrow money. The other was the politicians, who never gave him the powers he wanted to obstruct the anti-competitive mergers of electricity makers and electricity sellers.

In 1995, Scottish Power, which was integrated from the moment of privatisation – it both sold and generated electricity from the big coal stations at Longannet and Cockenzie – became the first privatised producer to take over a privatised seller when it bid for the former Merseyside and North Wales Electricity Board, renamed Manweb. Littlechild said he had tried to persuade

Tim Eggar, energy minister at the time, to intervene. Instead of worrying about the power over customers the takeover would give the Scottish firm, Eggar said he wanted to give Manweb 'a kick in the pants'. Both companies now belong to Iberdrola of Spain.

It seemed odd that Littlechild, the great free marketeer, should be upset about a private Scottish firm taking over a privatised electricity board, yet quite relaxed about a state-owned French company taking over the private London Electricity in November 1998. That first foray by EDF was followed in 2000 by its purchase of Cottam; in 2002 EDF added the old electricity boards in south-east and south-west England to its portfolio, and in 2008, with the purchase of British Energy, it bought most of Britain's working nuclear power stations. As age shuts them down the plan is to replace them, starting in 2023, with a French-designed reactor known as the European Pressurised Reactor (EPR). With the abolition of the CEGB, Britain no longer has the skills to design and build nuclear power stations.

'People naturally feel some pang of regret that something made in Britain is no longer made in Britain,' Littlechild said. 'But the reason it happens is that a better service has been provided elsewhere.'

Didn't it invalidate the privatisation of the CEGB and the old electricity boards if they could just be renationalised by the French, without British firms being able to do anything similar in France?

'People are better off,' he replied, 'even if it means some jobs move overseas, because we specialise in other industries and other sectors where we have an advantage, like financial services. The argument that Adam Smith and others made for free trade did not depend on other countries accepting it as well. You appear to think that you should not let foreigners compete in this country unless our companies are able to compete in their country. I'm saying we stand to gain by letting anyone who wants to compete in this country – at least customers stand to gain.'

Littlechild seemed reluctant to accept that EDF's move into Britain undermined the rationale for electricity privatisation and I was surprised, just before I left, when he looked at me sadly and said that, yes, he did regret what had happened, only a month before his term as regulator came to an end. 'I think it was not possible for the regulator to stop it ... I didn't want an important reform being compromised by a company from overseas that was still state-owned, very large, not subject to competition, its actions not determined by meeting the needs of customers but by, well, its plans.'

It wasn't that nobody tried to stop EDF's move into Britain. But in 1998, Labour was working with the set-up it had inherited from the Tories. In her notorious Bruges speech ten years earlier, Thatcher had warned overweening Eurocrats: 'We have not successfully rolled back the frontiers of the state in Britain, only to see them reimposed at a European level.' The same year, in another, forgotten speech, she boasted to an audience of businessmen that her government had forced Europe to break down the barriers to cross-border business. By supporting a single European market in goods and services, she said, the Conservatives were taking action 'to secure free movement of capital throughout the Community'. She saw no contradiction: those who claim to be her heirs still don't. But implicit in Thatcher's support for the single market was acceptance of a single Brussels-based regulator as the ultimate arbiter of fair competition in Europe. Since then the EU Competition Directorate has had more impact on Britain than any other EU body. And France has proved an adept lobbyist. Brussels lets the French protect EDF from competition at home, allows EDF to borrow money at low government rates, and lets it expand into the open arena of Britain.

A strong, cunning negotiator capable of schmoozing the Eurocrats was required if the Department of Trade and Industry was ever to make the case in Brussels against the EDF takeover of London Electricity. On 30 November 1998, when news of the deal broke, exactly such a man was in charge at the DTI: Peter Mandelson. New in the job and eager to prove he was more than just a master of the political dark arts, he claimed he modelled himself on a Tory predecessor, Michael Heseltine, who had pledged to 'intervene before breakfast, lunch and dinner' on the side of British industry. But Mandelson never had a chance to put the case. A few weeks after EDF made its move, he was on the brink of tears, listening to Tony Blair telling him over the phone that he must resign. Details had emerged of an undeclared £373,000 loan Mandelson had taken from the Treasury minister Geoffrey Robinson to buy a house in Notting Hill, an untenable conflict of interest. Mandelson quit, and after a sojourn on Corfu with his 'old and good friends' from the Rothschild banking family, passed into his personal Golgotha: a small flat, a Fiat Punto instead of a ministerial car and Friday nights shopping in Hartlepool Tesco's.

Had his desire for a nice house not forced him out of office, would Mandelson have made the effort to lead a concerted lobbying effort in Brussels against the EDF takeover? We'll never know. He was, proudly, the grandson of a patriarch of nationalisation, Herbert Morrison, and as such a kind of familial opponent to George Osborne, son-in-law of David Howell, patriarch of privatisation. Mandelson claims in his memoirs that his house purchase was 'nesting, rather than socialising'. But by moving to Notting Hill and hanging out with the Rothschilds he passed into Osborne's territory.

Tucked away in Mandelson's account of his 1998 downfall is a tortured paragraph, part confession, part self-justification, which could stand as the heart's cry of New Labour – the agony that wells up in the soul of an ambitious, sensitive socialist who suffers because he can't live like the hedge fund people, those people who are so much more charming than one has been led to expect, who are so groomed and well dressed and go skiing every winter. 'A bit of high living had definitely crept into my soul,' Mandelson wrote.

> I saw what others enjoyed and I wanted to share it. Not glamour, or luxury, or swank. Just comfort and smartness. I had absolutely no desire to show off. Social life was always secondary. Work always came first. But I cared about money because I didn't have it. I wanted my own savings, my own ability to spend on myself and others. I have never been greedy for riches. And yet it was my eyes getting too big for my stomach that brought me down.

With Mandelson gone and his replacement, Stephen Byers, coming to terms with the job, the baton passed to civil servants and to a junior minister responsible for energy, John Battle. Battle was from Leeds, a Catholic and an activist for social justice whose life until that point – studying the poetry of William Empson, training for the priesthood, setting up Church Action on Poverty to campaign for a minimum wage and mastering Labour's housing brief in opposition – hadn't obviously pointed him towards the energy portfolio in government. Today he is no longer an MP, and has returned north to a life of good works. I met him in the Tiled Hall Café in Leeds. He recalled the day in 1997 when he first walked into the DTI building as minister. He was greeted by a reception committee of civil servants.

'I was asked which room I wanted, and whether I needed anything. I remember asking for a whiteboard, and being told I wouldn't need one. I asked for a bookcase and they said: "Minister, if there are any books you want to read, you've got civil servants now, just get one of them to read the book and they'll give you a précis." I didn't understand that "Is there anything you need?" was code for "What do you want in your drinks cabinet?"' He asked the civil servants if they would draw up a report on the new energy markets and fuel poverty. 'I was told fuel poverty was not a concept recognised in the department; it was the concern of the Department of Social Security.'

Battle was well aware of the unfairness of the French takeover, but was under the impression that Littlechild was happy to see it go ahead. The civil servants who might have told him otherwise don't seem to have made a fuss about it; the DTI's permanent secretary at the time, Michael Scholar, told me in an email that the EDF takeover 'was not in the department a cause célèbre'.

Battle now regrets not challenging Littlechild and the other regulators. 'The regulator was completely fixed on price mechanism as the be all and end all, and opening up to new entrants. On paper it sounded fine. But in the real global economy, we couldn't buy a French power station, and they could buy ours. We didn't get a grip on the regulators. We left the framework to them. We should have changed the remit. We were too cautious and nervous about questioning the market. Why was it that we had to lose our nationalised industries in order to hand them over to nationalised industries from other countries? They could buy into us, but we couldn't buy into them. The French said they wanted to open up their markets but they never did.'

The DTI asked Brussels to let Britain's own competition authorities decide on the EDF bid. The European competition commissioner, the late Karel van Miert, refused, and soon afterwards issued an eight-page judgment clearing the EDF takeover. Ignoring EDF's monopoly in France, he focused instead on the cross-Channel cable through which EDF already sold Britain a relatively small amount of power. Such a piddling market share, he concluded, hardly threatened dominance. It was as if UEFA had been asked to consider the fairness of a French football team becoming the twenty-first member of the Premier League and, after scrupulous examination of the relative strengths of the existing twenty English teams, announced that the French would have no special advantage playing in England, ignoring the detail that when the English teams visited the French side at home, the French goal was boarded up with plywood. 'The DTI,' Helm writes,

> simply assumed that the British model was the one Europe should follow, and that its superiority would be evident from the results … The failure to prevent EDF's acquisition of London Electricity or its subsequent incremental acquisitions reflected not just an ignorance of how to work the Commission, but also of how to play the system.

Whilst RWE, Ruhrgas* and EDF invested in the politics and pro-
cesses of Brussels, the DTI relied on general principles. Its team was
systematically outclassed.

I arranged to meet some of the agents of the Robin Hood group,
L'Association des Robins de Bois – a clandestine network of
French subversives working within EDF on the company's home
territory – in Montbéliard, in Franche-Comté, where the Peugeot
family began making things for sale, starting with coffee mills
and bicycles in the nineteenth century. While I waited for my
contact outside the railway station, a freight train clanked past
bearing a seemingly infinite number of new Peugeots. Here was
France's well-lubricated machine a-running, its state-planned
network of nuclear reactors pouring out cheap, low-carbon electricity to power world-renowned Franche-Comté companies like
Peugeot and Alstom, and to power the network of state-planned
trains à grande vitesse that connects the country. 'Bienvenue à
Belfort Montbéliard – Territoire d'énergies' reads a poster at the
TGV station.

But Peugeot is struggling to compete at home and abroad;
France's fifty-eight nuclear reactors, all built between 1971 and
1991, are coming to the end of their working lives, with no
certainty as to how they will be replaced; and the new Belfort-
Montbéliard TGV station, which opened last year, deposits
arriving passengers in the middle of the countryside, several
miles away from both Belfort and Montbéliard. As for cheap
electricity, it is no use, if you are French, knowing that EDF
electricity is cheaper in France than EDF electricity in Britain
(which it is) if you can't afford it.

My Robin Hood contact, P, had worked directly for EDF for
fifteen years, then spent another fifteen in the CGT union, still,
under the French system, on the EDF payroll. Over lunch, he
explained the Robin Hood group: a loose association of electrical engineers and co-ordinators who step in when EDF managers

---

*   Now part of E.ON.

order a customer to be cut off for non-payment. In certain cases, if they can't help the customer any other way, a Robin Hood EDF engineer will return to the property and clandestinely, illegally reconnect the supply. Five years ago EDF electricians discovered that some government officials whose work was tied to the company were getting electricity for nothing. They promptly disconnected them. 'That was the birth of Robin Hood,' said P.

The group does what it can to protect its members and impoverished EDF customers from prosecution – making sure the reconnecting engineer is not the same as the disconnecting engineer, and that the meter never stops running, so that the bill continues to rise, at least nominally. Where possible they call in social services to help the customer rather than cut them off, or invent a reason not to do the job.

'We want an engineer to have the right to refuse to cut somebody off,' P said. 'It used to be easier to come up with excuses not to do it, because there weren't so many jobs. Now one engineer's doing ten disconnections a day, you can't refuse them all.' It was dangerous work, he explained. 'You need to know how to do it. If you make a mistake when you try to restore electricity, you're dead. If you create a short circuit you can blow your head off. You need special gloves, a special mask, a visor.'

Rather than use the tactic EDF and other electricity firms have adopted in Britain – replacing non-payers' meters with a meter requiring power to be paid for in advance – the homeland EDF will sometimes install a 'trickle meter', rationing poor customers to a thousand watts at a time. 'A thousand watts. It's too little,' P said. 'You can't live with that. If you have the light on in the evening, the TV and the washing machine, that's it.'

P described the Robin Hood group's activities as 'a legitimate act of resistance', echoing the origins of EDF in the undercover planning for postwar France carried out by the National Council of the Resistance during the Occupation. At the CGT's headquarters in Paris, in a modern brick building hollowed out by a vast atrium, I found the same description of France's electricity supply as a part of *la patrie* that had somehow been taken over by outside forces. 'For us,' Denis Cohen, the communist head of the CGT until 2003, told me, 'energy is like culture; it's not a private good.'

It was puzzling. From this side of the English Channel, it had seemed clear enough: although some shares in EDF have been sold, and the management has been given a measure of commercial freedom, EDF looked like a state company, owned, controlled and supported by the French state, subject to French political control, and thus to the French electorate. It has taken over a large chunk of the British electrical system, though EDF doesn't answer to me and my fellow voters. Yet ordinary French people don't seem to feel it is under their control, either. My efforts to arrange an interview with the company's supposed owners, the French state, in the form of the Agence des participations de l'État, were rebuffed. As a last resort I turned up unannounced at the APE's headquarters in the government offices in Bercy, a forbidding building resembling a cliff face of beige stone and tinted glass. I was shown the door.

'It's a funny company,' Thibaut Madelin, energy correspondent of *Les Echos*, told me of EDF. 'Obviously it's a state-owned company, and you can argue it's controlled by the government, and the union plays a big role, but I think the real power is within EDF. I've covered energy for four years and I've found no one can actually challenge it. The civil service and the regulator try somehow to control EDF but they can't. It's very hard to define where the power comes from.'

One spring morning I took the train from London, north through Cambridgeshire and Lincolnshire, to Nottinghamshire. The trackside was sprinkled with blackthorn blossom and when the sun flashed between the rainclouds the fields of rape flowers shone a dizzy yellow. Just before Newark-on-Trent the track began to cross lines of six-armed National Grid pylons, heaving their cables over the sheep and hedgerows like devas converging on a sacred site. We passed between Sherwood Forest and the River Trent and clusters of steam-headed cooling towers rose on the horizon, signalling the approach to England's great electric estate.

The five coal-fired power stations that spread out in an arc along the Aire and Trent valleys have been there since I was a boy: the squat towers, seen from the window of express trains hurrying between London and Scotland, seem as natural in the landscape as flat green fields and comfortable houses of dark red brick. Most of them were built by the CEGB in the 1960s, in the heyday of state planning, to use local coal. The quintet of West Burton, Cottam, Drax, Eggborough and Ferrybridge still run. With their turbines spinning at full tilt, they can make a fifth of the electricity Britain needs on a cold winter's day.

Inside the noisy room at Cottam that houses four 164-foot high boilers, Stephen Rawlinson, the plant's mechanical maintenance manager, beckoned me up a set of metal steps and opened a tiny hatch. We were like insects under the grate of a coal fire, sparks and orange-hot cinders the size of my head shooting into heaps of ash. Looking up, I saw the inferno itself, a vast fireball coiling and erupting, fed by jets of pulverised coal, ground finer than talcum powder in enormous rotating drums filled with steel balls. Here was the elemental fury behind the green charging light and the whine of the washing machine.

Cottam coal station (there's also a gas station, owned by E.ON, on the same site) was privatised in 1991 and bought by EDF in 2000. When I asked the predominantly middle-aged engineers how they felt about working for the French, they told me their first loyalty was to the power station itself. But beyond that, working for EDF reminded them of the old British public service they started out in. 'It's very much along the lines of the CEGB as we knew it years ago – very structured procedurally, which is a good thing to have,' said Dave Owen, a boiler engineer. He took me inside a boiler that had been shut down for cleaning. The mass of hot dust had been vacuumed out but every surface was still covered in brown powder. A gut-tangle of tubes and steam condensers at the top resolved itself into a vertiginous shaft lined with a delicate layer of tightly packed tubes that parted at the base to take coal from the feeders.

'I don't mind it going to other countries, but I believe there should be an engineering base in the UK,' Owen said. 'As a country we're losing out, from engineers who design to people who maintain.'

Boyd Johnson, who looks after the mass of machinery – itself the size of a large factory – that strips polluting sulphur from the gas given off by the burning coal, said that Powergen, the company that inherited Cottam from the CEGB, hadn't seemed committed to the future: it never invested in the full anti-pollution gear. EDF was different. 'As engineers, we're all about investment in the kit.' Being with EDF, he said, was 'like going back to the CEGB, but a little bit crisper.' France, to be sure, had different priorities, but 'at the end of the day, the French are investing. OK, you could say that in the future, when all the nuclears are built, they'll get quite a large say in how the industry is run. But then we have government regulators.'

Chris Wild, in charge of milling the coal into powder, showed me the troughs where conveyor belts deliver the raw mined nuggets into the plant. I asked where the coal came from. The last deep mine in Nottinghamshire, Thoresby, is twenty miles away. 'We have such a varied diet,' he said. 'I think this is from Kentucky.' Wild was among the last batch of apprentices taken on by the CEGB before it was broken up and sold. 'It doesn't matter,' he said. 'I don't think "My boss is wearing EDF overalls" if he rings up at two in the morning and says some bit of kit's broken down.'

Cottam operates with hundreds fewer staff than it did in the CEGB days and no apparent problems. 'If this downsizing had been done under the auspices of the CEGB, would it have worked?' Wild asked. 'How do you measure the loss of such things as the Hams Hall workshops and the apprentice

workshops at Burton on Trent, or the CEGB engineering programme? It makes you wonder if it could have remained as a
privatised, streamlined CEGB. Would it have been better?'

The cumulative effects of Littlechild's RPI-X regime, two decades'
idealisation of shareholder capitalism, and the relentless promotion of the notion that it is socially acceptable for senior
managers to be motivated by nothing other than a desire for
personal enrichment, have left the electricity system on which
Britain relies worn out. A fifth of the British power stations
running today are due to close by the 2020s, and the government wants some mix of new nuclear, wind and gas, together
with a smattering of coal and a rejig of the Grid, to make good
the shortfall. In 2012 one government minister said the figure of
£110 billion often bandied about for how much this would cost
was only the beginning.

The new imperative to be good world citizens by burning less
fossil fuel makes matters harder. Our nuclear power stations are
clapped out, our coal and oil stations are greenhouse gas factories, and since we've burned through most of our own North Sea
gas reserves we've become reliant on shiploads of liquefied gas
from Qatar, routed through the Strait of Hormuz, which Iran
promises to close if foreign powers give it trouble. Onshore wind
farms are unpopular with rural Tories; offshore wind farms are
expensive and far from the Grid, and besides, wind power needs
to be backed up with alternatives, since the wind doesn't blow
all the time.

The three main sources of Britain's future electricity supply
are gas, wind and nuclear, with coal's weight in the mix supposed to diminish. There is an argument that the best way to
replace the climate-altering force of coal would be to simply
enlarge the network of gas-fired power stations and offshore
wind farms. The most modern gas plants can be built quickly,
started up from cold in half an hour and switched off when not
required. They can be run with a staff of a hundred. Proponents

of increased gas use argue that gas is environmentally friendly in the sense that it's less filthy than coal, and that it allows Britain to ramp up the number of wind farms without jeopardising reliability of supply. A gas–wind powered electricity grid would be a transitional system, like a hybrid car – green as far as it goes, but with a carbon fuel engine in there so you wouldn't get stranded. Yet despite the new technology of fracking, which promises to make natural gas cheaper and easier for Britain to buy, there's unease over reliability of supply. New nuclear power stations, always on, pouring out a steady baseline of electricity with one seventh the carbon emissions, watt for watt over their lifetime, of natural gas, remain central to the government's hopes.

The original idea, formulated under Labour and inherited by its successors, was to unleash the pent-up atomic yearnings of the private electricity sector by giving the go-ahead for four new nuclear stations, each with a pair of reactors. Two pairs would be built by EDF at Hinkley Point in Somerset and Sizewell in Suffolk; two would be built by the Germans, E.ON and RWE, at Wylfa on Anglesey and Oldbury in Gloucestershire. At least four and possibly all eight would be a single model, the efficient, super-safe EPR* designed by Areva of France. Making all eight of one type would reduce costs: they would effectively be mass-produced. It was argued by the nuclear lobby that since nuclear power stations, like wind farms, don't produce much in the way of greenhouse gases once they're up and running, they should benefit from the same sorts of subsidy as wind. If the French and Germans were being asked to pony up the billions, it was reasoned, they needed some guarantee of payback over the decades of the stations' working life. Hinkley Point would go online in 2023, and within a few years nearly a quarter of Britain's peak electricity demand would be supplied by safe, clean, reliable new nukes.

And what was wrong with that? Almost everything, it turns out. The triple meltdown of reactors at Fukushima after the

---

* European Pressurised Reactor.

earthquake in Japan last March prompted the German government to shut down its nuclear sector entirely, which in turn
led RWE and E.ON to abandon nuclear investment in Britain.
The Japanese firm Hitachi, which has taken over the Wylfa
and Oldbury projects from the Germans, now proposes building pairs of Advanced Boiling Water Reactors (ABWR), made
jointly with the US firm General Electric, on the sites. The
French achieved economies of scale in the 1970s and 1980s by
building nearly sixty reactors of identical design. Eight reactors for Britain already sounds more like an artisanal than an
assembly-line product; four of one and four of another sounds
frankly experimental.

And experimental is what the first of the new reactors is.
Four ABWRs were running, not particularly reliably, in Japan
before Fukushima. But no EPR is or ever has been operational.
Two EPRs are being built in China, one in Finland and one at
Flamanville in Normandy. The Finnish and French EPRs will
cost at least twice as much as they were supposed to. Flamanville
is running five years late, the Finnish station nine. The Chinese
versions are due to go online in 2015 and 2016, a year late.

The French themselves seem to be cooling on the EPR.
François Hollande wants to cut the nuclear component of
France's electricity from 75 to 50 per cent. In a 2010 report on
the future of the French nuclear industry François Roussely,
a former head of EDF, warned that the EPR was too complex
and needed a redesign. He said customers should be offered a
smaller, simpler reactor called the ATMEA. The previous year,
taking over as EDF's new boss, Henri Proglio* mocked Areva for
pushing the EPR abroad. 'Do you know how many companies
have just one product in their catalogue?' he sneered. 'There was
Ford and his Model T. But that was a hundred years ago, and at
least he knew how to make and sell it.' France now wants to build
EPRs in Britain. Poglio's comments were widely interpreted

---

* Replaced in October 2014 by Jean-Bernard Lévy.

in France as a power play within the febrile world of French industrial politics, and it is this world – a world over which the British electorate has no control – to which the British public is being shackled.

Britain's prospective investment in the EPR is disturbingly reminiscent of the prelude to the catastrophic demise of Railtrack, the privatised company that had to be renationalised in 2001. There, too, as we saw in Chapter 2, the government allowed a private network on which the country depended to invest in an unproven technological fix, despite warning signals from Europe that the technology wasn't ready. In the free-market utopia envisioned by Littlechild and Lawson, this shouldn't have been a problem. In their vision, state planners don't know what people want: people know what people want, and entrepreneurs will invest and compete to supply those wants. If the product or service supplied is underused, useless or too expensive, it's the entrepreneur who loses out, not the customers. This perspective takes no account of people's susceptibility to marketing, yet it's a reasonable principle, and applied to restaurants, or cars, or furniture, there's much to be said for it. Were banks to face real competition it would be a good thing. Applied to Britain's electricity industry, however, it gives rise to two formidable problems.

The first is that a nuclear power station isn't a restaurant. If I own a café on the market square and it goes belly up, my livelihood suffers, but the townsfolk won't lack for coffee. If the National Grid pencils in thirteen gigawatts of nuclear electricity for the 2020s, however, and it doesn't arrive, the country is in peril. It's a variant of the old joke about you having a problem if you owe the bank a hundred pounds, but the bank having a problem if you owe them a million. If Jean-Bernard Lévy plans to move into a new house by Christmas and it isn't ready, Jean-Bernard Lévy has a problem. If Jean-Bernard Lévy's new reactor isn't ready for 2023, Britain has a problem. A wind farm that is nine-tenths finished is nine-tenths operational. A nuclear power station that is nine-tenths finished is a white elephant – a £16 billion white elephant, in the case of Hinkley.

The possibility that companies might get part-way through building a set of new nuclear reactors in Britain and have to stop due to cost overruns is less likely than the other variant: that, once begun, the new nukes will be finished whatever the cost. Which is the second problem. Expensive to build and difficult to dispose of, nuclear reactors aren't profitable. The only reason nuclear power is on the table is global warming. The only way it can be financed is by government subsidy. And the subsidy the British government is offering EDF and its minority partners (Areva and two Chinese state-owned companies) to build Hinkley is gigantic: a guaranteed minimum price for the electricity Hinkley produces, indexed to inflation for thirty-five years, of £92.50 per megawatt hour – about twice as much as the average wholesale price of electricity in Britain today. They have given EDF an incredible nine years to start and finish the project (the Japanese ABWRs were built in four). The Treasury is also guaranteeing loans EDF and its partners will take out to fund construction. An analysis by Peter Atherton and Mulu Sun of the London brokerage firm Liberum Capital pointed out that just to get Hinkley up and running would make it the world's most expensive power station; once it was generating, the price of gas would have to have increased by around 130 per cent for it not to get subsidies. 'The UK government is taking a massive bet that fossil fuel prices will be extremely high in the future,' wrote Atherton and Sun. 'If that bet proves to be wrong then this contract will look economically insane when [the plant] commissions. We are frankly staggered that the UK government thinks it is appropriate to take such a bet.'

This subsidy won't come from general taxation. It will come, as wind farm subsidies already do, from British customers' electricity bills. It's a stark illustration of the realities of privatising essential services – that what is being sold is not infrastructure, but bill-paying citizens, and what is being privatised is not electricity, but taxation. Effectively the French and Chinese governments are buying the right to tax British electricity customers through their electricity bills; to use British money and British sites to finance a world showcase for unproven French nuclear technology. And because the unacknowledged taxes in electricity bills take no account of people's earnings, the poorer you are, the higher your tax.

That's not to say the French people will be winners as a result of the deal (although Hollande has at least acknowledged that in France electricity bills are a form of taxation, and should be adjusted according to income). There is tension between the British, French and Chinese partners. Given that all the options are expensive and politically charged, the British government might still decide the EPR is too risky and go for the gas–wind hybrid option – allow extra gas stations to take up the slack, while assuaging the green lobby with continued offshore wind subsidies and investment in more esoteric future technologies: tidal power, clean coal, thorium reactors, a European supergrid linking northern windmills and Mediterranean solar farms, a cable feeding green electricity from Iceland. In which case the French people would be on the hook for EDF's expensive acquisition of British Energy and its existing, worn-out British nukes.

Free marketeers like Littlechild and Lawson might argue that, left to its own devices, the market would never have built nuclear power stations; it would always have gone for the cheapest option. But this is disingenuous. With electricity, the market can never be left alone. Coal might be the cheapest option, but it's too dirty. Gas might be the cheapest option, but the more the country relies on gas, the more emergency reserves it will have to keep in storage – which the market won't pay for. Helm's most devastating point about electricity (and gas) privatisation in Britain is that these are not naturally public industries; nor are they naturally private. 'It is extraordinary,' he writes, 'that anyone could have regarded these as anything other than political industries.'

Electricity privatisation hasn't been a success in bringing down prices. Most recent figures suggest British prices are typically right in the middle of the European average – higher than France's, lower than Germany's.* It has been a failure in terms of British industry and management; the best measure of the scale of folly and betrayal by politicians of both parties is the simple fact that a reliable, badly run British electricity system was destroyed, rather than being reformed, only so that a large part of it could be taken over by a foreign version of the original. And it has been a failure in terms of clarity, in the sense that in order to fund investment, governments that boast about not raising taxes, or of taking low-earners out of the tax bracket, permit predominantly foreign owned electricity companies to collect flat-rate taxes that hit the poor disproportionately.

How to explain the sense in this country that EDF is a manifestation of the French state, and the sense in France that it is and it isn't – that by expanding abroad it somehow eluded the people who are supposed to own it? 'EDF is the biggest electricity company in the world but it is still Franco-French,' Denis Cohen said, expressing the paradox. 'The strategy of this company, even though it is Franco-French, is to try to get out of France.'

What matters about EDF's enormous acquisitions in Britain is not that it's French, but that by crossing the Channel so decisively it has become something that is neither altogether French nor altogether British. It has become one of those transnational entities that uses national jurisdictions as conveniences, in the same way as the wealthy use national jurisdictions as conveniences for tax avoidance. By presenting itself in France as a champion of French national interests, sheltering behind the shield of the French state, while presenting itself in Britain as committed to the global free market and fair competition, it is

---

* Germany's high electricity bills are a function of its political decision to subsidise massive investment in wind and solar energy, and to close working nuclear stations early.

taking advantage of the fact that the two countries' governments, electorates and media are separate: the two eyes of supervision are attached to divergent brains, and EDF can exist in a state of institutionalised hypocrisy.

EDF is still the French CEGB, though more technically skilled than its former British counterpart. Tony Cooper, who in the 1990s headed the union representing electricity managers, told me that when EDF took over Britain's old nuclear power stations in 2008, 'a lot of people were saying: "Christ, at last we've got someone who knows how to run these bloody things."' But by lurching into the tax-gathering business overseas EDF has become a hybrid – a French CEGB crossed with a French version of Enron. One long-time observer of the French energy scene described accompanying a group of EDF executives to an Enron trading room at the hubristic height of that company's success. She was taken aback by the gleam of fascination and envy in the eyes of the *énarques* as they watched their American counterparts trade gigawatts on the screens.

Just because EDF is beset by Robin Hoods in France and has planted its standard at Cottam, hard by Sherwood Forest, doesn't make it the Sheriff of Nottingham. And yet there is an echo, in the conduct of the electricity oligopoly, of the popular notion of medieval social injustice that has defined the background to the Robin Hood legend: a country where the symbol of the nation's best interests, in the form of the king, is nowhere to be found, and in his absence, a rootless elite that has no concept of duty or service except to itself is busy taxing the poor. It is as if national boundaries are for the little people, the global peasantry who pay their taxes, not for great men and the great transnational corporations they run.

Still, the lights haven't gone out. At least that's what an MP told Dieter Helm a few years ago when he was giving evidence in Parliament. People warned there would be blackouts the previous winter, the MP said, and there weren't. With unusual passion, Helm put him straight. If you define the problem as the lights not going out, he said, you misunderstand everything about the way the new world of electricity markets works. The ideal situation for private electricity firms is one where there is only just enough electricity to go round; where the lights are always just about to go out, but never quite do. Then they can charge as much as they like, and people will have to pay. 'People think insecurity of supply means will the lights go off or not – but that is not the issue,' he said. 'It is what happens just before the lights go off.'

More than twenty years after the great electricity experiment was launched, it can be seen that although it was an act of privatisation – of taxation, principally – it was most significantly an act of alienation, lowering an impenetrable barrier of complexity, commercial secrecy and sheer geographical distance between the controlling interests of electricity companies and the customers they serve. It's easy to switch suppliers. But behind that barrier citizens and small businesses have no way of knowing that they aren't being fleeced as egregiously by the cheapest provider as they are by the most expensive. The consumer-peasants of Britain bring their tithes to the locked gates of the great electrical estates and wonder who lives in the big house now, and whether they are at home, or in one of their other estates around the world. No wonder Denis Cohen, old communist, heir to the Communards and the sans-culottes, hates what the company that pays him is doing abroad. 'I was very surprised to see the British trades unionists were not very opposed to this,' he said, meaning privatisation and foreign takeover. 'We, with our culture, would have fought until death to prevent it.'

5. Multiple Fractures

Privatised health

Wrightington Hospital, in the countryside near Wigan, grew in fits and starts around an eighteenth-century mansion that Lancashire County Council bought in 1920 after the death of its last resident, a spendthrift with a fanatical attachment to blood sports. The hospital promotes itself as 'a centre of orthopaedic excellence'. National Health Service hospitals have to promote themselves these days. In 2011 it survived a brush with closure. It's neat and scrubbed and slightly worn at the edges, unable to justify to itself that few per cent private firms set aside for corporate sheen, although it does have a museum dedicated to John Charnley, who, almost half a century ago, invented a reliable way to replace human hips with artificial ones, creating a benchmark by which the success and failure of the NHS would always be judged.

They still do hips at Wrightington, and knees, and elbows, and shoulders. They deal with joint problems that are too tricky for general hospitals. There's a sort of blazer and brogues testosterone in the corridors, where the surgeons have a habit of cuffing one another's faces affectionately. At the end of a hallway lined with untidy stacks of case notes in wrinkled cardboard folders Martyn Porter, a senior surgeon and the hospital's clinical chairman, waited in his office to be called to the operating theatre.

He offered me his intense, tired, humorous gaze. 'The problem with politicians is they can't be honest,' he declared. 'If they said, "We're going to privatise the NHS," they'd be kicked out the next day.'

The patient Porter was about to operate on was a sixty-year-old woman from the Wirral with a complex prosthesis in one leg, running from her knee to her hip. She had a fracture and Porter had got a special device made for her at a workshop in another part of the NHS, the Royal National Orthopaedic Hospital at Stanmore in Middlesex. The idea was for the device to slide over the femoral spur of the knee joint, essentially replacing her whole leg down to the ankle. 'The case we're doing this morning, we're going to make a loss of about £5,000. The private sector wouldn't do it,' he said. 'How do we deal with that? Some procedures the *ebitda* is about 8 per cent. If you make an *ebitda* of 12 per cent you're making a real profit.' You expect medical jargon from surgeons, but I was surprised to hear the word *ebitda* from Porter. It's an accountancy term meaning 'earnings before interest, taxation, depreciation and amortisation'.

'Last year we did about 1,400 hip replacements,' he said. 'The worrying thing for us is we lost a million pounds doing that. What we worked out is that our length of stay' – the time patients spend in hospital after an operation – 'was six days. If we can get it down to five days we break even and if it's four, we make a million pound profit.'

I felt I'd somehow jumped forward in time. A year had passed since the 2010 election that brought the Conservative-Liberal Democrat coalition to power. The Coalition's programme promised: 'We are stopping the top-down reconfigurations of NHS services, imposed from Whitehall.' A few weeks after they gained power, a new health secretary, the Conservative Andrew Lansley, announced his plans for a top-down reconfiguration of England's NHS services, imposed from Whitehall. When I talked to Porter, Lansley had barely been in his job a year, and hadn't yet, supposedly, shaken up the NHS. But here was a

leading surgeon in an NHS hospital, about to perform a challenging operation on an NHS patient, telling me exactly how
much money the hospital was going to lose by operating on her,
and chatting easily about profit and loss, as if he'd been living in
Lansleyworld for years. Had the NHS been privatised one day
while I was sleeping?

When the NHS was created in 1948, it had three core principles. It would be universal: everyone would get medical treatment
whenever they needed it. It would be comprehensive, covering
all forms of healthcare, from dentistry to cancer. And it would
be free to use. No matter how much the system cost to run, no
matter how much or how little any individual had contributed
to those costs, no matter how expensive their treatment or how
many times they went to the doctor, they'd never be billed for it.
Through dozens of reorganisations since then, these principles
have remained, along with another: that it's never a bad time for
a fresh reorganisation. Otherwise, much has changed.

The main source of the money that funds the NHS is still, as
it was in 1948, general taxation. For the first thirty years of the
health service's existence, civil servants in Whitehall and the
regions doled out annual budgets to hospitals and GPs according to the populations they served. Money flowed down from
the Treasury, but it didn't flow horizontally between the different
parts of the NHS. Each element got its overall allowance, paid
its staff, obtained its equipment and supplies, and co-operated,
sometimes well, sometimes not, with the other elements, according to an overarching plan. The aim was fairness, an even spread
of care across the country. In a monopoly healthcare system,
competition has no place; on the contrary, it seemed sensible to
the planners to avoid duplication of services. It was patriarchal
and democratic, innovative and hidebound, cumbersome and
cheap. For the majority without private insurance, if you were ill,
you knew you'd always be cared for; if you were cared for care-
lessly, you had nowhere else to go.

Trying to describe in generally comprehensible terms how

money flows through the NHS today would be hard enough without the shifting channels of policy. In England – Scotland, Wales and Northern Ireland have gone along divergent health paths – the various parts of the NHS had already begun altering or abolishing themselves in response to the reorganisation announced in 2010 when the reorganisation itself was reorganised. In 2012, the Coalition responded to the clamour against Lansley's reorganisation by sacking Lansley and keeping the reorganisation. Truly you can't step in the same NHS river twice. The last period of relative stability was just before Lansley came along, when, crudely speaking, the money flowed like this. Every so often – perhaps every year, or every two or three – the Department of Health made its pitch to the Treasury for the amount of money it thought it should get from the overall tax pot, and was then told how much it would actually get. Most of the money came from general taxation – income tax, VAT, corporation tax, duties on booze and tobacco – but a proportion came directly from national insurance, a vitiated form of the link between that levy and the welfare state its architects intended. In the last pre-Lansley allocation, Health got £101.5 billion for the following year, a slight increase. Most of it – £89 billion – was divided up between about 150 local agencies called Primary Care Trusts, or PCTs, spread around the country. PCTs acted as the 'commissioners' of health services, ordering a community's medical care from hospitals, GPs and mental health professionals and paying them accordingly.

PCTs could use NHS money to commission care from the private sector. They weren't under any obligation to shop locally, either. Under Labour in the 2000s, NHS patients had been given the chance to choose private or far-away hospitals for treatment, which meant the PCTs were obliged to commission from them. Even before Lansley's changes, NHS hospitals like Wrightington had become dependent for their financial viability on the money they made from selling their services to the PCTs. Competition already existed.

The amount of money PCTs got from the government varied. The Department of Health had a panel of civil servants and academics called the Advisory Committee on Resource Allocation (ACRA), which came up with a formula for working out the health needs of each area based on population size and density, the proportion of elderly people, life expectancy and the degree to which their health varied from the mean. In the poorer parts of Merseyside, for instance, where male life expectancy is sixty-seven, men can expect to be incapacitated by disability of some kind by the age of forty-four. The corresponding figures for the richer parts of West London are eighty-nine and seventy-four. The variation in the sums different PCTs got relative to their population was, accordingly, considerable. In 2011 South Gloucestershire received £1,298 per head, Islington in London £2,268.

Primary Care Trusts were set up in 2002; they were abolished only eleven years later. Post-Lansley, money flows through the NHS differently. It still comes from general taxation, but most of the money that used to go to the PCTs is doled out by a new organisation, NHS England, to bodies called Clinical Commissioning Groups, essentially clusters of GP practices. Across England, groups of family doctors have become responsible for handling tens of billions of pounds of public money, using it to commission most of the medical care NHS patients receive, from major surgery to simple diagnostic tests. Lacking expertise of their own, most are paying private contractors to manage these funds for them, or hiring ex-PCT staff to do the same jobs they used to do.

At the same time a series of other changes have made 'commission' more of a euphemism for 'buy'. Not everything the PCTs commissioned came with a price tag. But increasingly almost all procedures, even those as seemingly amorphous and complex as caring for the mentally ill, have been coming in quantified, priced units – 'healthcare resource groups', each with its own code. Any hospital anywhere in England, NHS or private, that carried out procedure HA11C on an NHS patient in 2010 – treatment of a routine hip fracture – got a base payment of £8,928 from the outfit that commissioned it, and £9,373 if it followed 'best practice'. A maternity unit clocked £1,324 for a regular birth, NZ01B; putting in an artificial heart, EA43Z, earned £33,531. The sum was adjusted according to a local 'market forces factor', which took account of the variation in cost of labour and assets between different areas. The codes and prices were worked out, in turn, according to the actions taken and materials used by typical hospitals, with 'best practice' bonuses – if a hospital gave a stroke patient a prompt brain scan and had an acute stroke unit of a certain standard, for instance, it would get an extra £475 on top of the base payment of £4,095. If the actual cost to the hospital was less – if the hospital managed to send the patient home quicker than usual, for instance – the hospital would keep the difference. The notion of the profitable hospital within the NHS was born.

The new system takes this simulated privatisation, this enactment of commerce, further. State money 'follows the patient' wherever the patient chooses to take it, even when that is outside the NHS. Patients with chronic conditions like diabetes will not be given treatment, but money to spend on treatment. All NHS hospitals are obliged to become 'foundation trusts', turning them into semi-commercial operations, able to borrow money, set up joint ventures with private companies, merge with other hospitals – and go broke. The contracts they make with GP groups are legally binding. They now compete not only with other NHS hospitals and private hospitals but potentially with the GP groups themselves, who may set up local clinics to provide diagnostic tests or minor surgery. Alongside the NHS Commissioning Board two other quangos now supervise the new, competitive marketplace: the Care Quality Commission, there to make sure the players in the new marketplace don't harm patients, and Monitor, which, among other duties, will make sure that if a hospital goes bust somebody takes up the slack.

In 2011, it was announced that a billion pounds' worth of NHS services, including wheelchair services for children and 'talking therapies' for people suffering from mild depression, anxiety or behavioural awkwardnesses like obsessive compulsive disorder, were to be opened up to competitive bids from the private sector. The doctor and *Daily Telegraph* blogger Max Pemberton described it as 'the day they signed the death warrant for the NHS'. Now the NHS must compete with private outfits for MRI scans in Lincolnshire, glaucoma treatment in Cheshire, continence care in Stoke-on-Trent and psychotherapy in West Kent. Worried about the lack of competition in flexi-sigmoidoscopy in Bassetlaw? NHS England's website reassures you: it's coming soon.

Throughout the current debate on the health service's future, the Conservatives have praised it as an abstract concept, pledging to uphold 'an NHS that is free at the point of use and available to everyone based on need, not the ability to pay'. But it is quite possible to praise something even as you legislate it out of existence. Changes don't need to be advertised as embodying a cumulative destructive purpose for that purpose to be achieved. The fall of the Roman Empire was never announced, yet its fate was sealed once its rulers, no doubt for reasons of efficiency, introduced a choice of competing barbarians to defend its borders.

In their book *The Plot Against the NHS*, Colin Leys and Stewart Player argue that, having failed to persuade the public and the medical establishment under Margaret Thatcher that the NHS should be turned into a European-style national insurance programme, the advocates of a competitive health market gave up trying to convince the big audience and focused on infiltrating Whitehall's policymaking centres and the think tanks. As a result the government and the cast Leys and Player call 'marketeers' – private companies, lobbyists, pro-market think tankers – publicly praise the NHS, while taking incremental steps to turn it into an NHS in name only: a kitemark, as one prominent marketeer puts it in the book.

Yet there was a huge gap between the end of John Major's administration in 1997 and the Tory-Liberal pact of 2010. Labour, the party that created the NHS, that has pledged to defend it and has denounced the Lansley reforms, was in power for those thirteen years. So how did a surgeon like Martyn Porter end up, in 2011, so accustomed to the world of commercial competition and the bottom line? As Leys and Player show, it was the governments of Tony Blair and Gordon Brown that began replacing the public components of the NHS with private ones, the effect concealed by large spending increases, long before the Coalition took charge. If the Conservatives and their Liberal allies are dismantling the NHS, it was Labour that loosened the screws.

The first attempt to introduce market competition into the NHS was made by Kenneth Clarke in 1990, in the dying months of Thatcher's rule. An 'internal market' was rushed in, against the advice of the medical profession. It was watered down; it had less effect than its critics feared or its supporters hoped. Tony Blair's first health minister, Frank Dobson, read its funeral rites when Labour came to power seven years later. Yet at the turn of the millennium, Alan Milburn replaced Dobson, and Labour introduced a new, more radical version of that market.

It was Labour that introduced foundation trusts, allowing hospital managers to borrow money and making it possible for state hospitals to go broke. It was Labour that brought in the embryonic commercial health regulator Monitor. It was Labour that introduced 'Choose and Book', obliging patients to pick from a menu of NHS and private clinics when they needed to see a consultant. It was Labour that handed over millions of pounds to private companies to run specialist clinics that would treat NHS patients in the name of reducing waiting lists for procedures like hip operations. It was Labour that brought private firms in to advise regional NHS managers in the new business of commissioning. And it was Labour that began putting a national tariff on each procedure.

The more closely you look at what has happened over the last twenty-five years, the more clearly you can see a consistent programme for commercialising the NHS that is independent of party political platforms: a purposeful leviathan of ideas that powers on steadily beneath the surface bickering of the political cycle, never changing course.

A key source of those ideas was Alain Enthoven, an American economist. Enthoven spent most of the 1960s in the Pentagon, one of the cerebral 'whizz kids' on the staff of the defence secretary Robert McNamara. McNamara was a wonk, confident that no mystery could withstand statistical analysis, and Enthoven was the chief wonk's wonk, crunching numbers to judge whether the new weapons the generals wanted were worth it. In 1973, Enthoven reinvented himself as an expert in the economics of healthcare. He believed the US health system, as a whole, was a failure (he described tax relief for private health insurance as a disaster), but thought one part of it, a California-based outfit called Kaiser Permanente, was exemplary. His ideal was something called 'managed competition', and in 1985 he wrote a paper for the Nuffield Trust suggesting it could work for the NHS.

Enthoven himself seems to have been taken aback by the speed with which Thatcher's sunset coterie latched onto him. In an interview with the *British Medical Journal* in 1989 he said of the Conservative proposals: 'I was very surprised by the lack of detail … I thought that I was throwing out a general idea that needed to be developed.' It is eerie to read the interview now. Everything that Enthoven prescribed then was either brought in by New Labour or is being put in place by Labour's supposed opponents a generation later. 'I recommended that the district health authorities be recast as purchasers of services on behalf of the populations they serve, with choice of where and from whom they buy the services, rather than being cast as monopoly suppliers' – check. 'Another very strong idea is that money follows patients' – check. 'Pay hospitals prospectively by diagnosis-related groups as our Medicare programme does' – check. 'Self-governing NHS trusts' – check.

What seems to have happened since 1985 is that Enthoven's ideas have become embedded in individual careers, financial aspirations and personal relationships independently of the rise and fall of parties. For individuals, there is money to be made by promoting the market. In 2006, *Accountancy Age* reported that the NHS was spending more on consultants than all Britain's manufacturers put together. The figure for 2007–08 was £308.5 million. The post-political careers of the Labour cabinet ministers responsible for marketising the NHS don't make for comfortable reading. Alan Milburn became an adviser to Bridgepoint Capital, a venture capital firm backing private health companies in Britain, and to the crisps and fizzy drinks maker PepsiCo; for eighteen days a year advising Cinven, which owns thirty-seven private hospitals, Patricia Hewitt, one of Milburn's successors as health secretary, was paid £60,000. The revolving door has become a blur. Simon Stevens, Blair's special adviser on health, became a senior executive at UnitedHealth, one of America's largest private health companies; he is now back on the government payroll as head of NHS England. Mark Britnell, a career NHS manager who rose to become one of the most powerful civil servants in the Department of Health, upped sticks in 2009 to become global head of health for the consultants KPMG.

This last move did have the advantage of giving an insight into what had actually been going on in Whitehall and Downing Street. In 2010 Britnell was interviewed for a brochure put out by Apax Partners, a private equity firm: it had organised a conference in New York on how private companies could take advantage of the vulnerability of healthcare systems in a harsh financial climate. 'In future,' Britnell said, 'the NHS will be a state insurance provider, not a state deliverer … The NHS will be shown no mercy and the best time to take advantage of this will be in the next couple of years.' Responding later to the dismay his comments had caused, Britnell said in an article for the *Health Service Journal* that the NHS had saved his life in the year he left government service, that he would always support it, and that the quotes attributed to him 'do not reflect the discussion that took place' at the conference. But he didn't deny making the comments. 'Competition,' he added, 'can exist without privatisation.'

Yet Britnell had topped his own 'no mercy' line in an article he'd written for the same magazine the previous week. There he made the unremarkable if contentious point that 'all over the world, the size of the state has been increasing.' What furrowed the brow was the base year he chose for the comparison with today's level of public spending: the year was 1870, when infant mortality in Britain ran at 16 per cent, working-class men had just been given the vote, and four years had passed since a cholera epidemic killed 3,500 Londoners.

Critics of the NHS often cite Enthoven's favourite health organisation, Kaiser Permanente, as a model for efficient, integrated care. And yet from the British point of view Kaiser stands out among American providers not because it's better or worse than the NHS but because it looks a bit like it. It's huge: it provides medical care to a mainly Californian membership roughly the size of the population of Austria. Its doctors are salaried and its hospitals are non-profit. It offers patients a complete service of hospitals, labs and family doctors, as the NHS does, although it also has its own pharmacies. And one explanation for its efficiency, as with the NHS until a few years ago, is that it actually limits choice. Most Kaiser members have a health plan that offers them or their employers relatively low premiums in exchange for using only Kaiser facilities.

Kaiser is doing a lot right. Its model of 'integrated care' – where a single health organisation looks out for people not just during treatment but before, after and between, and hospital admission is seen as a failure – has long been a goal for progressives in the NHS. It seems to have done a better job than the NHS of getting medical information off paper and into computers. A 2003 study in the *British Medical Journal*, investigating the length of time the over-65s spent in hospital, found that for hip replacements, British pensioners went home, on average, twelve and a half days after admission; Kaiser patients were home after four and a half. Kaiser doesn't tie its consultants to its thirty-five hospitals; those who deal with chronic conditions are as likely to be in its 455 medical centres, alongside family doctors.

Getting ideas from Kaiser is one thing (as alluded to by Martyn Porter, NHS lengths of stay in hospital have dropped sharply since 2003); using it as a template is another. The major problem that militates against importing the Kaiser model to the NHS is money. England isn't the only country that has studied Kaiser. In 2011 a Danish think tank, the Rockwool Foundation, reported on its investigations. Its team, led by Anne Frølich, found that Kaiser was better than the Danish health service at getting its constituent parts to work together, at getting patients to take responsibility for their own health and at preventing unnecessary hospital admissions. Everything was great, except that for every krone Denmark spent on healthcare, Kaiser spent one and a half. According to the latest OECD figures, Denmark outspends Britain on healthcare, head for head, by 25 per cent. On the basis of the Rockwool study, the Kaiser system could be reproduced in Britain only if health spending were increased by 87 per cent. That is not going to happen on any Tory or Labour planet in this galaxy.

The curious thing about the Lansley plan is that it was supposed to save money, yet despite the increase in spending on the NHS under Labour, the organisation remains a bargain. The two foreign systems with which it is most often compared, the American and the French, are more expensive, are coming to be seen as unaffordable in their own countries and contain elements that it would be hard for Britons to accept. Kaiser works well and is cheaper than traditional American healthcare. But it reflects the US model. Although that model is being changed by the introduction of President Obama's Affordable Care Act, it remains idiosyncratic. Most people over sixty-five are eligible for Medicare, a kind of gold-plated American NHS for the elderly, but otherwise, if you have no insurance, you have no guaranteed access to medical facilities, including Kaiser's. If you fall seriously ill in the US, aren't insured and aren't rich, you have two main options: to go to a hospital's accident and emergency unit, where they're obliged to treat you, or to try to get Medicaid, a government programme to help the poor and disadvantaged run on a state by state basis. But the hospital will charge the full rate for treating you, which it will then try to recover against any assets you have, while Medicaid is means-tested. In other words, being uninsured and having a serious car accident in the United States is hard to make compatible with owning a house.

The Affordable Care Act (ACA) is a giant step towards equality of opportunity in America, though it falls short of a revolution. The new law proposes that all fifty states accept a more generous means test for households trying to enrol in Medicaid. The threshold depends on household size; in most states, a family of four could be earning up to $32,500 a year and still qualify. In many parts of the US, where the current threshold is less than $12,000, this is a massive increase, and should enable proper health care for the first time to millions of low-paid working Americans whose employers are too mean to cover them. But a swathe of southern and mid-western states with Republican legislatures, including four of the five with the highest poverty levels, Mississippi, Louisiana, Alabama and Texas, are refusing, with the approval of the Supreme Court, to implement the system.

For middle-class Americans, the new system is just as radical. Individuals still aren't forced to take out health insurance, but they now suffer a stiff tax penalty if they don't. In return, for middle-income households earning up to $94,000, the government offers hefty subsidies on a choice of health plans, and has abolished the brutal 'pre-existing condition' rule, which allowed insurance companies to refuse coverage to people who were already ill. All businesses above a certain size will be obliged to start offering their employees health cover. Supporters of the law believe it will more than pay for itself; its increased costs will be offset by thinning out the armies of walking wounded who throng hospital emergency rooms, and by spreading risk more widely.

But as many as thirty million people will still be left without medical cover – low-paid people in the pro-inequality states, illegal immigrants and people who gamble that they won't need a doctor and prefer to pay a tax penalty rather than a premium. And even if you are insured in America, and have access to some of the world's finest medical facilities, just paying the premium each month doesn't make healthcare free at the point of delivery. Two standard features of US health insurance, before the ACA and under it, are the 'copay', a fee for consultations or drugs, and the 'deductible', an amount the patient is expected to pay before the insurance kicks in, like the excess on car insurance. The lower the premiums, the higher the copays and deductible.

With the new subsidies Kaiser's Platinum 90 plan, for instance, costs $345 a month for a forty-year-old woman with one child living in San Francisco and earning $40,000 a year. Although much more affordable than it would have been pre-ACA, that's a high premium, and there's no deductible. But each year she has to pay $20 to see a doctor after the first visit; $150 for a trip to the emergency room; between $5 and $15 per prescription; $250 a day for a hospital stay, and so on up to a maximum of $8,000 a year. At the other end of the scale, there's a Bronze plan that costs $123 a month. That's a bargain if she doesn't get sick. But if mother or child falls ill, she has to pay the first $9,000 out of her own pocket. After that the copays kick in – two-fifths of the actual cost of everything from chemotherapy to x-rays – until she's forked out $12,700.

A Harvard-led study found that 62 per cent of all bankrupt-cies in the United States in 2007 were due to medical bills, an increase of 50 per cent in six years. Most of those affected were well-educated, middle-class homeowners. Astonishingly, three-quarters had their finances destroyed by medical costs even though they had insurance. In a significant number of cases, it was paying to look after a sick child that bankrupted parents. Among the common ailments were neurological conditions like multiple sclerosis, which left households $34,000 out of pocket on average, diabetes ($26,000) and stroke ($23,000). In his paper 'Sick and (Still) Broke', the lawyer Ryan Sugden points out that while the ACA puts a helpful cap on copayments, it doesn't eliminate them, and does little to help people who have to quit work through their or a child's illness. 'While the Affordable Care Act will reduce the overall number of bankruptcies, and arguably eliminate the most morally objectionable causes of medical bankruptcy, in a system based on market principles there will – and must – be consumers whose own bad choices spell financial trouble,' he writes. 'For society to "win" and receive the benefits of a consumer-driven system, there must be some who "lose".'

Latest figures from the OECD and the World Health Organisation suggest that the US spends 2.4 times more on health per person than Britain, yet Britons live slightly longer, on average, than Americans. British men can expect to live to be seventy-eight, two years older than American men; for women it's eighty-two versus eighty-one.

The US healthcare system is unique, as is the NHS. Most rich countries lie somewhere in-between the two, using mandatory insurance, with a mixture of state, for-profit and non-profit medical organisations providing the care. France, for instance, spends slightly more on health than Britain, and French women, though not French men, live slightly longer. French people of working age, together with their employers if they have them, pay into a social security fund that's supposed to cover healthcare, pensions, disability and child support. The poorest French people get healthcare absolutely free under a system called Couverture Maladie Universelle, or CMU. There is also a list of thirty conditions, known as Affections Longue Durée, which are treated free of charge for everyone: cancer, HIV, diabetes, Parkinson's, all the way to leprosy. Otherwise the relatively well-off, though shielded from ruin by the sickness insurance system, Assurance Maladie, are faced with a system of copays not much less onerous than America's. Where in Britain copays are restricted to dentistry and prescription charges, in France patients pay a fee each time they visit the doctor. They pay a percentage, known as the *ticket modérateur*, of hospital costs, ambulance bills and medical procedures. Each visit to your GP, for instance, costs €23 up front, of which €15.10 will be reimbursed. A replacement hip is free, but to get one put in you have to pay 20 per cent of the cost of surgery, lab tests, consultants' fees and the stay in hospital.

The huge sums France spends giving its citizens free, universal access to the latest cancer drugs and equipment are popular, but the country's lavish spending on extreme illnesses doesn't put it as far ahead of Britain as critics of the NHS claim. One recent study led by Philippe Autier of the International Agency for Research on Cancer in Lyon showed that the number of people dying of breast cancer in England and Wales fell by 35 per cent between 1989 and 2006, against an 11 per cent fall in France. France is still doing slightly better than England but the rates have almost converged.

Britons who idealise the French system imagine that in France anyone can see any doctor they like and that the state will pick up the bill, but if this were ever true, it isn't true now. The country's social security fund is chronically in the red. To see a consultant inside the Assurance Maladie system, patients have to get a referral from a GP, as in Britain. And there are two kinds of doctor. Only *secteur 1* doctors charge the Assurance Maladie fee. *Secteur 2* doctors can set their own fees, but the share reimbursed by Assurance Maladie doesn't change. An increasing number are taking out private health insurance to cover the gap.

All the rich world's diverse health care systems are struggling with ageing populations, with the diseases of plenty – obesity,

diabetes – and new, ever more expensive ways to treat their illnesses. But to speak in terms of 'health care systems' doesn't
accurately represent what's happening to the NHS. The NHS
used to be no more or less than a health care system; now it's a
health care system into which a whole other system, the system
of competitive consumerism, is pushing. A system that was
concerned first with making people well and, as a secondary pre-
occupation, looking after itself, is now trying to accommodate
competition. But competition between agencies for business,
even medical business, is easy to understand. The more insidi-
ous novelty is competition between patients. Once it used to be
enough to get help for what ailed you. Now patients are being
encouraged to think about how the NHS treats them in terms
of the discontent-fostering narratives of advertising: to imagine
other patients who are getting better or worse treatment than
they are, in prettier or uglier hospitals, with therapies that are
not necessarily more effective but are faster, more fashionable,
that come in a wider range of colours. The blurring of the distinction between health care and the maintenance of lifestyle
choices gives the enemies of the NHS another means by which
to accuse it of failure.

One dark Sunday afternoon in February 1982 Jill Charnley
waited at the wheel of a car outside a hospital in Mansfield.
Through the storm she saw her husband bustling towards her
with a plastic pail containing the haunch of a woman who'd just
died. 'Down the road he came with a triumphant smile on his
face and this bucket with a hip in it,' she told me not long ago.
'He put it in the boot of the car. I remember saying: "My God, I
hope we don't have an accident, if they look in the boot of the car
to see what's there …"'

John Charnley, Sir John as he was by then, managed to restrain
himself from dissecting the specimen, preserved under forma-
lin, until the next day. The dead patient's hip was, in a way, as
much his as hers. It was implanted in 1963, one of the world's

first successful total hip replacements, performed by Charnley using a hip of his own design. 'This is truly a marvellous climax to my series of more than seventy cases,' he wrote in his journal, referring to post-mortem examinations he'd already done on his early patients. To have his prototype hip work smoothly inside someone for almost twenty years and still be, as he described it, in perfect condition, gave him joy.

The first generation of NHS surgeons were front-line surgeons in a literal sense. In 1940, aged twenty-nine, Charnley went to France as a military medic with the makeshift flotilla evacuating British troops from Dunkirk. 'He didn't expect to survive,' his widow said. 'The boat he was in was bombed or shelled. I remember him saying to me that this was the point when he believed he'd been saved for a purpose.'

The foundation of the NHS in 1948 coincided with a golden era in the struggle against infectious disease. In postwar Britain, orthopaedic surgeons earned their spurs in hospitals built in the countryside as sanitoria, designed to deal with the bone and joint problems caused by tuberculosis and polio. But the incidence of these infectious diseases was dropping. Casting around for new reasons to be, the bone doctors fastened on arthritis.

Up to this point, the options for people with a dodgy hip were limited. Basic human actions – walking, getting up, sitting down – require smooth movement of the femoral head, the ball-like top of the thigh bone, against the cup-like socket in the pelvis known as the acetabulum. When it works as evolution made it, it is because socket and head are sheathed in a smooth layer of cartilage that secretes a natural lubricant called synovial fluid. Inflammation, fractures and swelling make the hip jam and chafe like a rusted-up hinge. The result is immobility and pain. By the 1950s, it was becoming fairly common to cut off the degraded top of a patient's thigh bone and replace the femoral head with one made of metal or ceramic. Other surgeons focused on the acetabulum: they lined damaged hip sockets with cups made of steel, chrome alloy or glass. What was missing was a reliable way of replacing both head and socket. It had been tried in the 1930s, with the two parts made of metal, but it had never really worked.

Charnley charged at the problem with zeal. A grammar school boy from Bury, he was a charismatic dynamo, a brilliant explainer given to anger when thwarted. He was so obsessed with bone growth that he got a colleague to cut off a piece of his shin bone and regraft it, just to see what would happen. (He got an infection and needed another, more serious operation.) Imbued with technocratic patriotism he carried a torch for the British motor industry and saw parallels between car and human engineering. Jill Charnley remembers him roaring down to London in his Aston Martin – 'a brute of a car, a good engineering car' – to visit her. He told her he was redesigning nature, and illustrated his theories with ball bearings from the British Motor Corporation's new Mini.

They were married in 1957 and Jill moved into his medical digs in Manchester, where the wallpaper had a bone motif. Keen to avoid the communal dining-room, with its clientele of fusty bachelor surgeons, she tried the kitchenette. 'I went in and opened the first cupboard,' she said. 'I was literally showered with old bones and all sorts of screws and bits and pieces.'

Human bones?

'Oh Lord, yes.'

After noticing that a patient with a French-made acrylic ball fitted to the top of his thigh bone gave off a loud squeaking whenever he moved, Charnley realised that a complete hip replacement would work only when the head was firmly held in place and when materials were found that mimicked the low-friction, squeak-free movement of a natural hip joint.

His first attempt was a steel ball, smaller than the usual prostheses, attached to a dagger-like blade that was pushed through the soft core of the thigh bone and held in place with cement, like grout round a tile. For the socket, he used a Teflon cup. He put the experimental hip in about 300 patients. It was a disaster.

After a few years tiny particles of Teflon shed by the cup caused a cheesy substance to build up around the joint. The blade came loose in the bone. Pain returned. Each one of the Teflon hips that Charnley had so laboriously put into his patients had to be removed and replaced. He did the work himself. His biographer, William Waugh, quotes a colleague as saying the sight of Charnley going to each operation was 'like observing a monk pouring ashes over his own head'. Punishing himself further, Charnley went around for nine months with a lump of Teflon implanted in his thigh to observe its effects.

In May 1962 a salesman turned up at Wrightington trying to flog a new plastic from Germany, a kind of polyethylene, used for gears in the Lancashire textile mills. It proved many times more hard-wearing than Teflon. Only after implanting a chunk of polyethylene into his much-scarred legs and leaving it there for months was Charnley prepared to risk putting it in patients. It worked. The procedure was taken up around the world.

Now, each year, hip replacements free millions of people from pain and immobility. The operation has a success rate of about 95 per cent. It lacks the life-saving glamour of brain surgery, resuscitation of car-crash victims or new cancer drugs. It is something more remarkable, a radical and complex operation – involving the sawing of bones, the deep penetration of skin and muscle, extreme measures to prevent infection and the replacement of a vital body part with a synthetic substitute – that transforms the lives of its beneficiaries, yet has become routine.

Making artificial hips – and knees, and elbows, and shoulders – has become a multi-billion-pound global business. But it was in the austere conditions of an old TB hospital in Lancashire, in the state-run NHS, not in the well-funded, commercially competitive world of American medicine, that total hip replacement was pioneered. To make the first machine to mass produce polyethylene cups, Harry Craven, a young craftsman who worked for Charnley, scavenged odds and ends from a local scrapyard. In their book *A Transatlantic History of Total Hip Replacement*

Julie Anderson, Francis Neary and John Pickstone argue that
by putting surgeons on state salaries, the NHS freed them from
dependence on private patients, giving the innovative among
them the security to experiment. Charnley was only the most
successful of a string of British surgeon-inventors who designed
effective hips in the 1960s and 1970s.

Born in the NHS, routine hip replacement, the small family
car of medical procedures (the first Morris Minor went on show
two months after the NHS began), became the marker of the
Health Service's life stages. Stoical postwar patients, grateful to
have their pain relieved and used to rationing and queues, gave
way to a less accepting generation comfortable with the label
'consumer'. Charnley described his first patients as 'pitifully
grateful' for the relief from pain his short-lived Teflon hips gave
them. By the end of his life, he was ranting against the 'crass
ignorance and stupidity' of Britain's consumerist 'peasants'.

People were living longer, so they were older for longer.
Demand for the procedure rose faster than the number of surgeons and hospital facilities to carry it out. In 1982 a fifth of
patients waiting for a hip replacement had been waiting a year
or more. Supporters of the NHS pointed out, correctly, that the
service wasn't getting enough money to satisfy patients, and
was underfunded compared to its European peers; yet the huge
waiting list for hip surgery, much greater than for any other procedure, was used by Thatcherites throughout the 1970s, 1980s
and 1990s as evidence that the NHS was inefficient. When
New Labour came in and hosed money at the problem, waiting
times fell. Private companies, rather than the NHS, picked up a
significant portion of the extra work. Hip replacements, the life-
enhancing procedure that came out of the Welfare State, became
one of the main points of entry through which private health
firms were undermining it.

Once you start writing about hip joints, you begin to notice
the number of people hobbling and limping. Everywhere you
look there seems to be an aluminium walking stick. On the train

from Liverpool to Birkenhead one day I got into conversation with a couple of women in their forties who'd got onto the train with the help of sticks. One of them was waiting for a hip operation. The procedure was delayed longer than usual because she was trying to align two specialists. She couldn't get an orthopaedic surgeon to do her hip until she'd seen an endocrinologist to sort out another problem. I asked her whether she'd heard of the new centre in Runcorn specialising in joint replacements. Her eyes lit up: brand recognition. 'People tell me I should go there,' she said. I had to tell her that the Runcorn centre had just closed, only five years after opening.

The costly fiasco of the Cheshire and Merseyside NHS Treatment Centre, to give the Runcorn clinic its proper name, was a typically post-Thatcherite episode. Governments now so idealise the private sector that just allowing private firms to compete isn't enough. New Labour believed it had to pay private companies to compete with their state rivals. The Runcorn clinic was one of a wave of 'independent sector treatment centres' – ISTCs – masterminded by a Texan private bureaucrat called Ken Anderson, recruited by the Department of Health in 2003 to shower private firms with gold in order to bring down NHS waiting lists.

A firm called Interhealth Canada was given a five-year contract to run the Runcorn ISTC, starting in 2006. It built a state of the art joint replacement clinic, designed and equipped to the highest standard, but it didn't have to pay for it: the entire £32 million cost was refunded by the taxpayer. In case this wasn't enough to keep the entrepreneurial tiger of Interhealth happy, the PCTs in Cheshire and Merseyside who were supposed to send NHS patients to the centre had to pay Interhealth 25 per cent more than the NHS rate to carry out the operations. If an operation went wrong, however, Interhealth wouldn't be expected to put it right. Initially, it wasn't asked to take any responsibility for training doctors either. The cherry on the cake was that it would be paid for a minimum number of procedures, no matter how many it carried out. Over five years, the firm happily accepted about £8 million for work it didn't do.

Once the five years were up, the PCTs decided they'd had enough, and told Interhealth its contract wouldn't be renewed. In 2011 the centre's 165 staff were made redundant and the ISTC closed. The building reverted to NHS control and was mothballed. When I spoke to Interhealth's boss, Fred Little, it hadn't been decided what would be done with it; Little said it would probably end up as a primary care clinic – 'like using a luxury hotel as a garage', he told me bitterly, denouncing the NHS as a Soviet relic. According to a spokesman for the PCTs, Interhealth was offered a contract extension in 2009 provided it accepted the NHS rate for operations. It declined.

Dr Abhi Mantgani, a GP in Birkenhead, used to send patients to the Runcorn centre. It was fifteen miles away but his practice laid on transport for patients. Mantgani didn't like it that local GPs weren't consulted before it was opened; nor does he like it that, just when patients were getting used to it, the place was shut down. 'The service at the ISTC was fantastic,' he told me when I visited him in 2011. 'Patients only had to go twice, first as outpatients for all the diagnostics, then they got a date for the operation and went in for surgery. Why can't NHS hospitals provide the same level of quality service?"

Mantgani, who was born in India, had been a GP in Birkenhead for twenty years. His base was a smart new medical centre, light, bright and clean. Ambitious and articulate, he had an air of busyness and impatience with institutional inertia. He'd been navigating local health politics for a long time. To GPs, patient choice was old hat already. He was eager to move on. Being able to choose a hospital wasn't enough if you couldn't also choose a consultant. Having the power to commission a certain number of hip operations wasn't enough, either. Mantgani wanted to be

---

* The Runcorn Centre was reopened in 2013 by Warrington and Halton Hospitals foundation trust to provide the same service as the ISTC, but within the NHS system.

able to commission 'packages of care': to get a hospital to assess a patient, take them in for surgery, make sure their home had any necessary adaptations and check on them regularly after the op, Kaiser-style. And he wanted to get more tests out of hospitals into local clinics. 'Waiting six or eight weeks for an endoscopy is just not appropriate in a Western democracy,' he said. 'I think the NHS is a great system but I don't think it can remain the way it is ... in vast parts of the country there is no proper choice and it is a cartel. And that leads to patients being given what clinicians think is the right thing to do. I'm not for wholesale creating this into some kind of private industry. But I think if various other models of working act as the grit in the oyster to stimulate better performance, better competition and choice for the patients, it's not a bad thing at all.'

Actually, there was no sign of a cartel in the Wirral. I punched the postcode for Dr Mantgani's surgery into the NHS Choices website, together with 'hip replacement'. Under the changes brought in by Labour, patients could choose from five hospitals within five miles and fifty-nine within fifty miles. Wrightington, nineteen miles away, was the twenty-first closest. The closest was the Wirral's NHS hospital, Arrowe Park, three miles away; just across the Mersey was the Royal Liverpool University Hospital; the closest private hospital, the Spire Murrayfield, was only slightly further away. The site suggested you'd have to wait eleven weeks from referral to treatment at Arrowe Park, seven weeks at the Royal Liverpool and only five if you went to Spire. On the other hand, Spire doesn't have the full range of emergency services should something go wrong; nor is it likely to take difficult cases. If my hip was hurting like hell, I'm not sure I would want to take these choices on myself. Why should I? Like most patients, I'm not a doctor. Dr Mantgani admitted: 'The patient often says: "You tell me where I should go."'

Dr Mantgani was a believer in the new order, and since I met him power has shifted his way. The websites of the PCTs that opened and closed the Runcorn ISTC have gone dark. Health services on the Wirral peninsula are now ordered up by a body called the Wirral Clinical Commissioning Group, which supervises three consortia of local GPs; Mantgani is chief clinical officer, ultimately responsible, with his chairman, another local GP, Phil Jennings, for a budget of £445 million. Just before the group began its work, its board agreed a pay rise for the two family doctors of 5 per cent, to £112,000 each. A few months later Jeremy Hunt, Andrew Lansley's successor, told rank and file English NHS workers that a one per cent pay rise was unaffordable.

After meeting Mantgani I got back on the train and went to Hoylake, on the western coast of the Wirral. At the ocean's edge an immense beach stretched out towards the horizon. I could just make out a line of wind turbines turning there, scratching the air as if it held an eternal itch. In a café I met John Smith, director of studies at Liverpool University Medical School, a shy, rather noble-looking man with shoulder-length grey hair. 'I'm not sure in many ways what choice means,' he said. 'Most patients might want to choose their consultant, but they want them to be in the local area, so actually choice isn't nearly as great as it might appear. As soon as you start introducing choice, you start introducing league tables, short-term targets and less of an overall pattern of healthcare. On the one hand, they want to say, "Let's have a market economy," but on the other they want to say: "Let's plan." Realistically, you can do one or the other reasonably well but you can't do both. As soon as you have freedom of choice the market will decide the outcome. Even when you give GPs budgets, what does the GP do if he gets several patients who demand very expensive treatments?'

Whomever I spoke to, and whatever they thought of the latest NHS upheaval, the conversation turned to the cruel paradox of the Health Service: the more successful it is in lengthening life, the more threatened it becomes. 'When the Health Service was started the average retirement age was sixty-five, and life expectancy was sixty-seven,' Smith said. 'Much as I hate to say it, the issue of pensions is the issue that pervades the whole political affordability question. Unless people become surprisingly more productive, we are all going to have to work longer in order to maintain our standard of living. Someone is going to have to pick up the costs of looking after people who are being kept alive but whose ability to look after themselves is declining.'

To respect the NHS isn't to love it unconditionally. There can be few people who haven't experienced a moment of uncaring-ness or worse somewhere in the system. Monopolies, state or private, get complacent, and can resist good changes; perhaps the general hospital is over-fetishised in this country. At Stafford Hospital, a small general NHS hospital, patients died unneces-sarily between 2005 and 2009 because they were neither cared for nor cared about. Robert Francis's last report into the horror for the government began by describing 'a culture focused on doing the system's business – not that of patients.' Patients went unwashed for weeks on end, went hungry and thirsty, were left to soil their bedclothes, were sent home before they were well. It was terrible. It was also exceptional. And as Francis made clear, for all the terrible failings of the NHS system and the per-sonal sins against human decency committed in Mid-Staffs, a significant factor in the catastrophe was hospital management's determination to conform, at all costs, to Labour's new competi-tive framework, a framework the Tories and their Liberal allies have embraced.

Past commercialisations and privatisations of state monopo-lies don't give confidence that a commercialisation-privatisation of the NHS would have a happy outcome. Competitive pressures can reduce choice as well as encourage it. You can give patients choice, but someone else chooses the choices. One of the things businesses do is merge and consolidate and already foundation trust hospitals are doing just that. In East London, for instance, six hospitals – Barts, the Royal London, Whipps Cross, Mile End, Newham and the London Chest – have merged to create Barts Health, the largest NHS trust in Britain, with a turnover in 2013 of £1.25 billion. The London Chest has long been scheduled to close, but the other five hospitals are only a few miles apart. It seems unlikely they will all continue to offer all the services they do now. Foundation trusts often consist of more than one hospital, and one of the hidden implications of the Milburn-Lansley programme is that a strong, solvent, ambitious foundation trust has as much incentive to shut down one of its hospitals (in order to remain solvent and grow elsewhere) as a financially weak one.

The more for-profit companies become involved in the NHS, the more public money will leak out of the health system in the form of dividends. And the government is taking a risk. When it privatised the water industry, it effectively farmed out to the water companies the tax increases needed to pay for the renewal of the country's Victorian water infrastructure. When it privatised the electricity firms, it farmed out the tax increases needed to fund wind farms and new nuclear power stations. By commercialising the NHS, but promising to keep on paying for it, it doesn't leave room for manoeuvre in the health marketplace when competitors start encouraging patients to demand more expensive procedures.

One day I visited Edward Atkins, a retired bank manager, at his home in East Molesey in Surrey. The modern redbrick bungalow where Atkins and his wife live is about twenty minutes' walk from Hampton Court station, long enough for me to appreciate the boon of properly functioning hips and knees. Atkins answered the door, a tall, solidly built man with a full head of hair who could easily pass for sixty-five. In fact he's eighty. He'd still be playing tennis if he could. As he describes it, much of his life seems to have run on rails, making all the stops and adhering to the timetable of respectable, decent, middle-class life in the comfier corners of postwar southern England. Born in Portsmouth, he did National Service, then got a job as a trainee at Lloyds. He married, had children, got a mortgage, rose through the ranks and retired on an indexed pension at two-thirds of his final salary. His retirement began well. He played badminton, golf and tennis. Then, in his early seventies, he felt aches and pains in his right knee and groin. A cyst was removed from his knee, but he was told the knee was fine; perhaps the problem was his hip? In 2005, with the groin pain getting worse, Atkins, who has private insurance, went to see a consultant, Andrew Cobb.

Cobb, a distinguished orthopaedic surgeon doing a mix of private and NHS work, recommended a hip replacement of a new design called ASR, produced by the American company DePuy, a subsidiary of Johnson & Johnson. Apart from being more expensive, the ASR hip differed from the total hip replacement pioneered by John Charnley in two ways. Both surfaces, ball and cup, are made of cobalt-chromium – a so-called 'metal on metal' hip. And instead of cutting off the top of the thigh bone and pushing a spar deep inside the bone to hold the ball of the joint in place, the ball is a hollow hemisphere with a short stalk, like a mushroom, designed to cover the ball at the top of the femur rather than completely replace it. Hence the claim that the hip is not being replaced, merely 'resurfaced'.

Resurfacing means less bone is lost than in a full replacement. Even the most successful conventional hip replacements seldom last much beyond ten years, and it's easier and safer to put in a total hip replacement after a resurfacing than to put in one replacement after another. In other words, hip resurfacing is seen as ideal for the young and the active, people who are generally healthy and are likely to wear out at least one hip device. The DePuy ASR hip was marketed aggressively as a hip hip. A device with its origins in the basic need to eliminate pain and enable movement seemed to be entering the realm of lifestyle marketing.

Cobb pitched hard for the ASR hip, as Atkins remembers it, telling him the hip had 'just come out', that in a matter of six weeks he'd be playing golf again, even tennis. 'He said I wouldn't be able to play properly unless I had this operation.' But the clincher, for him, was a marketing video from DePuy showing a series of real people who were seemingly thriving with ASR hips. 'There was a golfer putting putts down from twenty-five yards. At the end there was this guy, apparently the coxswain of a West Country lifeboat, at the wheel of the actual lifeboat in very rough seas.'

What Atkins didn't know was that Cobb had helped design the hip he was promoting. Impressed by the video, he signed up for the operation. He was about to become a victim of what has been called 'one of the biggest disasters in orthopaedic history'. From the moment he went home, he felt something was wrong. 'All I know is my hip started clicking like mad after I got in a certain position. It was never really right.' The hip became inflamed, and the pain began. If he exerted himself – went out on his bike, for instance – his hip would swell up afterwards and start to hurt. He kept making appointments to see Cobb, who would reassure him. Atkins had already paid £2,000 for the operation, the part of the £14,000 procedure his insurance wouldn't cover. But every time he went to see Cobb, he had to pay more than £200 for a consultation. In the end, on his GP's advice, he ambushed the surgeon at a walk-in NHS clinic he ran. Cobb agreed to replace his ASR hip with a regular, Charnley-style hip, using NHS money. By this time Atkins had been living with the pain for four years: 'Four years that blighted my life and that of my wife. I couldn't sit; I couldn't stand. I was on 500 mg of ibuprofen twice a day. Since that operation I really haven't played any sport at all.'

The ASR hip wasn't the only resurfacing option for Atkins in 2005, but he didn't know this. The John Charnley of hip resurfacing is a Birmingham-based surgeon called Derek McMinn. In 1997, after six years of trials, he put a hip resurfacing device, the Birmingham hip, on the market. Now made in Warwick by the British multinational Smith & Nephew, it has been used with relatively few problems around the world. The DePuy hip was designed explicitly to compete with the Birmingham hip – a device that did the job perfectly well. It could have been an improvement; it turned out to be anything but.

In 2005, the year Atkins was given the ASR hip, McMinn made a prescient attack on the rival product at a conference in Helsinki. He warned that the groove DePuy had cut around the edge of the metal hip socket meant greater pressure on the rim as patients moved around, making it more likely metal debris would shear off and enter soft tissue. It might have been dismissed as the posturing of a rival, but disturbing reports were beginning to come in from Australia about problems with the hip.

The French authorities rejected the ASR in 2008, and though US regulators never approved it, the rules allowed American surgeons to implant it anyway. In Britain, the feeble agency that is supposed to monitor medical devices, the MHRA, didn't act. An investigation by the *British Medical Journal* pinpoints an early adopter of the ASR, Tony Nargol, a surgeon in North-East England, as one of the first to question its safety. He began getting bad feedback from patients in 2007. When he opened them up to investigate he was shocked to find that flesh and muscle around the hip had been destroyed; in some cases bone, too, was damaged.

Just as McMinn had warned, the ASR was shedding tiny fragments of cobalt-chromium, producing a devastating reaction in some patients. Further trouble was caused by individual atoms of cobalt and chromium leaching into patients' blood and spinal fluid. The evidence against the ASR began to escalate, but it was only in August 2010 that DePuy admitted defeat and issued a general recall of the hip. By that time the company had sold tens of thousands of the devices around the world. As lawyers began to gather clients for litigation, the scale of the disaster became apparent. Some of those who had signed up for the ASR in the hope of another twenty years of dancing or running or tennis may be permanently disabled. In March, British surgeons who had studied more data on the ASR suggested that a second version of the hip, designed for total hip replacement, would probably fail in half of cases after just six years. About 10,000 ASR hips were implanted in the UK. 'The really unlucky ones are those about fifty or fifty-five who had it done to extend their working careers,' Atkins said. 'There's no way they're going to work again.'

'I never made any secret of the fact that I had been one of the six surgeons contributing to the design of the ASR,' Cobb wrote to me in an email: 'Certainly, most of my patients were aware of this. I can't remember exactly what was said to Mr Atkins before his first operation but I usually discussed the proposed use of the ASR, the advantages I perceived to be offered by it over the Birmingham device, and the further information available on the Internet. I have no knowledge of a lifeboat coxswain featuring in any advertisements.'

The disturbing issues raised by the ASR hip fiasco – why was DePuy not obliged to test the device more rigorously by the authorities in Britain? Are other metal on metal hips a risk? – obscure a deeper question. Why are medical implants being marketed like iPhones, as in Smith & Nephew's video for the Birmingham hip at rediscoveryourgo.com, where to the accompaniment of a driving guitar track, strong, shadowy dudes with artificial hips ski, play football and climb rock faces?

The progressive justification for the current changes to the NHS, expressed by people like the former Blair adviser Julian Le Grand, now on the board of trustees at the King's Fund, is that the only true recourse for patients who experience incompetence, rudeness, slovenliness, patronising behaviour and uncaringness by public servants is the power to send a message to the offenders by taking their custom elsewhere. Hence the ideal of 'choice'. But the weakness of the British authorities in the face of the ASR hip, and the ease with which DePuy salespeople persuaded British surgeons to use the ASR implant when tried and tested alternatives were available, doesn't suggest the people who run our health system have a clear idea of the difference between 'choice' and 'marketing'.

In 1993, an op-ed piece by three surgeons in the *BMJ* pointed out that a significant cause of long waiting lists for hip replacements was that hospitals blew their orthopaedic budgets on expensive new kinds of joint implant whose increased cost couldn't be justified on medical grounds. Much of the cost of the latest medical devices, like the cost of a can of Coca-Cola, went towards the marketing propaganda without which it would never occur to you to buy them. The article's parting barb – 'the implant industry remains a haven for all the excesses of free enterprise' – still applies. A recent report by Audit Scotland (where the NHS more closely resembles its pre-Enthoven form) noted that in Lothian, the average cost of a hip implant was £858. In neighbouring Forth Valley, NHS joint buyers were paying more than twice as much. In the US, a basic Charnley-style hip implant will now set you back $10,000, or £6,100. Another type of hip has gone up in price there by 242 per cent since 1991, when inflation has been only 60 per cent. The authors of *Transatlantic History* point out that some of the cheaper hips used in Britain aren't sold in the US, even though they're made there. Many surgeons and consumers want the best, they say, 'but when that which is properly known to be "the best" is ipso facto old technology, the best may come to mean "the latest", and the latest may prove to be expensive failures.'

'There is no reason,' Aneurin Bevan wrote to doctors as the NHS came into being, 'why the whole of the doctor-patient relationship should not be freed from what most of us feel should be irrelevant to it, the money factor, the collection of fees or thinking how to pay fees – an aspect of practice already distasteful to many practitioners.'

I asked Martyn Porter how a place like Wrightington could survive in the marketplace if Porter the commercial manager failed to stop Porter the surgeon carrying out loss-making operations rivals wouldn't do. 'I came into medicine because if someone's injured, I want to fix them,' he said. 'Someone's going to fix them. Why not us? Secondly, you never get good, you get a little bit better. It's necessary at my age not to get bored. I'm just getting warmed up. However, the most important issue is the finance. We get a lot of money from the cheap and cheerful procedures, we take a hit on others. The managers are cool with that, as long as we're getting a reputation as a centre of orthopaedic excellence.'

The phone rang. The patient was ready. Porter wanted to talk some more about the Lansley project. 'I think there's a model there, but it's whether it can be delivered and won't be corrupted. I can see a very idealistic model, but by God, it's vulnerable to people ripping it off.'

Jill Charnley, now in her eighties, is the contented recipient of two artificial knees. They've lengthened her life, she says. Her shoulder gives her trouble and she could, if she wished, have a prosthesis put in for that, too, but she's made the choice not to. She's drawn the line, partly because of the physiotherapy involved and partly because she knows there's a limit to what medicine can achieve. 'We are all getting old,' she said, 'and bits of us wear out.'

There is only money in more, or in getting something. There is no money in less, or in getting nothing, even though less and nothing is everyone's eventual fate, and may be desirable long before that. The NHS can't avoid dealing with the financial consequences of its own success in enabling people to be old for longer and longer. But it can avoid becoming a victim of marketing.

In *The Charterhouse of Parma*, Stendhal wrote: 'The lover thinks more often of reaching his mistress than the husband of guarding his wife; the prisoner thinks more often of escaping than the jailer of shutting his door; and so, whatever the obstacles may be, the lover and the prisoner ought to succeed.' In the governance of Britain, it is as if the marketeers have internalised a modern version of this. The salesman thinks more often of making a sale than the consumer thinks he is being sold to; the lobbyist thinks more often of his loophole than the politician thinks of closing it; and so, whatever the obstacles may be, the salesman and the lobbyist are bound to succeed.

6. No Vacancies

Privatised homes

A housing shortage that has been building up for the past thirty years is reaching the point of crisis. The party in power, whose late twentieth-century figurehead, Margaret Thatcher, did so much to create the problem, is responding by separating off the economically least powerful and squeezing them into the smallest, meanest, most insecure possible living space. In effect, if not in explicit intention, it is a let-the-poor-be-poor crusade, a Campaign for Real Poverty. The government has stopped short of openly declaring war on the poor. But how different would the situation be if it had?

Look at things from Pat Quinn's point of view, for instance. What's being done to her is happening quite slowly, over a period of months, and is not the work of a gang of thugs breaking down her door and screaming in her face, but is conducted through forms and letters and interviews with courteous people who explain apologetically that they're only implementing a new set of rules. At the age of sixty, having worked for thirty years before being registered as too unwell to work, Pat Quinn is effectively being told that she's a shirker, and that the two-bedroom council flat where she's lived for forty years and where her husband died is a luxury she doesn't deserve. She's been targeted for self-eviction. Essentially, the government is trying to starve her out. Without the government allowance she receives in the form of housing benefit, she cannot pay her rent, and the government has cut the allowance so it's no longer enough to cover the rent on a two-bedroom council flat. It's just enough for a one-bedroom flat – a theoretical, but actually non-existent, one-bedroom flat. This is what the 'bedroom tax' means.

'It's just very, very hard to deal with,' Quinn told me when I visited her. 'This is my home, this isn't just a council place where I live. They can only do it to me because I have nothing. I'm sure if they had their way they would cull us. I really believe that.'

It wouldn't be so tough on Quinn if her municipal landlord, the borough of Tower Hamlets in East London, or one of the local housing associations – not-for-profit groups offering low-rent homes – or their counterparts in neighbouring boroughs, or the private sector, had affordable one-bedroom flats to spare. They don't. As I write this, the cheapest one-bedroom private flats in Quinn's area cost £240 a week including council tax, at the very edge of the new maximum the government is willing to subsidise for a single person. Demand is intense – they don't stay on the market for more than forty-eight hours, as a rule – and since, under the new rules, housing benefit will be given to the tenant rather than directly to the landlord, private landlords will be warier than ever of letting to benefit claimants.

The old council house waiting list no longer exists. Now areas run waiting lists for 'social housing', a pool of council and housing association properties at subsidised rents. In Tower Hamlets, there are 22,000 people on the list. A significant number of them will have families, so it's hard to know how many individuals the figure represents, but it corresponds to a fifth of all households in the borough. Of this 22,000, 10,000 are waiting for a one-bedroom flat. Five hundred of them have been waiting twelve years or more. How many one-bedroom flats became available in Tower Hamlets in 2012–13? Just 840. Supply and demand have floated free of each other, and not only in the category of social housing. In the same year, the price of private flats for

sale in Tower Hamlets went up by 5 per cent; in neighbouring Hackney, which has a similar demographic, it was a wild
15 per cent.

There aren't enough homes in Tower Hamlets. There aren't
enough homes in London, in the South-East, in Britain.
The shortage gets worse. Each year, population growth and
the shrinking of average household size adds a quarter of a
million households to the twenty-six million we have now. The
number of new homes being built is barely above a hundred
thousand.

To understand how it came to this, you have to go back to
1979, when Margaret Thatcher began forcing local authorities
to sell council houses to any sitting tenant able and eager to
buy, at discounts of up to 50 per cent. It was one of those rare
policies that still seems to contain in its very name the entire
explanation of what it means: 'Right to Buy'. Cherished by Tories
and New Labour alike as an electoral masterstroke, it offered
a life-changing fortune to a relatively small group of people, a
group that, not by coincidence, contained a large number of
swing voters.

Right to Buy differed from the period's other privatisations in
many ways. It was tightly linked to the buyer's personal use of
the asset being privatised. If the Royal Mail had been sold on the
same principle buyers would have got a discount on the share
price based on the number of letters they'd posted over their lifetime. According to Hugo Young, Thatcher had to be talked into
Right to Buy by a desperate Edward Heath, then her leader, who'd
been persuaded by his friend Pierre Trudeau after his electoral
defeat in February 1974 that he needed a fistful of populist policies. No wonder Thatcher baulked. Right to Buy violated basic
Thatcherite values: that self-reliance was good, state handouts
bad. Right to Buy was a massive handout to people who weren't
supposed to need handouts. In fact, that was why they got the
handout – because they were the kind of people who didn't need
handouts.

It was Britain's biggest privatisation by far, worth some £40 billion in its first twenty-five years. But the money earned from selling Britain's vast national investment in housing – an investment made at the expense of other pressing needs by a poor country recovering from war – was sucked out of housing for ever. Councils weren't allowed to spend the money they earned to replace the homes they sold, and central government funding for housing was slashed. Of all the spending cuts made by the Thatcher government in its first, notoriously axe-swinging term, three-quarters came from the housing budget.

What you think the Thatcherites expected to happen once they'd set Right to Buy in motion depends on how cynical you are about their motives. The most benign view is that they thought supply and demand was a straightforward elastic law, and that the market would take up the slack: private housebuilders would build more homes, for both sale and rent, as the number of new council houses being built waned. A dwindling number of the poorest people would be catered for by residual council stock, by the non-profit housing associations – which would still get state grants to build houses for the less well-off – and, for those who were really hard up, by an obscure welfare top-up called housing benefit.

It didn't happen that way. One outcome can be seen starkly in a recent online manifesto for self-builders of private homes, *A Right to Build*. Published in 2011 by Sheffield University's school of architecture and the London architectural practice 00:/, it was designed as an attack on the dominance of the big seven private housebuilding companies – in descending order of size, Taylor Wimpey, Barratt Homes, Persimmon, Bellway, Redrow, Bovis and Crest Nicholson – who between them have almost 40 per cent of the market in new homes. But the most striking thing in the document is a chart displaying the history of Britain, in housebuilding and house prices, since 1946.

It shows that in the 1980s, as the construction of new council houses shrank to almost nothing, there was a slight rise in the number of private homes being built, peaking at around 200,000 homes a year at the end of the decade. Then it fell back – and stayed fallen. Between the early 1990s and the onset of the financial crisis in 2008, supposedly a boom time in Britain, the number of new private homes built each year didn't go up. It barely budged from the 150,000 a year mark. The market failed. There was increasing demand without increasing supply. Mid-boom, as the imbalance between the number of people chasing a house and the supply of new homes reached a tipping point, average house prices took off like a rocket, trebling between Tony Blair's accession and the 2008 crash. (In Tower Hamlets, prices went up three and a half times.) Even allowing for inflation over that period of time (36 per cent) it's a terrifying increase.

The chart only shows part of Right to Buy's drawbacks. Those tenants who didn't buy their houses, either because they didn't want to or because they couldn't afford to, had their rents jacked up. At the same time, because of the growing shortage caused by the inability of councils to build, the failure of private builders to build enough, and weak government support for housing associations, rents in the private sector went up. The poorest and most vulnerable members of society, the sick, the elderly, the unemployed, single mothers and their children, were shared between a shrinking stock of council housing – the council housing least likely to be sold, that is, the worst – and the grottier end of the private rental market.

Much of the rent in both types of tenure had to be covered by housing benefit, and as council houses continued to be sold, the proportion of the poor and disadvantaged claiming housing benefit in expensive privately rented property rose. Many people who bought their council houses sold them on to private landlords, who rented them to people on housing benefit who couldn't get a council house, at double or triple the levels of council rent.

Right to Buy thus created an astonishing leak of state money – taxpayers' money, if you like to think of it that way – into the hands of a rentier class. First, the government sold people homes it owned at a huge discount. Then it allowed the original buyers to keep the profit when they sold those homes to a private land-lord at market price. Then the government artificially raised market rents by choking off supply – by making it impossible for councils to replace the sold-off houses. Then it paid those artificially high rents to the same private landlords in the form of housing benefit – many times higher than the housing benefit it would have paid had the houses remained in council hands.

In other words, since Thatcher, the British government has done the exact opposite of what it has encouraged households to do: to buy their own homes, rather than renting. Thatcher and her successors have done all they can to sell off the nation's bricks and mortar, only to be forced to rent it back, at inflated prices, from the people they sold it to. Before Right to Buy, the government spent a pound on building homes for every pound it spent on rent subsidies. Now, for every pound it spends on housing benefit, it puts five pence towards building.

The response of the current government to the housing crisis is to try to make it worse. It is taking steps to increase house prices, without taking steps to increase supply. The coalition's two most explicit interventions in the housing market have been to restrict supply and raise prices: the first when it cut, by two-thirds, the grant given to housing associations to build new homes, and the second with its mocking parody of Right to Buy, 'Help to Buy', offering already well-off people cheap loans to overbid for overpriced houses they couldn't otherwise afford.

Those who believe the aim of Britain's private housebuilders is to build as many homes as possible, and that they are only pre-vented from doing so by a cranky planning system, could say I'm being unfair and point to another coalition intervention. In 2012 the old rules governing what could get built where were replaced with a streamlined model called the National Planning Policy Framework, NPPF, which put the onus on councils to allocate enough land for new houses – including farmland, if necessary – to meet demand five and a quarter years ahead. Councils who

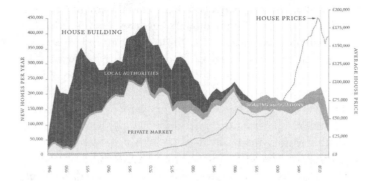

don't comply face, in theory, being overruled on appeal if they try to stop speculative development. But putting aside land for houses isn't the same as building them. The historical evidence suggests Britain's private housebuilders have been driven less by the urge to build the maximum number of new homes than by the urge to make as much (or lose as little) money as possible.

Pat Quinn was born into the final waning of the old East End, where working-class Londoners rented rooms in cramped, crowded, badly maintained terraced houses with poor plumbing and sanitation. Aged twenty, just married, Quinn and her husband, like hundreds of thousands of others, swapped their private landlord for a tenancy with the state. Long before the Luftwaffe and Hitler's V-weapons knocked jagged holes in the soot-blackened brick of Bethnal Green, Stepney and Poplar, the three London boroughs that would eventually be merged to create Tower Hamlets, the municipalities had begun knocking down old streets and moving their residents into newly built council houses, bigger and lighter than anything they were used to, with modern kitchens and indoor lavatories. When the Second World War was over, the bulldozers returned to clear bombsites and slums all at once, and the construction of new homes went on.

The pattern was repeated across the country. There was a difference, however, between council houses built in the 1920s and 1930s and those built after 1945. The interwar municipal housing estates were focused on the poor, on replacing the worst slum housing, even though, in practice, the poorest of the poor could seldom afford the rents, and moved to another slum instead. The politicians who got the interwar houses built were motivated by the fastidious, paternalistic, missionary zeal of their nineteenth-century reformist forebears, together with a contrary mixture of fear that socialism would come (so we'd better show the workers that a capitalist society cares) and hope that socialism would come (and this is what it will look like).

After 1945, as the scale of council house building increased in the hopeful atmosphere of the budding welfare state, the builders' masters voiced more ambitious aims. In 1946, Aneurin Bevan, minister for both health and housing, told Parliament that having the better-off catered for exclusively by speculative builders while the poor were set apart in council housing was wrong.

> You have castrated communities. You have colonies of low income people, living in houses provided by the local authorities, and you have the higher income groups living in their own colonies. This segregation of the different income groups is a wholly evil thing, from a civilised point of view ... It is a monstrous infliction upon the essential psychological and biological one-ness of the community.

Bevan's stance had all sorts of implications, but the most significant was that there was no limit to the number of houses the state was prepared to build, that building would continue until there was a home for everyone – a point effectively reached in the 1970s, at about the time Quinn and her husband moved to their new council flat.

Until then Quinn – father a long-distance lorry driver, mother a worker at the Bryant & May match factory – and her husband had rented the downstairs floor of a private terraced house in

Usher Road, Bow, a land of cobblestones, cigarette smoke, crowded pubs and crowded bedrooms, backyard privies and tin baths filled with water heated on the range. Usher Road was the kind of place the authorities considered a slum, and it was decided to knock the old terraces down. Residents were offered a choice of council house. Quinn chose a flat in a small new block near the Royal London Hospital in Whitechapel, two miles closer to the centre of London. Her husband was sceptical – Whitechapel had a reputation as a rough area where the sex trade flourished – but he went with her choice and they settled in. It is a measure of the relative value of private and council rentals in those days that their rent went up from £1 a week to £4.

I met her at a public meeting in Bethnal Green called to discuss ways of combating the government's welfare changes and went to visit her at home a few weeks later. Her flat is one of ten in a plain, red-brick, three-storey block; five one-bedroom places on the ground floor and five two-bedroom flats on the upper storeys, one of which is Quinn's. It was summer and red and white roses were blooming in the block's communal gardens. Quinn showed me the fruit and vegetables the residents had planted in the spring: raspberries, strawberries, lettuce, onions, peas, beans, radishes. 'Very optimistically a gentleman is trying to grow kiwis,' she said. 'The cherries aren't quite ripe enough to give you one … there's an aubergine there but I don't think it's going to make it.'

Only three of the ten flats still belong to the council. The rest have been sold off. Four are lived in by their owners and three are let out privately. Students share one of the flats, and in the others there are bankers (the flat is two tube stops from the City; you could walk to the Lloyd's building in half an hour), an immigration lawyer and an accountant working in one of London's temples of public art. 'Irish, Welsh, Iraqi, Bengali … three Bengalis. And myself, English,' Quinn said. It's the sort of diversity that might have pleased Bevan. But the government wants Quinn out.

In the 1990s, Quinn was officially recognised as too sick to work as the result of a bundle of ailments (she lists them: joint pain, migraines, gastritis, bouts of depression, underactive thyroid) and since then has had her rent and council tax, currently £120.39 a week, covered by housing benefit. For living expenses, she received £112 a week in incapacity benefit. (The Joseph Rowntree Foundation reckons £200 a week, excluding rent, is needed to maintain a decent life.) But last spring, everything changed. The bedroom tax – which effectively fines Quinn for losing her husband – slashes her housing benefit to £97.15 a week, leaving her to make up the £23.24 difference out of her incapacity payment. Except now she's not getting that either. At the same time she was hit by the bedroom tax, she was called in for a medical to reassess her fitness for work under the government's new, tighter incapacity rules. The assessment consists of ten checks on physical ability, such as:

> Can you move more than 200 metres on flat ground? (Moving could include walking, using crutches or using a wheelchair.)
>
> Can you usually stay in one place (either standing or sitting) for more than an hour without having to move away?
>
> If you experience fits, blackouts or loss of consciousness, do they happen less than once a month?

Then there are ten checks on your 'mental, cognitive and intellectual functions': 'Can you deal with people you don't know?' or 'Can you usually manage to begin and finish daily tasks?'

Each check answered 'no' scores points. The more points you get, the more likely you are to continue to be recognised as disabled. Quinn got zero points and a message telling her that the government accepted she was ill, but that she was not ill enough: she would have to start looking for work, and as long as she was unemployed, she would be switched to the Jobseekers' Allowance – a cut in the money she lives on of 40 per cent, down to £72 a week. But because of the bedroom tax, £23.24 of that has to go towards her rent, leaving her with just £48.76 a week to live on; £22 comes out of that for gas and electricity, which leaves about £27 a week for everything else. She doesn't drink, she doesn't smoke, she doesn't go to the bingo, she doesn't have a car, but that £27 has to cover the TV licence and her phone, as well the dozens of small items everyone needs, like toothbrushes and soap and light bulbs and postage stamps.

And food.

Britain's ever helpful banks have contributed to the picture. They have permitted Quinn to build up a debt of £6,000 on three credit cards. 'It's a nightmare,' she said. 'I had to apply for crisis loans. I haven't paid the rent, the electric or the gas. At my age it's embarrassing to be in this position.' It wasn't that she didn't want to work, she said; she left school at fifteen, on a Monday, and got a job on Tuesday. She does unpaid volunteer work as a local health champion. 'I can't do the heavy stuff. I'm not saying I can't work at all but they want you to work a full forty-hour week. They should prepare you for work and find out what you can do, instead of saying you've got to be prepared to work from now, without any preparation or anything.'

She will get a state pension, but not until November 2015. If she can hang on to her flat until then she'll be exempt from the bedroom tax. But it isn't clear how she will survive in the meantime. 'I think there should be a fairer way of asking people to leave their accommodation,' she said. Council tenants face a jail sentence if they try to sublet. I asked Quinn if a relative could move in so as to avoid the bedroom tax. 'That defeats the purpose of having a second bedroom,' she said. 'Why shouldn't I have a home I don't have to share with anyone? I could have my granddaughter move in. But if I had her, my daughter would have to give up the family credit. There's a way round it but somebody else has to lose money.'

One of the curious things about Quinn's situation is that the government would love to give her £100,000, but she's not prosperous enough to qualify for it. That figure is the maximum discount on the market price a council tenant who exercises Right to Buy can now claim in London. Given that her flat would be worth at least £300,000, Quinn could, in theory, buy it, sell it on and pocket the difference. But then she'd have nowhere to live; and she can't raise the missing £200,000, because she has no money for a deposit and no way of getting a mortgage. She and her husband didn't have a principled objection to Right to Buy. They just never got rich enough to get richer.

In most people's understanding of the world I'd be considered a homeowner, although since I have a mortgage I am, for the time being, renting it from the bank. I was born at my grandparents' house in Blackheath in the middle of the great London smog of December 1962, and since then I've had about thirty different homes: private flats my parents rented in London, a housing association property in Nottingham, state-owned homes in Lanarkshire during my father's years working for the Scottish prison service, a council house in Dundee, then a private terraced house there (the first home my parents owned, bought when they were in their early thirties), student digs in Edinburgh and London, private rentals in Northampton, a flat of my own in Edinburgh bought when I was twenty-seven, various rentals in the Ukrainian equivalent of privatised council flats, residency in Moscow apartments belonging to Russia's Diplomatic Corps Administration, two floors of a Georgian terraced house in North London bought with my then wife, a post-divorce rental in the East End, and now, my third tilt at home ownership, a flat in a converted school in Bethnal Green (Pat Quinn's old school, as it happens).

I don't expect to find myself living in a council house in the traditional sense – that is, a household dwelling owned and run by the state – any time soon. But that's more to do with the shortage of council houses, and the way they're run, than with any objection on principle, or a conviction that council houses are doomed to be ugly and uncomfortable. None of the things tenants found repellent about life on some council estates in the 1970s – the crime and anti-social behaviour, the damp, the powerlessness in the face of council bureaucracy, the noise, the distance from children's playgrounds, the difficulty of imposing personal style on a habitat you didn't own, the penny-pinching bodgery of council repairs, the obstacles to moving – is inherent to municipal tenure; they're the result of incompetence, carelessness and unreasonable economies.

Councils made some terrible mistakes in their postwar housebuilding programme, partly because of pre-Thatcherite Conservative populism. The Tories started a race with Labour over who could build more houses, abandoning Bevan's conviction that numbers weren't enough, that the homes had to be spacious and well built, too. The worst blunder involved the use of a Danish system of prefabricated concrete panels to build tower blocks three times higher than they were designed to be, assembled by badly supervised, badly trained workers and engineers. Hence the Ronan Point disaster in 1968, when a twenty-two-storey block in East London partly collapsed after a gas explosion, killing four people. The block was finally demolished the year before the great storm of 1987, which might literally have blown it down. Ronan Point was designed to withstand winds of up to 63 mph; some of the gusts during the storm reached 94 mph.

As the decades pass and the council homes of the 1950s, 1960s and 1970s grow into the urban landscape, as their brick and concrete weathers, as they benefit from comparison with the mean little boxes being built by private housebuilders, as a mix of new management, new investment and funds from the last Labour government have dealt with some of the backlog of repairs and design flaws, as the original intentions of architects become unexpectedly visible to a new generation, they are beginning to look like more attractive places to live. Too late for the less well-off; just in time for the hipsters. Rural peers now snap them up for their London pieds-à-terre. Wealthy parents buy them for their children. Buy-to-let investors cram them with students. I might have bought one myself, to live in; friends have done so. Once privatised there was no chance of the councils getting them back. I was shown plenty by estate agents in Tower Hamlets when I was looking for a place to buy – the agents call them 'ex-local', as in 'ex-local authority'. They were among the few places of any size I could afford, and they still sell for slightly less than homes built for the market. This is unlikely to last. In the capital, council houses have gone vintage; council houses in inner London are the new lofts, to be boasted about and refitted with salvaged Bakelite and Formica by the trendiest of their new inhabitants. In addition to all the other indignities the poorest of the poor in London suffer, they now have an extra one: the implication that they never saw the potential.

From my window, council houses – many of them privatised – are what I see. On the far side of Roman Road are the barracks-style brown brick walkways of the Greenways estate, built in the 1950s, solid and unremarkable, renovated not long ago, providing homes for hundreds; beyond them, its crown poking up beyond the Greenways roof, is Denys Lasdun's listed Sulkin House, built on the site of a bombed church, twin stacks of council maisonettes at an angle to each other, linked by a central, cylindrical shaft, like an open book propped on end – an early attempt to create a vertical street. But the main vista is on an altogether more epic scale, an inhabited twentieth-century Stonehenge, a seventeen-acre site of six towers and five lower blocks, widely spaced apart and angled in such a way that at least one face will always be catching the sun and the shadows cast by the towers will rotate like the spokes of a wheel. This is the Cranbrook Estate.

Cranbrook calls attention to itself. It's startlingly different from other estates. The piloti – stilt-like struts cut in from the building's outside edge at ground level – of the high towers are shared with Le Corbusier's modernist *étalon*, the Marseille Unité d'Habitation (which is smaller), but the most striking feature of the blocks, to the non-architect, are the superfluous details that depart from Le Corbusier's functional modernism: the flying cornices, concrete frames like giant handles that jut from the tower roofs, and the frog-green bosses studding the beige brick façades. The initial effect is of some vast, elegant set of combination locks, or duochrome Rubik's cubes, poised at any moment to whirr and counterspin, floor by floor, to trigger the catch on some deeper, hidden secret. Yet familiarity human-ises it. You become aware not only of how soaked in light it is but of the architects' legacy to the people who live there. Close to Roman Road is a crescent of red brick bungalows for the elderly, grouped around a garden with a fountain and a bronze sculpture by Elizabeth Frink, *The Blind Beggar and His Dog*. The toy-like bungalows are superficially so different from the beige and green high-rises behind them that you might assume they had nothing to do with each other, yet they were part of the plan from the start.

The architects hired by the then Bethnal Green Council for the project, built between 1955 and 1966, were the trio of Francis Skinner, Douglas Bailey and an elder mentor, the legend-ary bringer of the torch of modern architecture to Britain from Europe, Berthold Lubetkin. There's a received idea that Lubetkin was only peripherally involved in the design of Cranbrook. He was living in rural Gloucestershire, where he'd been based ever since evacuating his family there in 1939, farming pigs and brooding over the collapse of his hopes of becoming the master builder of a new town for coal-miners in Peterlee, County Durham. Yet as his biographer John Allan has shown, Lubetkin didn't step back from his vocation till much later. Indeed, he was responsible for the overarching design of Cranbrook. Each month he would come up to London, sketchbook bulging with plans.

Lubetkin and his protégés, backed by the public purse of Bethnal Green and London County Council, make an easy target for haters of publicly subsidised housing, for haters of the experimental in architecture, and for those more nuanced sceptics who believe with great passion in state housebuilding but condemn the execution of the great concrete monuments of residential modernism. The argument is that councils treated their tenants like factory-farmed livestock, stacking them on top of one another in concrete boxes in defiance of their traditional British desire for two-up, two-down homes with a patch of garden; that they left them prey to the visions of egotistical architects, who thought only of the grandiose shapes they would carve in concrete, shapes they would never imagine themselves inhabiting, or their children, or anyone they knew. There's much truth in this. In her book *Estates* (2007) Lynsey Hanley, who was brought up on a council estate on the edge of Birmingham, mocks architectural critics who describe various notorious London council tower blocks as inspiring 'a delicate sense of terror' or 'incredibly muscular, masculine, abstract structures, with no concession to an architecture of domesticity'.

'After all,' Hanley remarks, 'domesticity is the last thing you need when you have a family to raise.' The professional avant-garde's take on residential modernism, she argues, 'seems to fall for the idea that housing should be art. It ought to be beautiful, yes, but not at the expense of the people who have to live in it.' She doesn't explicitly mention the work of Bailey, Skinner and Lubetkin in Bethnal Green, but Lubetkin and his work on Cranbrook would seem, on the face of it, to conform to her archetype of the selfish modernist. Her critique is from the democratic left, but the legacy of Lubetkin and Cranbrook could just as easily be damned by conservative aesthetes in the mould of Prince Charles as having yoked the English working man to alien, totalitarian forms of dwelling.

Lubetkin, who died in 1990, gave his critics plenty to work with. He did have an ego; he deployed his enormous intellect with more force than tact. He and his wife, Margaret, were life-long communists, and his early designs for Cranbrook were sketched under the influence of a trip he had made to his native

Russia in 1953, after the death of Stalin, where the superhuman scale of state planning's achievements thrilled him:

> The broad expanse of the Volga drawn into the composition of rebuilt Stalingrad by a wide cascade of gigantic granite steps; the huge stadium which seems as broad as it is long; the ribbon of the Volga-Don canal in the midst of the arid steppe, with its sparkling foaming sluices; the generous openness of the forecourts and parks on which the new university building is presented to old Moscow, where the limitless parklands merge with the sky, and the horizon, as at sea, is imperceptible; these are sights that no architect who has been fortunate enough to see them will easily forget.

In reality, Lubetkin was too idiosyncratic to be a modernist, too liberal to be a Stalinist. Far from being a harmonious and cynical collaboration between municipality and architect, the Cranbrook Estate bears the mark of Lubetkin's despair at Bethnal Green and the London County Council, for which housebuilding had become a numbers game, where architectural vision and the sense of building a better world for working people had shrunk to sheaves of norms, regulations and pro formas – the first signs of an entry point for the privatisers (Harold Macmillan coined the phrase Right to Buy in the 1950s). Lubetkin had been thwarted in his desire to ally his ego and talent to progressive causes ever since he arrived in Britain from Paris in 1931. His early commissions were private flats for the wealthy and zoo buildings, including the extant penguin pool at London Zoo. Only for a brief time, when he worked with Finsbury Council in mid-century, did he come close to what he wanted: to listen attentively to the needs of residents and workers, then interpret their commission in his own way, with the support of secure, trusting patrons. Even then he was hobbled by postwar parsimoniousness.

When Lubetkin first expounded his vision for Cranbrook to his council backers, he started with medieval metaphysics and moved through to the Enlightenment via Copernicus, Descartes and Tintoretto. Was this the ludicrous self-importance of a man out of touch with working-class realities, or the sense of responsibility of an artist-craftsman who, despite his disillusionment, couldn't but take seriously the job of building homes for more than five hundred families? I prefer the second version. These were the days when councils' idea of consultation with future residents was to find out how many bodies there were and produce a piece of paper for the architect called a 'surrogate briefing' which listed the number of units required to put them in. Seen in that light the secret message of Cranbrook *is* its stand-out otherness. The sense it offers to the passer-by that whoever was responsible for it was striving with unusual mental ferocity to realise an obscure and arcane task he considered incredibly important is exactly the sign Lubetkin and his collaborators wanted to draw. A sign that read 'No council block must be just another council block'; a sign that read 'This matters'. He doubted even then whether it would be read. Towards the end of his life, he'd come to feel, he told Allan, that

> the public themselves became more and more disillusioned with any idea that art or architecture could lift them up or foreshadow a brighter future. Instead of looking at architecture as the backdrop for a great drama – the struggle towards a better tomorrow – they began to see only the regulations, housing lists, points systems, et cetera, and so expect only 'accommodation' … it made all our efforts seem so hollow.

Doreen Kendall was one of the original tenants of Puteaux House, one of the tower blocks on the Cranbrook Estate, completed in 1964. She's lived there ever since, in a two-bedroom, two-storey flat on one of the high floors; she and her late husband raised a daughter there. The common parts of Puteaux House are a little down at heel but the spaces are generous and light. Looking up from the lobby you can see the teardrop cross-section of Lubetkin's stairwell stretching up to the heights. In the early days children used to slide down the bannisters non-stop from the fifteenth floor to the ground. There's an intimacy and a familiarity within this vertical community. When I visited, we could hear somebody vacuuming the floor of the flat upstairs. 'She does all the corners every Friday,' Kendall said.

With their discount and an inheritance, the Kendalls were able to buy their flat in 1984. Rents had been going up and they thought they'd have a more powerful voice in dealings with the council if they became leaseholders. On the estate as a whole, about a third of the flats are in private hands. Kendall was astonished when I told her that councils had been forced to use the money they got from Right to Buy to pay down their share of the government's general debt. 'I thought it was in a pot, waiting to be used again,' she said. 'I thought there was a housing account that everything went into and they were just waiting for the government to release it.'

One by one, the original Right to Buyers are checking out of Cranbrook. 'There's about fifteen that have bought and they've died off and the flats've been sold. Arthur downstairs died over Christmas, and his flat's for sale. Sonny over in Offenbach, he died just before Christmas and his flat's up for sale. They'll be bought by people to be relet on short tenancies. You get to know people, they're very nice, then all of a sudden they're gone.'

Kendall is a fisherman's daughter, born in Milford Haven in 1929, who got her school leaver's certificate and moved from Pembrokeshire to the eastern edge of London to stay with her aunt and look for work. There she met John, a tailor in Bethnal Green, and moved in with him to a private rental in the East End. They were offered a place on the Cranbrook Estate after their old house was demolished.

The standard left-progressive history of what happened in Bethnal Green is that democratically elected, enlightened municipal authorities rescued the poor citizens of the borough from insanitary, crowded slums and gave them modern, healthy places to live at a reasonable rent, places that often delighted their new tenants, before institutional neglect, competitive consumerism and budget cuts took the shine off estate life. But there's an alternative, subversive account, which suggests that at some point – perhaps the 1950s, perhaps even earlier – 'slum clearance' began to merge into something else, the needless destruction of fundamentally sound old terraced houses which councils could have bought and modernised.

Kendall, who happens to be secretary of the East London Historical Society, subscribes to both versions of events. She and her husband adored the old two-room private flat they rented in St Peter's Avenue, and fought a long, bitter and unsuccessful battle with the council to prevent it and the neighbouring homes being knocked down. 'It was a lovely house,' she said. 'These days they would have done them up because when you go down Columbia Road the houses aren't as nice. It had a huge old garden. The toilet was just outside the back door. It didn't worry us. It had shutters and brass fittings – it wasn't a slum. We were absolutely heartbroken when they cleared the houses from there.'

Rather than seeing the move from St Peter's Avenue to the Cranbrook Estate as an expulsion from Victorian East End Eden to concrete council tower block hell, however, Kendall embraced her new home with the same fervour. 'I loved it,' she said. 'I absolutely adored it. We had central heating so we didn't need to light a fire any more. My husband thought we'd moved into a ship. All the walls were painted grey, battleship grey. Everything was grey except the wall where my books are and the bathroom, which was red, a dusty red.' The Kendalls avoided the alienation from the familiar rhythms of the city experienced by other East Enders who moved out to suburban council estates. 'You knew everybody anyway because you'd moved in with them. It wasn't a case of making new friends.'

Kendall pointed to the armchair where I was sitting and told me Lubetkin had sat in that very place, asking how she liked her new digs. I was sceptical: perhaps it was Skinner, or Bailey? But Kendall insisted it had been the old man himself, strong Russian accent and all. 'I always had the impression that he was the boss.

We all used to come, all the mums, and meet him and he'd say: "How's things working?" He'd come in and have a biscuit and a cup of tea and he'd say that no matter what flat he went into, his décor went with the furniture. He was very proud that everything went together.'

What Kendall has taken from the ruins of her previous home is a determination not to let the authorities mutilate the grandeur and pleasingness of her habitat a second time. She pointed out all the ways the council has departed from Lubetkin and his partners' design. The blocks used to be heated from central boilers, but these were shut down and replaced by individual boilers for each flat; as a result ugly white pipes now hang off the towers, like sheets knotted together by escaping prisoners. Originally the façades of the towers were cut into by deep openings that left the broad hallways between flats open to the air and gave Kendall a view of St Paul's Cathedral; after the 1987 storm, the council replaced them with blank steel shutters that close off the view from inside and, from outside, echo the bleak appearance of a row of shuttered shops. The green bosses studding the façades of the towers were originally made of concrete faced with glass beads that glittered in the sun; the council replaced them with aluminium boxes. Now when it rains, residents are driven mad by the sound of the drops rattling on metal. The Historical Society's repeated efforts to get Cranbrook listed have been rebuffed. 'The council doesn't realise what wonderful buildings they've got here,' Kendall said. 'We're just the Cranbrook Estate.'

Lubetkin's last artistic statement to the world was his finishing touch to the estate. In his vision, a broad, tree-lined pedestrian boulevard was to lead from Roman Road through Cranbrook to the great open space of Victoria Park. The boulevard exists, but the council refused to buy the last sliver of land blocking Cranbrook from the park's chestnut trees and ornamental lake. Lubetkin filled the melancholy dead end that resulted with a trompe l'oeil sculpture of a ramp and receding hoops, which,

as you approached it, seemed to take you towards some mys-
terious, hopeful future point. It's gone now; the council failed
to maintain it. When I saw her, Kendall had just had a circular
from the council announcing a new initiative to give children 'a
sense of ownership' of the estate by encouraging them to express
themselves freely with paint on the walls around the old sculpture. The project was to be called 'Bling My Hood'.

In 1963 the anarchist housing writer Colin Ward took a
walk through Bethnal Green. He saw one of Denys Lasdun's
new council blocks, admired Britain's first ever large-scale
council housing, the handsome, Hanseatic-looking Boundary
Estate, and saw the demolition of the area's first great effort at
philanthropic housing, the gloomy Victorian model workers'
tenements of Columbia Square, funded by Baroness Burdett-
Coutts under the badgering of Charles Dickens. The square was
being knocked down to make way for another Bailey, Skinner
and Lubetkin project. Ward saw temporary wooden housing,
the 'prefabs', some old enough to have gardens round them,
some new. Bethnal Green's prefabs were, Ward wrote, 'simply
the latest, temporary exhibit in what is not only a sociologist's
zoo, but an architectural museum. It's all there, every mean or
patronising or sentimental or brutal or humane assumption
about the housing needs of the urban working class.'

Bethnal Green is still an architectural museum, or perhaps,
now that Tower Hamlets is officially Britain's fastest growing
borough, an architectural gallery, a showroom for housing
policies. New housing versions emerge. Converted schools.
Converted churches. Converted synagogues. Converted hospitals. Since Pat Quinn moved to Whitechapel the match factory
where her mother worked has been turned into private flats. The
factory's old water tower was the platform from which the army
proposed to shoot down airborne threats to the 2012 Olympics,
which were held a mile from Quinn's old house. The borough
teems with estate agents. Private developers are building and

marketing flats along the Tower Hamlets stretch of the Regent's Canal – which not that long ago was a derelict, post-industrial, don't-go-there-after-dark place – as if the canalfront were the Côte d'Azur. And yet there are still an awful lot of poor people living here, old, sick, unemployed or just badly paid, in the economic shadow between London's two financial districts, the City and Canary Wharf. As everywhere in the South-East, there is a huge, growing, unsatisfied need for housing that doesn't require you to earn an above average income to afford. With the original council housing stock still dwindling and not being replaced, how is that need going to be met? One possibility is that slums will come back. Already 40 per cent of homes let at below market rents in Tower Hamlets are officially classed as overcrowded. Tower Hamlets has been less forthcoming about overcrowding in the private sector than its eastern neighbour, Newham, which has proclaimed a crackdown on 'beds in sheds', but the problem exists. In 2011 a private landlord was fined £20,000 for ignoring orders from Tower Hamlets to improve two ex-council flats he'd bought and rented out. Each flat had two bedrooms and a living room: the landlord had split each living room in two to create, in all, four tiny bedsits. At one flat he'd tried to expand further by building what inspectors describe as a 'lean-to'. One of the flats – damp, cold and unsafe, infested with roaches and bedbugs – had seven people living in it. A new fad is 'rent to rent', where somebody will rent a flat and then squeeze subtenants into the available floor space till they're making a premium on the rent they pay the original landlord.

Another possibility is that housing associations will come to the rescue. They now let to many more households in England than councils. What are they? And how did so much come to hang on them?

One of the oddest things about the privatisations of water, the railways, electricity and the rest is that they were framed as binary possibilities: stay or go, stick or twist. Those who had a stake in the outcome were either for privatisation, or for the persistence of state ownership. Other forms of organisation weren't considered. If there were proposals for another way that was neither the nationalised status quo nor stock market flotation, they went unheard. With housing, when Right to Buy came in, an alternative already existed, alongside private and state ownership. Housing associations had existed in various forms since the Middle Ages, philanthropic organisations set up to house the needy. They aren't always charities, though sometimes they are. Technically they're both 'industrial and provident societies' and 'registered social landlords'. They're run on commercial lines – they borrow money at commercial rates, they may build houses for sale or for market rent, they strive to avoid losing money – but they're forbidden to make a profit, they don't pay dividends and they don't have shareholders. Whatever surplus they make is put back in service of their primary function, which is to provide low-rent homes for the less well-off.

Some of the early housing associations are still around: the Peabody Trust, for instance, set up in the 1860s by the Anglo-American businessman and philanthropist George Peabody, which now rents out more than 20,000 homes in London; and the Joseph Rowntree Housing Trust, which originated in a trust set up by the chocolate-maker in 1904 to administer the model village of New Earswick near York. New Earswick is still there, still offering homes at below market rent. In the 1960s, idealists in North and West London reacted against the slum landlords' petty exploitations and the demolition-happy dogma of the state. In 1963, Bruce Kenrick – who would a few years later set up the homelessness charity Shelter, just as the nation was absorbing the shock of *Cathy Come Home,* Ken Loach's film about homelessness – founded the Notting Hill Housing Trust, which today, as the Notting Hill Housing Association, has 27,000 homes in London. In 1968 the architects David Levitt and David Bernstein and the planner Beverly Bernstein set up Circle 33, now part of a consortium of nine housing associations across England called Circle Housing.

The shift of housing associations away from their philanthropic, idealistic and anarchic roots began in 1974, when the government of a more statist era started giving them grants to build more homes than their modest means would otherwise have allowed. But the transformational step came in 1988, amid the hubris and anti-statist zeal of Thatcher's radical third term. Right to Buy was faltering; the best-built and most attractive council houses had been sold, leaving councils still responsible for millions of tenants who, lacking the means or desire to buy their homes, continued to live in vast estates that the councils had been starved of the funds to maintain. And because the Treasury had captured the councils' sales receipts and diverted the rents of their most prosperous tenants to mortgage lenders, the councils lacked the financial muscle to correct, by refurbishment, or demolition and replacement, the design flaws blighting so many estates.

Huge sums were needed to bring these decayed or badly built forests of brick and concrete up to a decent standard. Barring a tax increase, the money could only be got by borrowing, and the stream of revenue from council tenants' rents made excellent collateral. But the government of 1988 didn't want to let councils borrow. Partly this was because of a belief that the public sector was incompetent; mainly it was because the sums needed would have to be added to Britain's total government debt, exposing how the Thatcher-era tax cuts had put the country's finances in jeopardy. So they turned to the housing associations. First, non-profit making as they were, they were formally designated part of the 'private sector', making it possible for them to borrow on the open market without the debt showing up on the government's books. Then, the government made it possible for councils to sell their housing stock wholesale (or estate by estate if they preferred) to housing associations specially created for the purpose. The only obstacle to a council shedding its municipal housing was a clause, grudgingly added after parliamentary pressure, making it obligatory for tenants to be balloted before a stock transfer could go through.

The first wave of stock transfers was relatively small-scale: mainly rural Conservative councils, starting with Chiltern District Council in Buckinghamshire, which transferred its entire stock of 4,650 houses to the new Chiltern Hundreds Housing Association (still operating today under the name Paradigm). It was under New Labour that the policy took off. Tony Blair and Gordon Brown intended to do the right thing by their party's natural supporters, the remaining millions of council tenants, and renovate their decaying homes. But they didn't intend to let Britain's municipalities take on extra debt to bulk the government's grants up to the levels required. Pressure was put on councils to offload estates and tenants, and the councils, in turn, put pressure on tenants to vote in favour. 'Yes' campaigns got public money; 'no' campaigns didn't. It was made clear to tenants that a 'yes' vote would result in money being made available quickly to renovate their homes, while a 'no' vote would put refurbishment in doubt. The government spent billions of pounds easing the way for the new housing associations by wiping out the debt attached to the homes they acquired. Council after council went through the process. Glasgow shed its 80,000 council houses; Sunderland disposed of 36,000; in the spring of 2003, Walsall and Coventry sold 43,000 between them. By the end of 2008, there were 170 councils with no council houses left.

In 1985, housing associations ran only 13 per cent of all social housing. The rest were council houses. By 2007, it was half and half; by 2012, only 1.7 million homes were still in council hands, against 2.4 million owned by housing associations. The housing associations seemed the ideal embodiment of Third Way economics, motivated neither by profit nor by state command, a parallel to academies in education and foundation trusts in health, yet with an old and noble pedigree. At a ceremony marking the handover of 17,000 homes in Tameside in 1999, Tony Blair said stock transfers 'buried for good the old ideological split between public and private sector'.

On the face of it, by ploughing what surplus they make back into building more homes, and doing so, on the whole, with efficiency and respect for tenants, housing associations represent a setback to the prevailing neoliberal consensus that the lust for personal gain embodied in shareholder capitalism is the only deep motivator that can make an organisation succeed. A study by the Joseph Rowntree Foundation in 2009 found that most housing associations which took over and renovated council estates had exceeded the official standards for good homes, in terms of facilities and living space; had given tenants a bigger say in estate management compared to supposedly more democratic councils; and had gone beyond their remit to invest in community facilities like libraries and schools. Lynsey Hanley, who bought a previously privatised council flat on an ugly, decayed estate in Tower Hamlets and became involved in a successful campaign to have the estate transferred to a housing association, knocked down and rebuilt from scratch, wrote:

> It's a testament to the sheer horridness of many estates that their tenants have, like us, elected to have their own homes destroyed in order that something better might replace them, that crime and anti-social behaviour might be designed out and that overcrowded households might finally be able to offer their children a room of their own ... tenants not only voted for it, but designed it themselves. The one complaint that was raised most often in our steering-group meetings was that 'the council has never listened to us.'

Opponents of stock transfers argue that they were simply a second attempt to purge the country of direct state responsibility for an essential human need after the first attempt, Right to Buy, slowed down; that they were, in effect, another privatisation, and one that cost the state dear. A report on stock transfers by the National Audit Office in 2003 judged the programme a success but conceded that if councils had been allowed to use grants and loans to renovate a million homes themselves, it would have cost £1.3 billion less than getting housing associations to do it. The

NAO said there were other benefits: shifting risk from taxpayers to the housing associations, getting repairs done faster and giving tenants a bigger say (as a rule housing associations give tenants a third of the seats on the boards running their estates). Yet as the social-policy thinker Norman Ginsburg put it in his article 'The Privatisation of Council Housing' (2005), 'There is no question that improvements have been accelerated by the transfer, but that is only because local authorities were prevented from doing them. There is undoubtedly increased tenant participation ... but whether tenants exert any more collective influence than they did within local electoral politics is highly debatable.' As for the notion of risk transfer, he said, was it such a wonderful thing to transfer risk from taxpayer to the assumed-to-be-too-poor-to-pay-taxes tenants? 'It appears to be celebrating the loss of a public responsibility for meeting basic needs.'

Whether councils, given the chance, could have carried out the vast renovation programme that the housing associations are successfully pursuing (few who have lived in British cities for a generation, even if they don't live on a council estate, can fail to have noticed how much less grotty the estates look) is a question that can't be answered. The successful renovation of 70,000 council houses carried out in Birmingham after its council tenants voted against stock transfer in 2002 suggests that they could. But housing associations are dominant now in the place council housing used to be, and as the effects of Right to Buy, increasing population and the failure of the market to build enough houses to cope with it have become apparent, successive governments have turned to housing associations to fill the gap. In 2005, the housing association wave came to the Cranbrook Estate.

Rather than try to transfer its stock in one go, Tower Hamlets has done it estate by estate. Its preferred bidder for Cranbrook was Swan Housing Association, created in the 1990s to own and run a set of former new-town homes in Basildon, Essex.

Headed by an experienced housing manager, John Synnuck, the organisation began to expand, building homes and acquiring them from councils in stock transfers. They were opposed by an organisation called Defend Council Housing, rallied locally by George Galloway, who after his expulsion from the Labour Party over his anti-Iraq war activities had fought and won the parliamentary seat of Bethnal Green and Bow under the Respect banner. Defend Council Housing claimed that the Swan takeover amounted to a privatisation of the estate by a rapacious corporation. They won the argument and got the votes. Cranbrook is still in council hands. But supporters of the housing association claim residents made a terrible mistake; that the housing association takeover wouldn't have been, and couldn't have been, a privatisation at all; that the residents were deceived into opting for a bleaker, more insecure future. 'Defend Council Housing caused real damage,' David Orr, head of the National Housing Federation, the umbrella body for housing associations, told me. 'They persuaded people to vote against their own best interests in pursuit of an ideology about council housing. And I think that's unforgivable … a hundred years ago, 90 per cent of us lived in private rented housing, and most of it was squalid, and it was council housing that changed that. But the idea that the way you defend council housing and its place, not just in history but in the present and in the future, is by attacking housing associations, and by persuading people not to vote for things that were clearly in their interests – I just think that's crass.'

In the course of the Cranbrook campaign – one of many contested by Defend Council Housing activists around the country – Galloway wasn't always scrupulous about the facts. Like virtually all housing associations, Swan doesn't pay dividends and doesn't have shareholders. It was therefore inaccurate for Galloway to say of Swan: 'These organisations exist for their own corporate reasons and their own corporate benefits, including their shareholders, to whom they distribute a dividend.' Glyn Robbins, a housing theorist and part-time political activist who chaired the meeting where I met Pat Quinn, also took part in the anti-Swan campaign at Cranbrook. He doesn't go as far as Galloway, but still calls housing associations 'private companies, run as businesses'.

We met for the second time in his office at Quaker Court, the Islington council estate where he works as a housing manager. Speaking with his activist's hat on, he told me that the promotion of housing associations as benign, philanthropic organisations was a trick. 'They had this kind of cosy, non-threatening image. At times some were benign and did good deeds but as they became more and more reliant on private sector finance and more and more commercially oriented they have become, for people in most housing need, far more similar to the private sector. Where do we draw the line between not paying dividends to private investors and paying housing association chief executives quarter of a million pound salaries? If you want to work in the public sector, aren't you beholden to accept a different kind of reward that reflects that ethos?'

I went to see Swan at work renovating a council estate it has taken over in Bow, another part of Tower Hamlets. Three enormous, decayed tower blocks are being refurbished inside and out in a site hemmed in by railway lines. Swan's architects have used the space at the foot of the high-rises to build hundreds of low-rise new flats and houses that compare favourably in size and appearance to others being built by private developers elsewhere in East London. Any council tenant on the estate who wants one of the new or refurbished flats, at a rent similar to the one they were already paying, will get one. The homes left over will be let at market rents, sold as shared-ownership properties, or sold outright; Swan will use the proceeds from these commercial activities to cross-subsidise its social housing. The reason Doreen Kendall was against the Swan takeover of the Cranbrook Estate wasn't some erroneous idea that Swan was a for-profit company, but that Swan intended to finance the refurbishment of the estate by obliterating Lubetkin's design: their plan was to build new homes on top of and in the gaps between existing ones, gaps which, for instance, contain the Cranbrook residents' community centre. Some of these homes would have been sold, or let out at market rents.

Even as governments have courted and flattered the housing associations, they've chivvied them into becoming financially more creative in finding ways to go about their business. They've cut the grant they give them to help them build, forcing them to use whatever extra space they can carve out of each council estate they take over, or out of each new development they start, to build houses for sale or private rent for the purposes of cross-subsidy. By encouraging the housing associations to take on more private debt and to carry out more and more private work to fund their altruistic activities, the government makes them look more and more like for-profit companies. The danger is that social housing might ultimately become a philanthropic stub on a private body, like the donations a bank makes to charity.

There have been some troubling instances of fat cattery at the housing associations. None of the hundred names on the most recent list of housing association chief executives' salaries published by the journal *Inside Housing*, which keeps them under fantastically detailed scrutiny, earns less than £100,000 a year; sixteen of them (including Synnuck of Swan) earn more than £200,000. In 2010, the association Housing 21 gave its retiring chief executive, Melinda Phillips, a package worth more than half a million pounds – salary and pension worth £207,000, and what was effectively a farewell gift of £300,000. In August 2013, Great Places Housing Group showed similar generosity to its retiring chief, Stephen Porter. Along with £204,000 in wages, pension payments and bonus, the board handed him a parting gift of £245,000. Altogether it was the equivalent of £28 from every Great Places tenant household.

Housing associations have diversified furiously. The Gentoo Group, created out of the transfer of Sunderland's council houses in 2001, has gone into construction, facilities management, solar panels, bulletproof glass, train windows and a software package called Streetwise that helps housing managers track and control estate troublemakers ('Streetwise can calculate the cost of each type of intervention or legal action taken, allowing an organisation to identify the most cost-effective way of dealing with anti-social behaviour'). A third of Gentoo's £175 million turnover is unrelated to social housing, although the company assured me that it doesn't subsidise its other activities from tenants' rent. At the same time, Gentoo, whose chief executive, Peter Walls, almost doubled his salary at transfer when he switched from being the council's director of housing, struggles to find ways to build new homes for the less well-off. Sunderland's population is falling, and it was always part of the plan to demolish 5,000 homes by 2021. But the result of knocking down 4,000 former council houses, selling 4,500 to Right to Buyers and building 1,500 affordable rent replacements is a net loss of 7,000 affordable homes.

In 2013, an over-ambitious housing association, Cosmopolitan, would have gone bust had it not been taken over by another large association, Sanctuary. It turned out that Cosmopolitan had used its social housing assets – most of which were the 7,000 former council houses of the borough of Chester – as collateral to guarantee loans it took out to fund a student housing business. Accounting blunders meant Cosmopolitan breached its loan covenants. If Sanctuary hadn't come to the rescue, Cosmopolitan's tenants might now have large financial institutions as their landlords.

In recent years Swan has set up spin-off companies: Swan New Homes to build houses for sale, a private residential care company called Vivo and a property management firm, Hera. If Vivo and Hera make good profits, fine – that will go into the social housing pot. If they lose money, however, there's a danger that Swan's surplus will be diverted to shore up these for-profit arms. For now, three-quarters of the new homes Swan builds count as social housing. But it seems that every time the housing associations show they can deliver with reduced government support, the reduced support becomes the new norm, ready to be cut again. If there were any doubt about the way all this is heading, a rule change made in 2008 under Labour made it possible to set up for-profit housing associations – as if the party's policy people had listened to George Galloway's misrepresentation of what housing associations were and thought it was a good idea.

'Housing associations, particularly some of the bigger ones, have now reached the stage where they have assets and knowledge and expertise that allow them to operate in a rather different market and start looking at building for sale – not just riding on the coat tails of developers but being the lead developers themselves,' Orr told me. 'But here's the rub: when we move away from the model of up-front capital investment to provide social rental homes, and do things that are more commercial, that's the point where people on the left say see, we told you, they're all just greedy bastards who want to build and they only care about development. Which is not true, but it's a narrative that follows.'

Government leverage over the housing associations derives above all from the fact that Whitehall sets the rents housing associations may charge, most of which are actually paid via housing benefit. There are now three different kinds of rent in Britain: market rents; 'social rents', which is what council tenants pay, in London typically about half market rent or less; and 'affordable rents', currently pegged at 80 per cent of market rents. When in 2010 the coalition cut by two-thirds the grant it gave to housing associations, it still wanted them to build the same number of houses. The only way the housing associations could do that was by borrowing more money on the market. The only way they could finance that debt was by charging higher rents. Fine, said the government, from now on, whenever you build new social housing, you'll have to make them affordable tenancies, with those 80-per-cent-of-market rents. The indirect consequence was that the housing benefit bill went up.

'The part of the government that's interested in building new homes has an absolute requirement to see rents going up,' said Orr. 'The part of the government that's interested in housing benefit has an absolute requirement to see rents coming down. And the bit of government that's meant to manage all the finances, the Treasury, want to see both of those mutually contradictory things happen at the same time.' He might have added another contradiction – that the government agency encouraging housing associations to come up with ever more financially inventive ways of squeezing more homes out of their limited budgets is called the Homes and Communities Agency. The regulator supposed to make sure housing associations don't take on excessive financial risk is … the Homes and Communities Agency. The policy gets more knotted still on the former council estates taken over by housing associations, where the coalition is demanding that when a social tenancy ends – when a former council tenant dies, for instance – the property is relet on an 'affordable' tenancy. But with the coalition's own changes to housing benefit, poorer tenants in 'affordable' tenancies are finding it harder not to fall into arrears, meaning the revenue stream to the lenders the housing associations borrowed from is jeopardised – making it impossible to get further loans.

The direction of social housing policy since 1979 has been to gradually remove the state from the business of building houses, and now to gradually remove the state from the business of subsidising rent. You can imagine free marketeers believing the market can house the poor in decent comfort without the better-off being forced to chip in, although there is no evidence that it can. This is the benign view of the Thatcherites' motive. But it is easier to believe that the actual intention – not formally designed in some conspiratorial way, and never openly described as such – is to demonetise that part of general taxation on the well-off that goes towards evening things out for the poor and replacing it with a tax in kind, a tax on conscience. To permit the gradual re-emergence of slums, in other words, in order to keep income and corporation tax low, and to make the threat to the well-off an easily ignored threat to their conscience, rather than to their wealth. To settle for history as wheel rather than ascent, in which it will eventually be time for Dickens to come around again.

There is a substantive obstacle in the way of that descent back into squalor: there is no neat way to separate the shortage of social housing from the shortage of housing in general. The government is pulling back in the face of a market that is failing across the board. Matt Griffith, author of an incisive paper for the think tank IPPR about the housing crisis, *We Must Fix It*, points out that the interconnecting problems afflicting the private house-building industry do not reflect a deeper economic malaise; they *are* the deeper economic malaise. Britain's established housebuilders, Griffith reckons, no longer have housebuilding as their primary function. They've essentially become dealers in land. Griffith estimates British housebuilders have enough land to build 1.5 million houses. This is much higher than most estimates because he includes not only land that has been given planning permission for homes to be built on it but also the shadow land bank: the vast stretches of agricultural land that housebuilders' canny local agents guess will get planning permission in future, and have tied up through confidential option deals with landowners.

Why is this land not being built on faster? Because the price the builders paid for the land is tied to the price they expect to get for the houses when they do finally build on it. In boom times, they build more homes, but tend to be over optimistic about the prices they will fetch, and overpay for land accordingly. In lean times they can't build, because to do so would be to acknowl-edge that they overpaid for the land, which would threaten them and the banks that lent to them with massive losses through the devaluation of their assets. Instead of competing to build the most attractive houses, the firms in the private housebuilding oligopoly compete over who can best use their land-banking skills to anticipate the next housing bubble and survive the last one. The whole system incentivises land hoarding and an under-supply of new homes compared to demand, to keep prices high. This, in turn, incentivises banks to favour property loans over other forms of lending. An incredible 76 per cent of all bank loans in Britain go to property, and 64 per cent of that to residential mortgages. That is money that could be spent on lending to other, more productive businesses. Yet it is so large a share of banks' assets that the kind of radical reform of the planning and land ownership system Griffith wants to see might, by lowering house and land prices, bring the banks to their knees again. As Martin Wolf wrote in a despairing attack on Help to Buy in the *Financial Times*, 'a deregulated and dynamic housing supply could spell financial and political Armageddon.'

Against this is David Orr's prescription: to increase housing supply at the other end of the market with a relatively small increase in government funding to housing associations, and to hand council housing over to a new set of European-style municipal housing agencies that could borrow money without adding to the national debt. Housing associations and councils have land banks of their own and every reason to build on them. 'What is the thing that most characterises subsidised housing? Answer: subsidy,' Orr says. 'If we had a government that wanted to see a significant increase in the supply of new homes they would stop asking "Can we do it?" and they would start asking "How can we do it?" Right now we spend £10.5 billion per annum on housing and transport – £9.5 billion on transport, and £1 billion on housing. If we decided to spend £8.5 billion on transport and £2 billion on housing it would still be £10.5 billion, and with that extra billion, we would be building 40,000 new homes a year before they even got High Speed 2 anywhere near a planning application.'

Making space for everyone in the crowded southern end of an island with a growing population is likely to involve everyone giving something up. No one knows the fate of the Cranbrook

Estate; like Doreen Kendall, I would like to see it remain council property, yet somehow restored and properly maintained the way Skinner, Bailey and Lubetkin designed it. That's what I think should happen. But I'm not sure how. And suppose Tower Hamlets decides, like Swan, that it wants to increase the number of homes on the site by building over its green spaces or knocking it down and starting from scratch? The council, working with Swan, has already begun doing exactly that on another estate, the brutalist concrete Robin Hood Gardens near the Blackwall Tunnel, claiming, against the aesthetic objections of Richard Rogers and Zaha Hadid, that it has the support of the majority of residents. If we campaigned against a similar project for Cranbrook, would we be righteous campaigners fighting to save the nation's artistic heritage, or Nimbys obstructing urgently needed new homes?

The broader battle is to fight for the ideal embodied by Cranbrook: the ideal of social housing supported from general taxation on the better-off, the ideal that it is not only the prosperous who matter. Glyn Robbins's father was born in 1929 in a slum in Limehouse, since demolished. There was no hot running water there and no bathroom. Three families shared a single house. Robbins's father's family of four slept in a single room. In 1936, they were offered a council house in Dagenham, a suburban house with front and back gardens. The result was a bequest of stability to their children and grandchildren. 'If I'd said to my Nan and Grandad that they might even think about buying their house it wouldn't have made sense. They had no reason to,' Robbins said. 'It was only after 1979 that that temptation was dangled. With some pride they were adamant they wouldn't buy it and never did and so when Nan and Grandad died the house got given back to the council and it should have been left to the next family on the list. But I went back recently, and of course it's been sold, and it's in a shit condition.'

You could see Robbins's lament as nostalgia. After all, the slum-to-council-house journey was a one-off, exclusively for two past generations. There are no slums in Britain now, no favelas. But that would be to assume the journey couldn't go in the other direction. One kind of move back to the early twentieth century has already begun. Throughout the 1980s and 1990s we thought the proportion of homeowners would keep going up as the number of council houses went down. But since 2004 home ownership has been in decline in Britain. Since 1992, the number of people living as private renters has doubled. Julia Unwin, chief executive of the Joseph Rowntree Foundation, is pessimistic: 'At the turn of the twentieth century, the free market had provided squalid slums. We undoubtedly face the re-creation of slums, the enrichment of bad landlords, the risk of people being destitute. Beveridge had soup kitchens. We have food banks. We've got something that *does* take us back full circle, a deep divide in way of life between people who are reasonably well off and those who are poor. There's always been a difference, but the distinction seems to be more stark now.' The advent of the age of gentrification doesn't preclude the advent of slumification, and nostalgia becomes prophecy.

7. In Farageland

Private island: No trespassing

Thanet, the location of Nigel Farage's 2015 run for a seat at Westminster, lies nicely along the axis of his commute between his home in South London and his office at the European Parliament in Brussels. If Kent, cartographically speaking, is England's right foot, the Isle of Thanet is its big toe, pointing east into the sea towards Belgium. It hasn't been an actual island since the fifteenth century, when the channel separating it from the English mainland silted up, but it's still surrounded by water on three sides, and when the sun shines in summer, the light suffusing the air over the chubby peninsula has a vertiginous depthlessness, as if you'd come to the rim of the world and a few steps forward would take you into some infinite, radiant void. It's easy to see why Turner told Ruskin that the skies over Thanet were the most beautiful in Europe.

Thanet has two parliamentary constituencies, North Thanet and South Thanet, and a single local council, also called Thanet. Otherwise 'Thanet' is a concept linking three seaside towns that live side by side without surrendering their individuality, like three people sharing a flat. There's Ramsgate, a former ferry port on the south side of the peninsula; Broadstairs, a genteel resort facing east; and Margate, the faded one-time summer playground of industrial Britain, to the north. Farage will contest

South Thanet, which comprises Ramsgate, Broadstairs, a sliver
of coastal Margate called Cliftonville, and a swathe of extra-
Thanetary land to the south that includes the town of Sandwich.

One evening in the early summer of 2014, before Farage
had confirmed he would run, I took the train from London to
Ramsgate, where a local secondary school, the Ellington and
Hereson, was staging a version of *Question Time*, with the Ukip
leader on the panel. The high-speed train from London, which
has been running since 2009, is a twenty-first-century thing, fast,
air-conditioned and made in Japan. The new service doesn't have
first- and second-class carriages: instead, it's overpriced to all,
without favour. The trains shoot out of concrete-and-glass metropolitan halls and streak through Kent along the Eurostar track
at 140 mph, reaching Ramsgate in an hour and twenty minutes.
Soon they will be faster still. Yet when my train hummed into
Ramsgate and I stepped out into the stillness of the seaside
suburbs I felt I'd journeyed to the England of the 1970s. An air
of homely neglect hung over the broad avenues of large semis.
In London there is more money than space, or time; here, it was
the opposite.

The Ellington and Hereson School is a set of shining white
blocks built in 2007 as part of Labour's PFI programme. As well
as Farage, Charlie Leys, the sixth-former who had organised and
was chairing the event, had managed to pull in South Thanet's
sitting Tory MP, Laura Sandys, a believer in EU membership who
is standing down at the next election, and the candidates from
Labour, the Liberal Democrats and the Greens. I watched Farage
while the others were taking their turns to speak. Photographs
and news footage always show him goofily grinning or laughing;
it was strange to see him without a smile. I remembered watching Gordon Brown at a press conference once while Tony Blair
was PM, curious about what he would do with his face while
Blair was taking questions, and I saw Farage was doing what
Brown had – looking away from the other speakers and the audience, not reacting to jokes or thrusts, managing to make it look

as if he was giving the minimum attention necessary to prove his assumption that nothing interesting was being said, while he devoted the greater part of his mind to the future of Britain. It's hard to do that without looking aloof, and Farage did look aloof.

In his answers he hopped through his populist, contradictory programme, in which all problems – except drugs, where he's open to liberalisation if experts recommend it – lead back to the European Union. It was the EU that wouldn't want the government to subsidise the local airport. It was the EU that'd damaged the economy by giving workers too many rights. It was the EU's fault that British companies didn't export more to India. European immigrants were to blame for the shortage of social housing.

What does South Thanet want from Nigel Farage? As an individual, he's a celebrity: he has the potential to put Ramsgate and Broadstairs on the map. But do voters think leaving the EU is the priority for Britain? Do they want Ukip to run the country? Or do they simply want Farage floating into Parliament, like the astronaut at the end of Stanley Kubrick's *2001: A Space Odyssey,* to start methodically extracting the circuits from the out-of-control controller's brain?

There's plenty of evidence in Thanet to support Ukip's general proposition that local power is being diminished while the power of remote, faceless authorities is growing. But the overwhelming might of those remote, faceless authorities has little to do with Brussels. It has to do with global business and chainification. It has to do with the neoliberal political agenda: privatisation, jurisdiction-hopping, protection of inherited wealth and a shift of taxation from rich to poor. The Ellington and Hereson School supposedly belongs to Kent County Council, but in fact, until 2032, the premises are owned, maintained and controlled by a Luxembourg-based investment vehicle called Bilfinger Berger Global Infrastructure, which also owns hospitals in Canada and prisons in Australia. Bilfinger Berger, in turn, subcontracts the job of running the school to the outsourcing company Mitie, which, among its many other deals, has the government contract for the forced removal of immigrants through Heathrow. The school is obliged to rent its own buildings, and to pay Mitie's charges for maintenance or alterations. 'Every time we want to change a light bulb, it costs £25,' Colin Harris, the deputy head, told me. Ellington and Hereson has been trying to break away from Kent's traditional selective education system – the county retains the 11-plus – by becoming an academy, which would result in its being funded directly from central government. But it would still have Bilfinger Berger as its landlord. Ellington and Hereson's bid for academy status has been held up because Whitehall and Kent County can't agree on who should pay the rent and service charge to Bilfinger Berger's diffuse cloud of global investors.

This year Ann Gloag, the Perthshire castle-dwelling Scottish demi-billionaire, bought Thanet's airport at Manston for £1, then closed it down; 144 people lost their jobs. Hornby, the model-train maker, which has been in Margate for sixty years, moved its distribution warehouse to another part of Kent, but there was little hullabaloo: the trains themselves have been made in China for a long time. Another part of the constituency, Sandwich, is still trying to pick itself up from the blow inflicted three years ago by the US drugs group Pfizer when it closed down most of its vast research lab, leaving only six hundred scientists where there had been 2,500. The most promising development site in Ramsgate, the one-time Pleasurama amusement park on the seafront, has been left derelict by its absentee leaseholders for a decade. Of the fifty-three shops and restaurants in Broadstairs's new Westwood Cross shopping centre, only two – a burger joint and a store selling boast-brand accessories – aren't part of retail chains headquartered elsewhere. Westwood Cross has sucked the life out of Ramsgate's high street, where the branches of the big banks look isolated among derelict shopfronts, charity shops, junk shops, pound shops and Bright House hire purchase, which offers a washing machine for £6 a week, at an annual interest rate of 65 per cent. Westwood Cross belongs to the London-based mega-landlord Land Securities, owner of thirty-five shopping centres and retail parks around the country.

Along the horizon offshore are the spinning turbines of Thanet Wind Farm, the world's third largest. It belongs to Vattenfall, Sweden's state electricity company. The monopoly on the power cables under Thanet's streets belongs to Asia's richest man, Li Ka Shing. Thanet's water supply and drainage system belongs to Southern Water, which is owned by a consortium of Hong Kong investment funds and Australian and Canadian pension funds, advised by an American and a Swiss merchant bank. Sewage spills by Southern regularly force the closure of Thanet beaches.

The growth of absentee landlordism and privatisation in Farage's chosen battleground, the alienation of its economy and infrastructure from the people who live there, is overwhelmingly to do with choices made by successive British governments. To the extent it has anything to do with the EU, it's the part of the EU that was designed by people like the former commodities broker who said recently at the Euromoney Global Borrowers and Investors Forum: 'If, post-EU … we come up with a regulatory framework which is cheaper and more competitive, but retains the confidence of the customers, we can actually make London a more competitive marketplace for foreign banks from all over the world.' The ex-broker was Nigel Farage.

The evidence at street level from Thanet is that while a sense of being taken for a ride by remote powers – Brussels, Westminster, Holyrood, Pfizer – draws people to Ukip, it isn't the key attraction. Asked the morning after the Scottish independence referendum whether 'the English question' – should there be an England-only legislature to match those of Britain's other three constituent nations? – could garner Ukip more votes than Europe, Farage said it was another Westminster misgovernment issue, as good for Ukip as Europe and immigration. But there's no doubt which of those three Ukip is pursuing with most success in Thanet. The significance of the West Lothian question is as subtle and hard to grasp as the significance of those armies of Australian pensioners who benefit when the people of Ramsgate fill their kettles. Gloag's financial manoeuvrings over Manston airport are as complex and tedious as the Common Fisheries Policy. What's easy to understand is that, on the streets of Ramsgate, Broadstairs and Margate, people have appeared who speak Eastern European languages. This, according to Ukip, is the problem. 'The UK's population went up by *half a million* last year,' a Ukip handout blares, 'ENOUGH IS ENOUGH.' The handout shows a picture of the white cliffs of Dover with a sign hung on it reading, 'Sorry we're FULL.'*

'What we have here, and this is what irks the youngsters, is all the unskilled jobs are going to East Europeans,' said Martyn Heale, Ukip's campaign manager in South Thanet. His logic was that the number of people from mainland Europe working in Britain and the number of unemployed indigenous Britons was about the same. His solution was a job swap: expel the Europeans and put Britons in their place, coercing them, if necessary. 'Over two million Europeans are working in this country,' he said. 'The sensible way, over a two-year period, would be to train our people to replace Europeans in the jobs they're working in. We would turn round to unemployed people and say if they don't take the job, all benefits would cease. You have to encourage people to go back to work with a big stick sometimes.'

Heale was sitting behind his desk in Ukip's Thanet headquarters, a narrow shop freshly painted in the party's purple and yellow livery on a run-down thoroughfare off Ramsgate High Street. He's a comfortably spread man with a Tudor beard and a permanent gentle smile of reassurance. I met him in high summer, weeks before Farage went public on where he would fight, but Heale and his deputy, Aaron Knight, were already on full salaries.

---

* The population of the UK increased by 400,000 between mid-2012 and mid-2013, according to the Office of National Statistics. Of the increase, more than half was due to births outnumbering deaths. The increase due to immigration was 183,400.

Heale, originally from north Devon, has been many things: an apprentice chef after leaving school at seventeen, a prison officer. Most recently, he trained and provided a large door-to-door sales force as a subcontractor for the Scottish power company SSE. In 2011, SSE abandoned the doorstep selling of electricity when it was convicted of tricking customers into switching suppliers. Heale says that his salespeople didn't do anything wrong, that they were made scapegoats for the actions of other SSE staff. He is proud of the way he trained his troops to make a tough sell on the doorstep. 'If you accept every time you get a no you're a little bit closer to getting a yes, you're closer to getting a sale.'

Heale was one of seventeen Ukip members elected to Kent County Council in 2013, making them the second biggest party. (Of the eight seats in Thanet, Ukip won seven.) Before that, in 2003, Heale stood as an independent against a Tory councillor but lost. Before that, he was a Conservative for twenty years. Before that, living in London, he was in a group called the Progress Party; before that, he hung out with the anti-immigrant fringe politician Dennis Delderfield; before that, in 1978, he was a branch organiser with the National Front. 'I met a lot of people in the prison service and families who were ex-forces,' he said. 'It was a bit of a social club. Initially the National Front was just a group of retired people and soldiers.'

In 1978, a trades union report catalogued more than a hundred violent racist attacks on Bengalis in the East End of London: 'Hammer attacks, stabbings, slashed faces, punctured lungs, clubbings, gunshot wounds, people beaten with bricks, sticks and umbrellas, and kicked unconscious in broad daylight'. The report didn't attribute the violence directly to the National Front, but accused them of encouraging it. That year, under the leadership of the anti-Semitic former neo-Nazi John Tyndall, the Front launched a racist campaign aimed at schoolchildren called How to Spot a Red Teacher: 'You can recognise them when they sneer at our White race and nation and everything that has made Britain great.' In view of Ukip's insistence that it isn't a racist party, I thought Heale might be defensive, or embarrassed, or apologetic about having been a member of the NF in 1978. To my surprise, he came to its defence. 'There's been an attempt by many people to associate the National Front with the far right,' he said, 'but that's not fair, that's not true.' Heale left the NF when he fell in love with and married an Egyptian woman. After some ugly encounters with other ex-members who were unhappy that he'd married outside his race, he moved to the coast.

Much of Heale's organisational work is devoted to trying to broaden the party's base beyond the middle-aged and the elderly. He's had some success. The combination of Farage's personality and the appeal of blaming Europe for Britain's problems has drawn some young people to Ukip, among them the organiser of the school debate, Charlie Leys. Leys, who has just turned eighteen, hands out Ukip leaflets first thing each morning, goes to school, then works on the fish counter at the Ramsgate Waitrose in the late afternoon. Next year he'll run for a seat on the local council.

I arranged to meet him again at the branch of Caffè Nero on the high street. He told me he'd experienced no hostility at school, though on the street he'd been called a racist, a homophobe, a bigot and a sexist. His career in politics began after a classroom session just before the 2010 election, when it became clear his teacher didn't have a good grip on what a hung parliament was. Leys hit the Internet. For the whole of his childhood up until then, he had known no government but Labour, and the economy had crashed; he concluded that it must be Labour's fault, so couldn't support them. He credited the Conservatives with putting the economy back on track, and did an internship with Laura Sandys, but couldn't back the party fully because they were in favour of continued EU membership. Then, in his own words, he 'found Ukip when they were still quite repressed'. 'Repressed', he meant, in the sense of being belittled and trivialised in the media. He finally joined the party in July, just after the school debate. Unbeknown to either of them, his father had joined Ukip at the same time.

I asked whether he or any member of his family had ever been obstructed or harmed by the European Union. 'Personally, it's never affected me,' he said. 'But it may well affect me in a negative way. In trying to get jobs. If we have an open door to Europe there's potential for millions of people to come over.' Leys was a fortnight shy of eighteen at this point, but he voiced the same sentiment about Farage's approachability you hear from older men: 'I think the fact you can go and sit down in the pub and have a drink with Nigel is brilliant.'

For now, Farage has managed to maintain the perilous balance of seeming both a cheery squire from a pre-Blair pastoral – a comfortingly old-style conservative figure for old Conservatives, a kind of Denis Thatcherite – and a radical who annoys the establishment and wants to smash things up. In the absence of a populist left-wing party wanting to build a new world on the ruins of the old, the Ukip idea of rebuilding an old world on the ruins of the new is exciting enough to draw the young. But the closer Ukip gets to anything resembling power, the more it will be forced to channel rebelliousness into policy. Everyone in the party is bound to like it when Charlie Leys says about the European Union: 'I don't agree with most of our laws being made outside our country, and us having no say."* Not everyone in the party will like his uncompromising support for gay marriage ('I don't like being told what to do').

One evening I went for a drink with Aaron Knight, Martyn Heale's twenty-eight-year-old assistant. His little cousin came with him and they both drank juice. 'Martyn said I'm his secret weapon,' Knight said. 'I'm charismatic … I understand what Ukip wants to achieve. I truly believe I will be one of their key assets.' But not unconditionally. 'I said if the path they're going

---

* A 2010 House of Commons research paper concluded that, depending on how you measure it, anything from 15 per cent to 50 per cent of new British laws and regulations come from Brussels. Euro-legislation can't pass without consent from representatives of national governments, including Britain, and MEPs, including British MEPs.

on I deem not to be right I will walk away. I'm not there to pledge allegiance through light and darkness, I'm there to fight the noble cause.'

Knight is another Ramsgate native. His father died when he was fifteen. He began studying media at Thanet College, dropped out, moved away, did various jobs, moved back. 'I don't want to join the slave industry,' he said. 'I don't like the concept of money. It seems to bring out the worst in people. I'm very much against it. I delved into conspiracy theory. Instead of listening to what everyone told me I decided to stop, listen and look at things from outside. I started to see patterns. I'm very interested in history, so I did a lot of reading history, science, religion. I kind of came up with a conception about how the world worked ... I was very anti-politics for a long time. I decided to look at all the parties and see which ones aligned themselves with me in terms of how best for the future. I read a lot about them. I listened to Nigel Farage.'

Knight said he didn't believe in all conspiracy theories, but there were 'certain things where there is an alternative view of what occurred,' like the attacks of 9/11, which he believes were carried out by the American government to create an excuse to invade Iraq, not for oil, but for archaeology. 'I think they're trying to dig up the ancient world,' he said. I asked Knight where he gets his information. He tends to begin the day, he said, with a Hungarian website called RSOE EDIS, which provides a map of newsy emergencies like earthquakes or Ebola outbreaks around the world – 'just to keep track'. He uses the BBC. He regularly glances at Disclose.tv – 'that's my conspiracy forum I used to be on'. He doesn't tweet, but he does use Facebook. He expressed the orthodox purple and yellow creed on immigration – 'British people, the natives, have become an underclass. The opinions we have are branded as racist' – but without the bitterness that often accompanies it. 'Ukip are genuinely the best option for here,' he said. 'I'm not saying countrywide.'*

---

* Knight was fired in October 2014.

In 2012, Lord Ashcroft, the former deputy chairman of the Conservative Party, published a report called *They're Thinking What We're Thinking: Understanding the UKIP Temptation*, based on a poll of 20,000 people and fourteen focus groups. He concluded that people were drawn to vote Ukip not because of its policies on Europe or immigration, but because it was the only party that gave voice to the cloud of fears, grumbles and prejudices they had previously been too afraid to utter:

> Schools, they say, can't hold nativity plays or harvest festivals any more; you can't fly a flag of St George any more; you can't call Christmas Christmas any more; you won't be promoted in the police force unless you're from a minority; you can't wear an England shirt on the bus; you won't get social housing unless you're an immigrant; you can't speak up about these things because you'll be called a racist; you can't even smack your children. All of these examples, real and imagined, were mentioned in focus groups by Ukip voters and considerers to make the point that the mainstream political parties are so in thrall to the prevailing culture of political correctness that they have ceased to represent the silent majority.

Ashcroft warned against panic in Tory ranks, and against trying to emulate Ukip. 'The Tories said once before that Britain was becoming a foreign land,' he wrote, referring to William Hague in 2001. 'We told those who agreed that if they came with us we would give them back their country. As we found, there is no future in that kind of approach for a party that aspires to govern, or appeal beyond a disgruntled minority. We cannot "dog whistle" to them that we share their view, in the hope that nobody else will notice.' Ashcroft predicted Ukip's triumph at the European elections, and the Tories' drubbing. But it was nothing to be alarmed about: people had told his researchers that the European elections had as much meaning as the Eurovision song contest, and their votes were just a way of making a protest.

Ukip's county council advance in 2013 was harder to dismiss. In Thanet, the history of the established parties is blighted by treachery, malfeasance, bullying and incompetence: fertile territory for an insurgency. In 1983, Cyril Hoser, a senior Conservative on the council, was jailed for six years for fraud and forgery. In 1999 Jonathan Aitken, Tory MP for South Thanet for fourteen years, got eighteen months for perjury. In 2013, the former Tory leader of the council, Sandy Ezekiel, was sentenced to eighteen months for abusing his powers to buy two neighbouring properties in Margate, one of them owned by the council, for himself. In the same year a company called Transeuropa, which operated a ferry from Ramsgate to Ostend, went bust after a secret conclave of senior Labour and Conservative councillors had allowed it to build up £3.4 million in unpaid harbour fees. The council had to write off the debt. In 2012, a Tory member of the council, Ken Gregory, was cautioned by police after he left a voicemail message on the phone of a fellow councillor, the independent John Worrow, who is bisexual, saying: 'With a bit of luck, you'll get AIDS.' Not long afterwards the police called on a Labour councillor, Mike Harrison, who had described the bisexual Green councillor Ian Driver on Facebook as a 'shirt-lifting gender bender'. When last year the council's own standards committee noted the collapse of trust between the people of Thanet and the hung council, and the vindictive, aggressive atmosphere between the parties, the council rejected the report, and all four independent members of the standards committee resigned.

Driver is a defector from Labour. In the noughties, the head of the council's planning committee was a Labour councillor, Ken Gregory. When Labour lost power and the Tories came in, Gregory left Labour, joined the Tories and kept his post. The candidate the Conservatives have selected to run against Farage, Craig Mackinlay, is a founder member and former party leader of Ukip. Some have wondered whether Ukip's recent success might cause the Conservative Party to split. In Kent it's already happening; many of Ukip's councillors are defectors from the Tories.

'In seaside areas, traditionally, politics have been quite fluid,' said Norman Thomas, who produces *Thanet Watch*, a local investigative magazine. 'There's a feeling that lots of Tories are waiting

to see which way the wind blows before jumping ship to Ukip.'
Ukip voters, said Thomas, belong to one of two groups. The first
is white flight migrants from London. 'They thought London
was this idealised place of jellied eels and pearly kings and
queens and then these black people and other minorities came
in and spoiled things so they came to places like Broadstairs and
Margate. Thanet was seen as a sort of white enclave where they
could be happy again. Lots of these people are still here and will
be voting in their droves for Ukip – reasonably well-off, probably without a personal axe to grind, but historically prejudiced.
I've spent many an hour selling magazines in the town centre
and inevitably, especially in Ramsgate, I won't be there very long
before someone comes up and starts telling me how wonderful
the country was before all these foreign people came here.'

The other group is those trying to get work. Unemployment is at
10 per cent in Thanet; higher among the young. The coast is busy
with rumours of Britons being passed over for minimum wage
jobs in favour of East Europeans. Many people mention Thanet
Earth, a set of four giant greenhouses in the countryside west
of Ramsgate where in computer-controlled conditions Dutch
industrial farmers grow tomatoes, peppers and cucumbers for
British supermarkets. The scale of the operation is gigantic: they
have nearly a million tomato plants. 'Thanet Earth was opened to
great acclaim,' Martyn Heale said. 'It was going to provide hundreds and hundreds of local jobs. These jobs have gone entirely
to people from Eastern Europe and Holland.' I asked Thanet
Earth if I could visit, or at least talk to them about Ukip's claim.
The PR agent for the site's operators, Fresca, declined, and sent
me a bland statement: 'Thanet Earth has a diverse, cosmopolitan
workforce of which we are very proud … A candidate must have
a legal right to live and work in the UK, but their nationality is
not a relevant consideration for us.'

According to the government's migration advisory committee, half a million migrants from Eastern Europe have come to
Britain to do low-skilled jobs since the EU was enlarged from

2004 onwards. Since 2010 tens of thousands have come from
Spain, Portugal and Italy. The latest government estimate suggests that 4 per cent of the population of Kent is made up of
non-British EU citizens. The committee's most recent report is
much less bleak about the impact of immigration from Europe
than Ukip would like. Most of the problems, it suggests, are
caused either by government failures or by exploitative employers, or both: employers take advantage of lax enforcement of the
law to make cash-hungry, non-unionised migrants work exces-
sively long hours, in poor conditions, for less than the minimum
wage. In 2012 a chicken-catching firm in Kent, D.J. Houghton,
was shut down by government agents after it was found to be
treating its Lithuanian workforce like slaves, docking their wages
for the privilege of sleeping in a damp, rodent-infested house or
for spending a week living in a minibus roaming from farm to
farm, the length and breadth of Britain. There are so few inspectors monitoring whether bosses are actually paying the minimum
wage that at the present rate it would take two and a half centuries to get round every employer.

It's no consolation to an eighteen-year-old in Ramsgate who
can't find work, but it's hard to imagine Britain coping without
immigrants. With Britons living longer and longer, someone will
have to do the hefting and hauling. Since 1971, the population
of Britain has increased by 25 per cent, but the number of men
of retirement age has increased by 70 per cent.

Nonetheless, the immigration issue presents a challenge to
traditional left-wing thinking about the protection of hard-won
workers' rights in countries that have them, and how to extend
them to people from countries that don't. It's hard for liberals to
answer the question, 'If you don't believe in absolute freedom for
anyone in the world to live and work in Britain, where would you
draw the line?' The beginnings of an answer might be: 'Where
immigration is a means to undermine people's existing rights,
together with the rights of the people who are being used to
undermine them.'

In the decorous company of sixth-formers or international businesspeople, Farage will insist he isn't against immigration, or Europe, or Europeans – only against British membership of the European Union. Being anti-immigration, he has said, would be 'moronic'. He says he wants a Switzerland-style trade relationship with the EU, and an Australian-style immigration system, based on points, with the world: fewer Polish builders, more Indian scientists. But this isn't the message Ukip is putting out on the street, where, as Lord Ashcroft correctly noted, EU membership isn't an issue. Immigration is. All immigration. Foreignness. Otherness. 'Say no to mass immigration,' a Ukip flyer in Thanet says. Rumours and urban legends about victimised indigenous Britons and pampered foreigners fly across the Internet. Hate anecdotes in the right-wing press become generalised: if one foreigner is found to be cheating the system, there must be thousands like them, millions. Farage is the beneficiary. Ukip's discourse isn't so much a dog whistle as the full dog orchestra.

Whenever you mention Farage to people who like him, the conversation goes straight to immigration, without your having to mention it. I got chatting to two railworkers, Steve Hughes and Simon Breach, who were having a pint outside a pub on Ramsgate High Street. Both had it drummed into them by their fathers to vote Labour, with tales of the horrors of the Thatcher years. Both feel they were let down by their union, the RMT, in a recent dispute with their bosses. Both now intend to vote Ukip. 'Farage tells you as it is,' Hughes said. 'What he's for is a good thing because we are getting overrun. I'm not racist in the slightest. I've got a lot of friends who are black. But it seems like they're getting more rights than we have, the immigrants … I'm fifty-one years of age. In my opinion, in fifty years time, I think this country will be run by the Muslims. I actually do.'

'All this terrorism,' Breach said. 'There's a lot of them here to cause a lot of problems. In London it's one in three. It's scary.'*

---

* One in eight Londoners is Muslim

Each told me a story about a deserving Briton close to them who'd had trouble getting money out of the welfare system, and each told me a story they'd heard from a third party about an immigrant popping into a government office and walking out with a fat loan cheque.

'I've got a friend that runs a business,' Hughes said. 'He has about fifteen or sixteen Polish people working for him, because he only has to pay them £200 a week each. He doesn't have to give them holiday pay, sick pay, annual leave or anything like that.'*

'They're everywhere, the Polish,' Breach said. 'If they come over here and work for a living that's fine, but they're putting people out of work as well. You won't get a harder worker than a Polish, they'll work very hard and get paid peanuts. Who's going to turn that away?'

'We all know Ukip will never ever get into power,' Hughes said. 'But Farage is a fighter. He's a gentleman. He likes a beer.'

In her 1938 novel *The Death of the Heart,* Elizabeth Bowen describes a train trip from London to the Kent seaside. It's one of the most extraordinary journeys in English literature. Without stretching the bounds of the real, she takes her young protagonist, Portia, from a nineteenth-century milieu – a stuffy, oppressive, metropolitan townhouse, gloomy with servants, sexual frustration, snobbery, hypocrisy and heavy furniture – to a bright twentieth-century world of freedom, consumerism and erotic risk. For decades, until the advent of cheap package holidays to Spain put an end to it, versions of that journey – from Britain's dark, class- and custom-bound cities to the beaches, amusements and liberties of the South Coast – kept Margate going. Cliftonville, the easternmost part of Margate and the only bit that lies in South Thanet constituency, was the site of street after street of tall terraced lodging houses, where the funsters slept and, I suppose, a significant proportion of my peers were

---

* Employment law is the same for British and Polish workers.

conceived. 'The town used to double, treble, quadruple in size in summer,' said Clive Hart, one of Cliftonville's Labour councillors. 'Birmingham used to close down and send everybody here for a fortnight. I was born in a council house a mile from the sea. In the summer months my mum had to put a sign in the window saying "No places" because people were knocking on the door.'

In the early 1980s the holiday trade collapsed. The guesthouses of Cliftonville emptied out. Too big for family houses, their dozens of bedrooms, each with a sink in the corner, made ideal cheap bedsits. For the next thirty years, seized by the shifting tides of the economy or government policy, many of the most troubled inhabitants of south-east England washed up here, while Cliftonville decayed around them: refugees, victims of the bedroom tax, the unemployed, drug users, difficult neighbours other boroughs didn't want. In recent years, two new groups have moved in: immigrants from Eastern Europe, including many Roma from the Czech Republic and Slovakia, and middle-class migrants from London, looking to salvage, strip and repaint Cliftonville's vintage heart.

Cliftonville as a whole is historically a Labour area, but Hart admitted he was struggling to hold the line against Ukip. Until recently he was the leader of the council, but he resigned in May after a Saturday night Twitter brawl ended with him tweeting at his critics in block capitals. 'The working-class people, many of them are disgruntled, they feel let down by politicians of all sides,' he told me. 'I've done what I can for the underdog, the vulnerable. But I think they look at the three [national party] leaders and, you know, it's hard to tell any difference between them. Even I sometimes feel that way. It's all homogenised into the same type of person who's running the country.'

The line dividing South Thanet from North Thanet runs between Cliftonville and the east end of Margate's main beach, putting the pearl of Margate's recent revival, the Turner Contemporary art gallery, on the non-Farage side. The civic activists of the Ramsgate Society look with envy and admiration

at the way their counterparts in Margate encouraged the council
to back the project, the way it has acted as a gentrification bomb:
it has given impetus to other efforts on Margate seafront, like the
restoration of the Dreamland amusement park. They call it the
Turner effect. One much-talked-about scenario is of Margate as
the new Whitstable: first the artists come, then the commuters
and the tourists.

I walked up the hill from the Turner one blazing afternoon
and crossed into Cliftonville, into what may soon become
Farageland. The railings of the old guesthouses were hung with
black plastic rubbish sacks marked 'Reusable Seagull-Proof Bag'.
The streets had the shabby grandeur I imagine Notting Hill might
have had in the 1970s, and the sea was turquoise in the haze. I
walked into Athelstan Road, where at one end a grand Victorian
warehouse has been turned into studios for artists and craftspeople. Further on I started talking to the young men and women
sitting out on their steps in the sunshine; they weren't artists or
craftspeople.

It's hard to represent those conversations, because everyone
was talking at once, and only one of them told me his name, and
most of the men, stripped to the waist, flaunting their tattoos,
were drunk, emphasising their points with waves of the cans in
their hands. I only had to say I was writing an article about Ukip,
and they were off, saying how much they loved Farage, how they
wanted him to sort out the immigrants. 'I swear to God, Ukip
needs to do something,' said one man, who described himself as
a car dealer, and said he was trying to sell the silver car parked
at the kerb opposite. 'You live on this road for three months,
I'm telling you now, if you wasn't racist, you soon would be. The
Polish are all right, I've got time for them. At the end of the day
they're putting money in the till. Here, they sit outside their steps
drinking, spit bird seeds out, just a drain on our resources.'

'I'll vote Ukip,' the woman next to him said, 'because my little
boy, when I was younger, you would rarely see a black person,
and now it's "spot the white person".'

As I was leaving, one of the tipsy rhetoricians took me aside. His name was Chris. He'd had a good job working on the wind farms but something had gone wrong. As we talked his partner was weaving to and fro on the periphery, her face dark and blotched as a result of substance abuse, her calves below the hem of her dress complex with weeping sores. Chris told me how much better she was than she had been; it was only recently that she'd started wearing dresses again. He searched for the right euphemism to explain her plight. 'She's a former user of the brown,' he said. He took me to the alleyway leading to their basement bedsit. His neighbours threw trash down into the back yard, he said, and pointed to the line of pot plants he'd bought and arranged around their door. He must have been drinking all day, but he wanted to show that he was trying, that he cared.

Around the corner in the next street I met some of the neighbours. What may have been an entire family of Slovaks, perhaps a dozen of different ages, was sitting and standing out in front of their house. The only one who spoke English, a fifteen-year-old girl called Jessica, began to talk, then became hard and suspicious. 'Why are you talking only to Slovaks?' she asked.

A few doors along a group of Czech Roma guys, all sober, were chatting outside. Miroslav had a head of Christ with a crown of thorns on a thick silver chain around his neck, a tattoo of a pistol and roses on his left pectoral and, in the middle of his chest, the emblem of a Kalashnikov with the words '50 Gypsies'. 'I don't like them,' he said, referring to the Slovaks, 'because they make us look bad.' Miroslav had been in England since he was eleven. He'd just left a factory job and he was about to start work in a Mercedes showroom. 'I don't have a British passport, but I feel totally English,' he said. 'I don't think I am English, but because I've been here for such a long time, I feel part of the English.'

In Britain the Roma are often mistaken for people from South Asia. Miroslav told me he'd been randomly attacked in the street – for racial reasons, he assumed – but he didn't seem to see anything unusual about it. He made it sound as if it was just one of those things, like getting caught in the rain. The remarkable thing, and the only reason he mentioned it, was that after he was attacked a white English person came to his aid. He wove for me a touching imaginary scenario in which Farage might be attacked in the street, and one of the Czech Roma might come to his aid, take his bloodied body in his arms and comfort him. Like many working immigrants, Miroslav sympathised with some of Ukip's ideas without sympathising with the party. 'You've got to see who's trying to come to work and pay tax, and see who is coming here just to claim benefit,' he said. 'They're a racist party. You can't chuck all people in the same bag.'

Despite the widespread belief to the contrary, EU immigrants have to overcome extra hurdles before they can get benefits in Britain. In Broadstairs I met P., a twenty-five-year-old from Wrocław, who, after five and a half years in the UK and a masters in linguistics from King's, has acquired perfect English – good enough to get a job teaching immigrants the language. She works on a government programme called Conditionality. Claimants with poor English skills have two rounds of twenty-four weeks' teaching. If they don't show improvement, their benefits are stopped.

I showed her some of the milder Ukip literature, which she found unexceptionable. 'There are so many people who just stay here and stay on benefits and I'm also paying for their houses so I'm not supporting that, really,' she said. 'But at the same time there are many people who are trying to contribute to the taxes and the welfare of the country.' I showed her the 'Sorry, we're full' leaflet. She wrinkled her nose. 'That's horrible. I think it's targeted at not really educated people.'

Having lived in London for most of her time in England, P. felt she had emigrated all over again by moving to Thanet. 'When this came up I didn't even know where Margate was,' she said. 'This is my first encounter with the real English. All the little traditions. The things they talk about at work. Not about culture, nothing political, about families, about pub outings and karaoke nights and promotions at Iceland. And everyone eats really badly here. I thought it was just a myth people are fat here but they eat really badly and they don't cook.'

One of the ideas behind the design of the current EU was that, in terms of labour, it would become more like the United States; that people would be able to do exactly what they are doing, crossing the continent to where the jobs are, moving from Poland to England as easily as Americans move from Oklahoma to California. But even in America, 'as easily as' isn't always easy, and Europe's working class is far less culturally cohesive than its American counterpart. The US also has a federal minimum wage. Besides, a United States of Europe is exactly the dread spectre Ukip evokes in opposing British membership of the EU.

So far the Conservatives have suffered most from the depredations of Ukip, but Farage raises an awkward issue for Labour that it has yet to acknowledge: the EU is a hybrid project. It serves the interests of social justice and global capitalism simultaneously. The EU that forces mobile phone firms to lower their roaming charges and Britain to clean up its beaches is also the EU that is giving multinationals the power to sue governments. The EU that tries to give British workers greater rights is also the EU that makes it easy for employers to play national workforces off against each other. Reacting to this, in Britain, in France, in Sweden, in Finland, in Germany, in the Netherlands and in many other EU countries, an ad hoc pan-European alliance of right-wing anti-immigration parties is growing in strength. As a Europe-wide confluence of ideas and action, the progressive left is dallying in the coffee shop.

Afterword

Since the first edition of this book was published I've had the chance to talk about it with readers around Britain. I found there are many who share my belief in the need for a radical rethink of the privatisation project. Like me, they are looking for more than an account of what went wrong. We want to know how to put it right, but have lost faith in the prospect of fresh thinking from the established political parties about the fundamentals. We no longer want to tinker with the rules of the game; we want to change the game.

I can't fill this gap. I'm not a politician, an economist or a historian; I'm a writer. Yet the same sense of empowerment that the failure of career economists to foresee the crash of 2008 gave an inquisitive non-specialist like myself encourages me now to draw my own conclusions.

This book is not a call for wholesale renationalisation along mid-twentieth-century lines. The bizarre notion that the only alternative to private ownership is to turn water or train companies into opaquely subsidised government departments is kept alive not so much by left-wing activists as by right-wing commentators. Nervous of growing popular doubt about the prevailing economic orthodoxy, they want to frighten the public (and international creditors) with bogus spectres of a return to the 1970s or the Sovietisation of Britain.

The most absurd paradox of Britain's privatisation is that it has actually led to the *nationalisation* of British infrastructure by foreign governments: with parts of former British state firms becoming the property of the governments of France, the Netherlands, Sweden, China, Singapore and Abu Dhabi.

Nor do I attack private enterprise as such. I've not written about car manufacturers, or architectural practices, or restaurants, or delicatessens, or hairdressers, or nightclubs, or estate agencies, or farms, or pharmaceutical firms, or software design companies, or any of the thousands of manifestations of private initiative past and present. I've not even written about the big private oligopolies – the banks, the supermarkets, the accountancy firms. I've written about entities that are fundamentally unlike competing private firms; that can't, as Dieter Helm says of energy, be deemed naturally 'private industries' or 'public industries', but can only be considered *political* industries.

What I have written about is the privatisation of what many would call public services. It's a good term, and we should keep using it, because it captures the important idea of services provided for the common good. But 'public services' is too broad a term to fully reflect the nature of the grand privatisations, and too narrow to reference their history. It is also ambiguous, in the sense that it is easy, common and not necessarily a bad thing for a public service to be privately owned; think of taxis, airlines, plumbers, bakeries.

I'd prefer to describe what I've written about as the privatisation of universal networks. By 'universal', I mean a social and technological system that the society of a country has deemed essential to each citizen, and must be available to all, however little they're able to pay to keep it running.

There are about a dozen universal networks in wealthy countries. It's impossible to be precise, partly because the number varies from country to country. In Britain, health care is a universal network. In the United States, you could argue that it is, and you could argue that it isn't. Another cause of uncertainty is that new technology brings about the death of old universal networks and the birth of new ones. In our lifetimes it's possible we'll see the death of one universal network, the postal system, and the birth of another, Internet access.

The spread of Internet access is a good example of how a universal network comes about. Access to the Internet for regular citizens began as a gimmick and a curiosity which was also, in some sense, a luxury. It then became a useful luxury; transitioned to being simply useful; made the move to being popular; eventually became embarrassing to be without; then difficult to be without. Finally, it has become essential, in the sense that everyone is assumed to have it. If you're unemployed in Britain today, for instance, you won't get welfare payments unless you can show you're applying for seven jobs a day. The only way to do this is online.

The Internet began as a government project. Non-specialist access to the Internet then grew through private companies. Yet once a private, optional network makes the jump to being a universal network, it ceases to be possible for it to belong exclusively to that free market world. Once society deems that all its members must have constant access to a network, political pressure increases in the drive to make that happen. We can see this, for example, in the way the fervently pro-market British government has leaned on mobile phone companies to pool their competing private networks to provide better coverage, or, in the US, in President Obama's suggestion that the Internet be classified as a 'common carrier'.

Go back two centuries to early nineteenth-century Cheltenham, and you saw a similar process taking place with water. First came a state, or public, initiative – in this case, by municipal authorities – to set up a private company to provide water to clean the city streets. Once established, the private water company expanded and offered new services: running water, toilets. The take-up followed the same sequence as with Internet access – first water was a gimmicky luxury, then a useful luxury, then just useful, then popular. At this point political pressure began to build on the water company to become universal – to extend its service to parts of Cheltenham that couldn't afford it. In the end, after a long struggle, the running water network in Cheltenham did become universal, when enough people realised that making it available to everyone was not simply an act of charity but a means to enrich society as a whole, to the benefit of all.

The first universal network was security: the defence of the realm. It was also, because it transcended family and clan interests and involved defining what the realm was, the starting point of the modern state. It is no coincidence that two countries whose armies suffered devastating failures in 2014, Iraq and Ukraine, are among the countries that have been exposed most fiercely to the bad mentoring of outside agents promoting free market solutions to problems that could only have been solved by the state-led reconstruction of universal networks.

After defence, the universal networks are, depending on country: police and justice, transport, welfare, education, health, water, the postal service, protection against natural disasters like fire, flood and epidemics, energy, cash and payments, refuse collection, and now the Internet – of which the phone system has become, effectively, a branch. Food is not a universal network; most governments, including Britain's, elect to prevent starvation by making welfare payments. Nor is housing, although, in Britain in the 1970s, it almost became one. For the time being, the British state is under no obligation to provide a roof for a healthy, child-free homeless adult.

There are two striking things about the list of universal networks. One is that it pretty much corresponds to the list of portfolios in your typical modern government. Privatise them all, and what remains of government? What is government for? Does it protect, provide, shelter, guide, build? If not, what is a 'nation'?

The other is that most of the networks weren't networks, or universal, during the lifetime of many of the most prominent economists whose work provides the rationale for privatisation. When Adam Smith wrote *The Wealth of Nations,* the only universal networks in Britain were the same as in medieval times – defence, the justice system and the production of currency. (Some might include roads and the Poor Law.)

The logic of the privatising trajectory on which Margaret Thatcher and her heirs launched Britain leads to a new pre-industrial dispensation, where the state removes itself from all businesses except defence, the police-court-jail system, the issue of sound money, rubbish collection, workhouses and the upkeep of roads; where welfare payments are abolished and all other universal networks – medical treatment, education, gas, electricity, water, trains and buses, the Internet – are available only at market price, in other words, de-universalised. Poor Britons would, once again, be free to starve, to die of treatable diseases and to be illiterate, or to eke out a menial living in the workhouse.

There are, without doubt, some – mainly to be found within the ranks of the Conservative party, Ukip and the wealthy – to whom this logic appeals, for whom Georgian Britain is an idyll to aspire to. Yet the mainstream privatisers among politicians, economists and the percentage men of the City reject logic. Certainly there is an element of rational self-interest among privatisation's wealthy advocates: it makes it easier for governments to cut income tax on top earners. But most pro-privatisation voices either see the benefits to everyone of keeping the main universal networks universal, or understand that, as long as everyone in Britain gets to vote, there are simply too many beneficiaries of universal access to health, education and welfare to begin de-universalising them.

Defenders of privatisation, then, fall back on six lies. The first is that privately owned companies are structurally more effective than publicly owned ones. This is a belief more akin to religious faith than reality; part of the cult that has elevated the business executive to a new priestly caste. The truth is less exciting. Sometimes public agencies fail. Sometimes private firms fail. The pre-privatisation British Rail and post-privatisation Network

Rail, commercially run and publicly owned, were more effective companies than privatised Railtrack. Two of Britain's largest privately owned banks recently had to be rescued by public funds. The traditional failing of the old nationalised industries – that they struggled to match their staff profiles to new and better ways of doing things – are more easily fixed than the central flaw in privatised essential services, which is that their first goal is to serve their owners and directors, rather than the public.

Second, there is the lie that privatised networks compete in a free market. Some essential networks, like water and energy distribution, are natural monopolies, so for them, competition is non-existent. And once any network transitions to universality, in a democracy, it cannot resist political pressure, not just because it's regulated, but because the extreme ends of the wealth spectrum seek to drag it in opposite directions. The low paid, those who haul and scrub and nurse and tend and gather, demand – rightly – that the networks should either be free at point of use, or affordable, not just for their own sake, but to bring the prospects of their children level with those of their more privileged peers. The wealthy, who can afford to spurn some of the baseline universal networks on which the less well off depend, like health and education, seek to have the entire country subsidise the parts of the networks that advantage them – telecom coverage around their remote rural second homes, for instance, and fast roads to their third homes, and flood defences for their fourth homes.

The third lie is that shrinking the state means lower taxes. In fact, it simply means shifting taxes away from progressive income tax towards regressive flat fees that take little or no account of people's ability to pay.

Fourth is that in the face of remorseless benefit cuts, depressed wages for all but the wealthiest and ever-higher access charges to the networks, the networks can be affordable to everyone, and so remain universal.

Fifth, privatisation benefits British firms trying to compete abroad. In fact, most attempts by privatised companies playing a role in the universal networks to break out of Britain have ended in failure. The continuing transfer of ownership of the British water, energy and transport networks overseas, with parts of the health network likely to follow, means not only a loss of control and accountability on the part of the British public but the loss of skilled design, engineering and administration jobs to other countries.

Sixth, that the cultural destruction involved in privatisation doesn't matter, and that people don't care; that a power station, or the concept of a national postal system, or a city hospital, even the very notion of a sense of collective endeavour and achievement over generations, can't have the same imaginative hold over a people as the preservation of a charming Cotswold village or a national park. It can. It does. And it does matter.

What is to be done? These are my thoughts, starting with the terms in which the economy is discussed.

- Journalists, politicians and academics need to accept that fees to use privatised universal networks are taxes, and should be considered in any discussion of the overall tax burden on citizens. Similarly, journalists and politicians should treat excess pay, perks, abuse of office, waste and bad bureaucracy in the privatised universal networks in the same way as they treat them in state organisations.
- The infrastructure of universal networks, and the power to commission services within those networks, should be in the hands of commercially run, non-profit-making organisations, along the lines of traditional housing associations, through which all state subsidies are channelled.
- If extra money is needed for the infrastructure of universal networks, it should be borrowed directly, through the issue of bonds, and not gained by selling shares or retained shareholder equity.
- Private companies, independent non-profits and state-owned

foreign companies may compete to do work within the universal networks, but may not own them outright.

- There should be a presumption that, where practical, universal networks will be funded progressively, either along the lines of the NHS or through means-testing, as was done in the days when British students received not only free tuition but a living allowance.
- The commissioners of universal networks should be democratically accountable, possibly through direct elections, and should serve terms longer than the lifespans of any two successive governments, subject to recall by popular petition.

I can see problems with most of these ideas, but they do have the virtue of offending everyone. The notion of continuing to permit private companies to provide some public services, albeit under public control, is a tough one for the left to stomach, and most of the remainder – what, nationalise the fibre-optic network? Buy back the reservoirs? Ridiculous! Impossible! – will dismay the right. The last proposal, to disaggregate government and bring democracy more in line with the lifespan of big projects, seems likely to baffle across the board. But these are not so much proposals as directions for thought, informed by the experience of researching this book.

I'm not immune to the common notion among men of my age that everything is getting worse. Yet it sometimes seems to me that, as I get older, I get more naive, or more hopeful. If traditional socialism takes too benign a view of human nature, the prevailing economic and moral orthodoxy that I've endured with my fellow-citizens for the past thirty-five years – that personal greed and family interest, occasionally attenuated by personal pity, is all that makes the world run smooth and shiny for the greatest number – is too cynical. I don't buy it. The notion of 'care' has become so hollowed out from overuse in marketing by the companies who run the networks that it's easy to forget part of our motivation to do a job well, alongside the earnings, is we really do care. Not always, but more often than the cynics would hold, whether we're working for a private firm or a public firm or are self-employed, we care about the people we serve, and we care about doing the job well, in the eyes of our peers, and for its own sake. That cannot be bought, and that is not for sale.

January 2015

Acknowledgements

Versions of most of the chapters in this book first appeared in the *London Review of Books* and, in the case of 'Signal Failure', in the *Guardian*. I'm grateful to Mary-Kay Wilmers, editor of the *LRB*, for her support and patience, and for her consent to the breach of the norms of article length that publication involved. I extend the same gratitude towards Alan Rusbridger, editor of the *Guardian*. At the *LRB* I must also thank Daniel Soar, Jean McNicol, Paul Myerscough, Deborah Friedell, Christian Lorentzen, Joanna Biggs, Alice Spawls, Nick Richardson and Jonah Miller. I owe a particular debt to Ian Katz, then features editor of the *Guardian*, who first suggested I looked into the story of the West Coast Main Line and didn't complain when I took one and a half years to hand the piece in; to Charlie English; and to Rob Edwards, who helped with the Freedom of Information request for access to the consultants' report that doomed Railtrack.

I carried out more than one hundred and fifty interviews for this book. Some of the people I would have liked to interview wouldn't talk to me, or were prevented from doing so by the organisations they worked for. Others spoke on condition of anonymity. Where I've quoted people and could do so, I've identified them. But there were many who helped me with background information, or who spoke with me at a stage when I knew too little to ask the right questions, and so haven't been quoted. Rabina Khan falls into the latter category in respect of housing; David Worksett and Allyson Pollock, health. I'm grateful for their time and their help with context. I'd like to thank Peter Morris for his inexhaustible patience in helping me understand the numbers in annual company reports, and the mechanism behind private consortia takeovers of infrastructure. Alicia Weston, Keith Hill, John Bryant, Roger Harding, Neil Litherland and Stuart Macdonald offered insights into Britain's housing policy mess.

In an era where large corporations' trappings of openness – bright, friendly, content-rich websites and well-staffed PR operations – turn out to be facades for gagged workforces, denial of corporate history and a refusal to engage with sceptical questions, the generalist-journalist is grateful for the work of specialist journals whose reporters track narrow fields scrupulously week by week, and to whose presence shy executives have become habituated. I'm particularly indebted to the staff of *Inside Housing* and the *Health Service Journal*.

Two organisations I approached put me together with helpful, imaginative and articulate men with the authority and confidence to face my questions directly, answering them with intelligence and humour, acknowledging their critics, and accepting that they spoke to a corporate history going further back than the beginning of that financial year. These were David Simpson, then of Royal Mail, and Chris Green, then of Virgin Trains.

The more thorough and detailed a journalistic inquiry, the more likely the journalist is to have to demand of his interlocutors not only information about a situation but a kind of instant education into the most basic terms by which the situation must be framed. It is a great deal to ask of an interviewee in terms of patience, particularly when the questions stray towards the inquisitorial; I thank, in particular, Stephen Littlechild and Emma Cochrane for their readiness to stop and explain concepts to me.

I am grateful to Dieter Helm, who read through the original version of the 'Taking Power' article before it was published in the *LRB*; to Michael Pryke, who read 'Not a Drop to Drink'; and to Nick Timmins, who read 'Multiple Fractures'. Any flaws in these chapters remain my responsibility.

Examples of electricity market abuse were found in *Power Systems Restructuring: Engineering and Economics*, edited by Marija D. Ilic, Francisco Galiana and Lester Fink, and *Privatization, Restructuring, and Regulation of Network Utilities*, by David Newbery. *Right to Buy: Analysis and Evaluation of a Housing Policy*, by Colin Jones and Alan Murie, was an invaluable text, as was Matt Griffith's report *We Must Fix It*, available on the IPPR website (ippr.org). I am indebted to William Waugh's *John Charnley: The Man and the Hip* and John Allan's magnificent *Lubetkin*.

I would also like to thank Chloë Penman, Matthieu Le Goff, Joseph de Weck, Marc Francis and Stewart Smyth; my agent, Natasha Fairweather; my editor at Verso, Leo Hollis; and those loyal Dundonian readers of my articles, Russell and Susan Meek.